COLOSSIANS AND PHILEMON

John Woodhouse

'Over a period of several months at Moore College, Dr John Woodhouse preached a series of expository sermons on Paul's letters to the Colossians and Philemon which were clear, insightful and wonderfully refreshing. The publication and expansion of these fine messages in the Focus on the Bible commentary series will now benefit a much wider audience. Honest readers will be challenged by the gospel of God's gracious saving plan for the world, the place of the Lord Jesus within it, and how those who have been united with Christ are to live. May the God who is the Author of these two powerful letters use John's rich exposition to challenge and encourage us in the twenty-first century'.

Peter O'Brien,
Emeritus Faculty Member, Moore Theological College, Sydney

'This commentary by John Woodhouse is a rich source of biblical insight on the texts of Colossians and Philemon. This volume is a great resource for the pastor as he prepares to feed his flock, but it is equally helpful for students of the Bible who desire to understand better these magnificent letters. Maybe even more importantly, the text reflects the author's own love for the Savior. I can gladly commend it.'

Bill Cook,
Professor of New Testament Interpretation,
The Southern Baptist Theological Seminary, Louisville, Kentucky

COLOSSIANS AND PHILEMON

So walk in Him

John Woodhouse

CHRISTIAN
FOCUS

ISBN 978-1-84550-632-2

10 9 8 7 6 5 4 3

Published in 2011
Reprinted in 2021 and 2025
in the
Focus on the Bible Commentary Series
by
Christian Focus Publications, Ltd
Geanies House, Fearn, Ross-shire,
IV20 1TW, Great Britain
www.christianfocus.com

Cover design by
Daniel Van Straaten

Printed by
Bell & Bain, Glasgow

MIX
Paper | Supporting responsible forestry
FSC® C007785
www.fsc.org

Contents

Colossians

Philemon

To the students and faculty of Moore College, Sydney, who for a couple of years shared weekly with me in hearing the Word of God from Paul's letters to the Colossians and to Philemon. Thank you for your effective participation in the faith (Philemon 6).

Introduction to Paul's letters to the Colossians and to Philemon

Behind the letters of Paul to the Christian believers in Colossae and to one of their number by the name of Philemon is a wonderful story of evangelism, church planting and Christian growth. Some of the details of the story are a little unclear, and there are some gaps in the evidence, but the main lines are vivid enough. I will take the liberty of filling in some of the gaps in the following reconstruction of what took place.

The story begins with a rather well-to-do businessman who lived in the town of Colossae. His name was Philemon. It may have been his business that brought him one day in about the year A.D. 53 down to the coastal town of Ephesus, not far from Colossae. No doubt he had visited Ephesus many times, but on this occasion there was quite a stir – because a Jewish man, by the name of Paul, was gathering crowds in a hall in the town and arguing about one he called Jesus, who (he claimed) was not only the Messiah of Israel, but also the Lord and judge of all people everywhere (see Acts 19:8-10). Other astonishing things were happening around this man Paul: diseases were remarkably healed, evil spirits left people (Acts 19:11, 12). Like many others in Ephesus at the time, Philemon (though not Jewish himself) came to hear Paul. To his own surprise he was persuaded by this extraordinary message and came to faith in Messiah Jesus, the Lord. Philemon actually became involved in some way with Paul in his work. It is likely that he subsequently returned to Ephesus on a number of occasions over the next year or two, and supported and helped Paul in his missionary labours there.

At about the same time, another citizen of Colossae had much the same experience as Philemon. His name was Epaphras. (Epaphras, like Philemon, was not Jewish.) Unfortunately the details are vague, but both of these men returned home to Colossae, now believers in Jesus, the Christ and the Lord. We know that Epaphras told 'the word of truth' to many of his fellow citizens of Colossae, the gospel that he had learned from Paul. A number of them understood the truth of the grace of God and also came to faith in Messiah Jesus (see Col. 1:3-8). Epaphras went on with the same news to the nearby towns of Hierapolis and Laodicea, with similar results. In Colossae the new believers in Christ Jesus began meeting together in Philemon's house. No doubt Philemon, from his time with Paul, was able to provide some kind of leadership and encouragement to the growing gathering of new believers meeting under his roof.

Our attention must now turn to one member of Philemon's household, a slave named Onesimus. Onesimus, whose name meant 'useful', did not live up to his name. He was not the best of slaves, and does not appear to have got on well with his master. Not surprisingly, perhaps, Onesimus was not caught up in the strange ideas his master had brought back from his recent trip to Ephesus. The odd gatherings of people from different backgrounds that had started to take place in the house must have been perplexing to him.

Again we wish we had more details, but we don't. For some reason Onesimus chose to run away from his master and, in the process, may have robbed him. For slaves to run away like this was not unusual, but it was dangerous. It seems that Onesimus fled far from Colossae (for understandable reasons) and found his way eventually to far-off Rome.

Some years had passed since Paul had been preaching about Christ Jesus in Ephesus. It was now about A.D. 60 or 61. Much had happened to Paul through these years, but by the time Onesimus came to Rome, by a remarkable providence, Paul, too, was in Rome. He was there, however, as a prisoner. He lived in his own rented quarters, with a Roman soldier guarding him (Acts 28:16). The book of Acts tells us that he 'lived there two whole years at his own expense, and welcomed all who came to him, proclaiming the kingdom of God and teaching about the Lord Jesus Christ with all boldness and without hindrance' (Acts 28:30, 31). Once again we are tantalized with a lack of answers to many questions, but among 'all who came to him' was apparently Onesimus. What drew Onesimus to the friend of his former master, we can only guess. The fact is that Paul led Onesimus to Jesus. Onesimus became a believer! Furthermore, a deep affection grew between Paul and Onesimus, and he assisted Paul in various ways.

Some time passed. Then one day, there was another surprise for Paul. A familiar face from those years in Ephesus appeared among his visitors. It was Epaphras. Here the lack of detail is very frustrating. The circumstances of Epaphras' coming to Rome are unknown to us, as is the way in which he came into contact with Paul. However, it seems that he, like Paul, was (or became) a prisoner of the authorities, somehow in connection with his faith in Christ. What we know is that Epaphras shared with Paul news of the believers back in Colossae, and also in Hierapolis and Laodicea – news of their solid faith, their extravagant love, their confident hope, and their orderly lives (see Col. 1:7b, 8; 2:5).

Paul was, of course, overjoyed and full of thankfulness to God. Yet two things now needed to be done. First, he needed to make contact with this group of believers meeting in his old friend Philemon's house. He needed to ensure that they were firmly established in the faith, that they continued to walk in Christ Jesus the Lord. So he wrote a letter to confirm and strengthen and stabilize the faith of the Colossian believers. This letter has found its place in the New Testament, and is the concern of the first part of this commentary.

Second, what was to be done about Onesimus, the slave who had now come to faith in Christ Jesus, but who had run away from Paul's dear friend and brother in Christ, Philemon, in whose house the Colossian believers now met?

Paul carefully wrote another letter (the focus of the second part of this commentary). He sent the two letters off to Colossae by the hand of a long-time, trusted colleague,

Tychicus. With Tychicus he also sent (no doubt to everyone's surprise) Onesimus!

When Tychicus and Onesimus reached Colossae, word soon spread among the believers that a letter had arrived from Paul, the man who had taught Epaphras and Philemon the news about the Lord Jesus that they had all come to believe. They gathered (as I imagine the scene) in Philemon's house to hear the letter read, and Tychicus read the longer of the two letters he had carried from Rome.

I have tried to imagine what was happening with Onesimus. Did he join the gathering? Or was he kept out of sight for a while? We do not know. But when Tychicus finished reading the longer letter, I picture him saying, 'Brothers, I do have another letter from Paul that he wants you all to hear. It is brief, but important.' Tychicus then read the letter we know as 'Philemon'.

The account I have given includes a number of assumptions and other understandings that are not beyond doubt. Here I will briefly comment on the most important of these, but refer the reader to the more substantial commentaries for detailed discussions of the evidence.

1. The authorship of the letters

Since the rise of critical biblical scholarship in the nineteenth century questions have been raised about whether Paul really wrote Colossians. Arguments have been made about differences between the style, vocabulary and theology of this letter, when compared to other letters more certainly by Paul. These arguments are all indecisive, depending on substantial assumptions (based on a very small corpus of writings agreed to be by Paul) about what he could and could not have written.

Against these arguments stands the clear claim of the letter, not only in its opening words, but in many personal references to Paul and his circumstances through the document. Any suggestion that this evidence is not to be taken at face value calls for far more significant proofs than have been advanced.

The situation with Philemon is rather different. Few scholarly challenges have been mounted against the plain claim of that letter to have been authored by the apostle Paul.

In each case it is possible that the actual physical writing may have been done by another hand, under Paul's direction or dictation. This may be suggested by the way in which he draws attention to the points at which the words have in fact been written 'with my own hand' (Col. 4:18; cf. Philem. 19, but see our comments later on this verse). This, however, does not alter the fact that the 'I' of these letters is clearly presented as Paul himself.

2. The date and place from which they were written

These matters are related and the subject of considerable scholarly discussion. When he wrote both letters, he was imprisoned (Col. 4:10, 18; Philem. 1, 23). The letters, however, nowhere directly say where this was. There are two main possibilities. Paul may have been imprisoned during his three years in Ephesus, in about A.D. 52-55. The account of Paul's time in that city in the book of Acts does not mention a period of imprisonment, but it is possible. The book of Acts does, however, record Paul's two years of house arrest in Rome in about A.D. 60-62. Arguments in favour of the letters having been written during an imprisonment in Ephesus include the closer proximity of that city to Colossae, and the numerous movements of people indicated in the letters between where Paul was and Colossae. However (while certainty is not possible) I have assumed that the imprisonment from which these letters were written was the one described at the end of the book of Acts. This fits with all of the data that we have, and it is hardly ruled out by the difficulty of several trips by various persons between Rome and Colossae. Indeed the later date of the Roman imprisonment (compared to a hypothetical Ephesian incarceration) may better allow for the various things that appear to have happened between Paul's evangelistic work in Ephesus and the writing of these letters (see the reconstruction above).

3. Why was the longer letter to Colossae written?

The motivation for Paul writing his longer letter to the believers in Colossae has been the subject of a great deal of discussion and debate. Much of this has focused on attempts to discern a 'false teaching' present at Colossae and which Paul had presumably heard about from Epaphras. On this view, the letter was written 'to provide the resources that the Colossian Christians need to fend off some kind of false teaching to which they are exposed'.[1] The commentaries generally accept that there was such a teaching present in Colossae, and that Paul's letter was intended to address this problem.

The existence of what we may generally call 'false teaching' in many early Christian communities is beyond doubt. A number of Paul's letters have explicit references, not only to such teachings, but also to the false teachers themselves. One striking feature of the letter to the Colossians is that there is no direct reference to either false teachers or particular false teaching. This has led to a wide range of proposals concerning the kind of teaching that Paul may have been 'correcting' or at least responding to in this letter. The range of views is wide because there is such a lack of evidence to control speculations.

Another possibility is attractive. Perhaps Paul makes no direct and explicit reference to false teachers and false teaching simply because there was no such specific threat in Colossae, or at least none of which he had particular knowledge. If this were the case, Paul's letter would have the purpose summed up in the following words: 'Therefore, as you received Christ Jesus the Lord, so walk in him, rooted and built up in him and established in the faith, just as you were taught, abounding in thanksgiving' (Col. 2:6, 7).

In other words, Paul wrote to the believers of whom he had heard such a marvellous report from Epaphras, not because they were in some *particular* danger, but to confirm them in their 'good order and the firmness of [their] faith

---

[1] Douglas J. Moo, *The Letters to the Colossians and to Philemon* (Nottingham: Apollos, 2008), p. 47.

in Christ' (Col. 2:5b). Certainly Paul was aware of the many challenges to this faith in the world of his day (as in ours!). Therefore he warns them of dangers. However, these are not to be interpreted as clues about a specific 'false teaching' in Colossae, but to be understood as indications of the *kind* of threat that believers could be expected to face.[2] This view has been adopted in the exposition that follows, and will be explained more fully at various points.

In this commentary I have tried to imagine us joining the believers gathered in Philemon's house to hear Tychicus read these two remarkable letters. I invite readers to join me in this imaginative and highly instructive exercise.

Study Questions

1. Read the account of Paul's time in Ephesus in Acts 19 (where, we understand, Philemon and Epaphras were among those who became believers in Christ Jesus the Lord).
    a. Note the indications of the effectiveness of Paul's ministry among non-Jewish hearers. How was it, do you think, that such people came to believe in the Messiah of Israel?
    b. What was it about Paul's message that aroused opposition?
2. Read about Paul's time in Rome in Acts 28:11-31 (where the letters to the Colossians and to Philemon were probably written).
    a. What happened in Rome that emphasized, for Paul, the importance of the gospel going to the nations?
    b. How does Luke summarize Paul's teaching to those who came to him during his two years in Rome (including, we understand, Onesimus).

---

[2] A view along these lines is argued persuasively by Morna D. Hooker, 'Were There False Teachers in Colossae?' in Barnabas Lindars and Stephen S. Smalley, eds, *Christ and Spirit in the New Testament: Studies in Honour of Francis Digby Moule* (Cambridge: Cambridge University Press, 1973), pp. 315-31.

3. Read through the letters Paul wrote from Rome to the believers in Colossae and to Philemon (preferably at one sitting), noting everything we lean about:
    a. Epaphras;
    b. Tychicus;
    c. Onesimus;
    d. Philemon;
    e. the circumstances of the recipients of the letters;
    f. Paul's purpose in writing these letters.

Colossians

As you received Christ Jesus the Lord,
so walk in him.

1

A Letter from Paul
(Colossians 1:1, 2)

There is much we do not know about the circumstances on the day in the early 60s of the first century A.D.[1] when two men, named Tychicus and Onesimus, arrived in the town of Colossae bearing two brief letters. Colossae, located about 100 miles inland (as the crow flies) from the Mediterranean coast of modern Turkey, on the south bank of the Lycus River, was not a particularly important town at the time. We know little about the group in Colossae to whom the letter was addressed. Some of its members may have been ethnically Jewish, but most were not. From time to time they met, it would seem, in the house of one Philemon (see Philem. 2).

The only reason we know anything at all about this group of people is that the letters that arrived in Colossae that day are now to be found in the New Testament. They

---

[1] The precise date is far from certain, and depends among other things on whether the letter was written from Rome or Ephesus. The evidence for this question is also inconclusive (see the Introduction). These matters have very little bearing on our understanding of the letter, and so are not pursued here. I am assuming that the letter was written by Paul from prison in Rome in about AD 60. The case for this view is presented by Douglas J. Moo, *The Letters to the Colossians and to Philemon* (Nottingham: Apollos, 2008), pp. 41-46. The case for the letter being written from an otherwise unrecorded imprisonment of Paul in Ephesus between 52 and 55 is argued in N.T. Wright, *The Epistles of Paul to the Colossians and to Philemon* (Leicester:Inter-Varsity Press, 1986), pp. 34-39.

were written by someone very well known to us: the great apostle Paul.[2] Although Paul is one of the most influential figures of world history, his importance was far less obvious to his contemporaries. Indeed it is interesting to reflect on what the recipients of his letter that day in Colossae would have thought about him. Most of them had not seen him in the flesh (2:1), although some of them (including Philemon) had. Yet they had certainly heard of him. From the available evidence it seems that they had become Christian believers some time earlier as an indirect consequence of Paul's vigorous teaching about Jesus Christ in the coastal city of Ephesus, about 100 miles to the west (see Acts 19). Apparently among those who heard Paul then, probably in the hall of Tyrannus (Acts 19:9), and were persuaded and repented and believed, was Epaphras, a citizen of Colossae (Col. 4:12). Such was his joy at his new faith in Jesus Christ that he returned to Colossae, and to the nearby cities of Hierapolis and Laodicea, himself proclaiming Jesus Christ (see 4:13). One of the letters now borne by Tychicus and Onesimus from Paul (see 4:7-9) was addressed to those in Colossae who had come to faith in Jesus Christ through the efforts of Epaphras (1:7).

Although we do not know exactly what happened that day, I like to imagine the small group of believers called together, presumably to Philemon's house, with the rather exciting news that a letter had arrived from Paul – the man who had taught Epaphras about Jesus.

In the first part of this volume we will be listening to the letter that was read to the gathering that day in Colossae. Our purpose is strikingly like theirs. We will be hearing a letter from a man *we* have never seen in the flesh, but who has played a significant role in *our* faith in Jesus.

In my imagination I see Tychicus standing before the hushed gathering, taking out the parchment, and beginning to read: 'Paul, an apostle of Christ Jesus by the will of God, and Timothy our brother, To the saints and faithful brothers

---

[2] There is a debate among scholars about whether Paul the apostle was in fact the author of Colossians. However reasons for doubting the authenticity of the letter are not compelling. See the Introduction and Peter T. O'Brien, *Colossians, Philemon* (Waco, Texas: Word Books, 1982), pp. xli-xliv.

in Christ at Colossae: Grace to you and peace from God our Father' (1:1, 2).[3]

We who have the great collection of Paul's letters in the New Testament are a little spoiled. The first few lines of a letter from Paul begin to sound the same. Today's readers of the New Testament have heard something very like these opening words many times. But for the listeners in Philemon's house that day this was new. True, they were familiar with the form. Letters typically began in this way.[4] I doubt they thought twice about that. It was what was said that captured their attention.

In these opening words Paul summed up, in a way that the letter will more fully explore: (1) how they should think of Paul; (2) how they should think of themselves; and (3) how they should think of life.

1. How to think of Paul (1:1)

How do you think of Paul? After all these years, with the great volume of commentaries that have been written on Paul's letters, the vast tomes on Pauline theology found in theological libraries, as well as the smaller number of biographical works on this great man's life, we might well think that we are in a very different position from those who first heard these words that day in Colossae. While the obvious differences between now and then are considerable, I would like to emphasize the similarity of our situation. How *we* think of Paul is just as important as it was for those believers in Colossae.

a. Apostle of Christ Jesus

Paul introduced himself as **an apostle of Christ Jesus**. The message that Epaphras had earlier brought to Colossae was about *Jesus*. Jesus was a Jewish man, who had lived only a few decades earlier in a relatively remote corner of the Mediterranean world that was the Roman Empire.

---

[3] Except where otherwise indicated Bible passages are cited from the English Standard Version (ESV).

[4] The pattern was common in the opening of letters in Paul's world: name of sender, name of addressee, a greeting.

Through Epaphras' words those listening to this letter had come to believe something about *Jesus*. The message about Jesus claimed this title for him: Christ. *Christos* is Greek for the Hebrew title *Messiah*. This could only be understood by reference to the Jewish scriptures that we now know as the Old Testament. The promises and the hopes found in those scriptures were the basis for the message about Jesus. It was precisely because of *Christ Jesus* (Messiah Jesus, promised King Jesus) that Paul (himself a Jewish man, of course) had written this letter to the group of non-Jewish people (at least predominantly so) in Colossae, a city he had never visited (as far as we know).

These Colossians had already learned enough about Messiah Jesus to have their own lives radically changed. We will hear more about that in due course. For the present we notice that Paul introduced *himself* as one who had been sent ('apostle' comes from the Greek word meaning 'send') by the Messiah Jesus: Israel's King. Unless we see something of the peculiarity of this situation we will not appreciate the impact these opening words must have had on those who first heard them.

There are so many things to say about *Paul*. It has been plausibly argued that he was the greatest intellect of the ancient world, surpassing even Plato and others. Certainly his impact on world history has been immense, although largely unacknowledged. We could speak of his particular and profound insights, his extraordinary strategic missionary effort through the Mediterranean world, his capacity to address the needs of the churches he founded, and so on. Volumes have been written about Paul. Rightly so. We can study his brilliant understanding of so many things: the work of Christ, the justification of sinners, the church, eschatology, the Spirit. As Peter acknowledged, 'there are some things in [Paul's writings] that are hard to understand' (2 Pet. 3:16). There is certainly much to learn.

Nevertheless there is a fundamental question that can easily be overlooked. How do you think of Paul *himself*? As we listen to Paul, as we study his teaching, as we learn from him, it is very important for us to recognize that he is not simply another thinker or teacher, but that he addresses us as Jesus Christ's representative and spokesman: 'apostle'. He speaks not just *about* Jesus Christ, but *for* and *on behalf of, from* Jesus Christ. No less is meant by the introduction, 'Paul, apostle of Christ Jesus'.

There was, therefore, something special happening as this letter began to be read that day in Colossae. I suspect everyone would have sensed it as these first words were heard. They had learned well of Christ Jesus from Epaphras. They had (as we will see) come to true and marvellous *faith* in Christ Jesus through Epaphras' faithful testimony. But now the apostle of Christ Jesus himself was addressing them.

This certainly means that Paul speaks with *authority*, the authority of Christ Jesus. It means he has every right to claim a hearing from anyone who claims to take Christ Jesus seriously. Our attitude to the apostle of Jesus will reflect something of our attitude to Jesus. Yet it is more than that. We ought not to think of Paul *only* in terms of his authority. He was sent by our Lord Jesus Christ. We ought to be as thrilled, delighted and eager to hear Paul as we would be to hear Jesus himself. Indeed his words come to us from Christ Jesus.

b. By the will of God

Furthermore Paul is this apostle **by the will of God**. It will become clear in the course of this letter that this is more than a general assertion of divine providence over things that happen. In that sense you may be a student, a husband, a mother, an electrician (or whatever) 'by the will of God'. That is an important perspective for us to have on all of the events of life. God's good and sovereign hand does rule over all things. The implications of that for our Christian lives are huge. In the course of this letter we will see that *the will of God* of which Paul speaks is both more specific and more magnificent than general providence.

In 1:9 we will hear that he prayed for the Colossian believers that they 'may be filled with the knowledge of [God's] will'. That does not simply mean filled with the knowledge of God's providence over everything that happens. *God's will*, Paul will go on to explain, involves how all things were created for his beloved Son (1:16). *God's will* is that all his fullness dwell in him (1:19). *God's will* is to reconcile all things to Christ, making peace by the blood of his cross (1:20). In other words, *God's will* is his great purpose for the whole of creation, at the centre of which is Jesus Christ.

Do you think you are filled with the knowledge of God's will?

If you are (or if you want to be) then you need to understand that Paul is Christ Jesus' apostle *by the will of God*. The great plan of God, in other words, to reconcile all things through Jesus Christ, includes making Paul Christ's apostle. This will be explained more fully as the letter unfolds (see especially 1:23–2:5). As Christ Jesus' apostle, Paul was a servant of the gospel (1:23), he suffered (1:24), he was given by God the stewardship to make the word of God fully known (1:25). Knowing and understanding that Paul is Jesus Christ's apostle is part of knowing *the will of God*. Pay careful attention therefore: as we respond to what we hear from Paul, we are responding to the will of God.

All this casts an important light on what was happening on that day when the Colossian believers heard Tychicus begin to read this letter. As we begin to read Paul's letter it is important for us to recognize whose words these are.

c. Timothy our brother

Having introduced himself in such striking terms, Paul included another name with his own: **Timothy our brother**. We know that Timothy had been involved with Paul in the Ephesus ministry (Acts 19:22). Perhaps Epaphras had spoken of him. Certainly Timothy was a most trusted colleague of Paul; his right-hand man, we might say. Timothy was a *brother*, not only to Paul, but also to these Colossian believers (hence '*our* brother') even though, as with Paul, most of them had never have actually met him. The point of mentioning Timothy here will become clearer in a moment.

2. How to think of yourselves (1:2a)

The addressees of the letter are now identified: **To the saints and faithful brothers in Christ at Colossae.**

In many contexts Paul uses the expression 'the saints' to refer specifically to Jewish believers in Jesus.[5] It is possible that 'the saints and faithful brothers' refers to *the Jewish* ('the saints') and *the non-Jewish* (the 'faithful brothers') believers in Colossae. The non-Jewish believers have been brought to join the Jewish believers when they came to trust in Messiah Jesus, Israel's promised king. They became 'faithful (that is, believing) *brothers*'. They now belonged to the new family of God's people as fully as 'brother Timothy'. A little later, Paul will put it like this: '[God] has qualified *you* [Gentiles] to share in the inheritance of *the saints* [the Jews] in light' (1:12).

It is not clear that Paul means to make that distinction (between Jewish and non-Jewish believers) in verse 2. These words could be translated: 'To the holy and believing brothers in Christ at Colossae.' The original grammar slightly favours this and the following exposition understands the words in this way.[6] Yet the weight of what Paul is saying here does not depend on resolving this small ambiguity, for either way he is speaking of the astonishing new identity of the Colossian believers. We must understand that this is identical to *our* identity today if we believe in Messiah Jesus as they did. Let us notice carefully five things that the Colossians were being encouraged to understand about themselves.

a. Holy

First, Paul calls them 'holy'.[7] That is an astonishing thing for a Jew to say of non-Jews. *Israel* was God's *holy* people (Exod. 19:6). Within Israel the Levitical priests were the *holy* ones (Exod. 28:2). The '*holy* ones of the most high' in Daniel's famous vision were those of *Israel*

---

[5] D.W.B. Robinson, 'Who were "The Saints"?' Chapter 10 in Peter G. Bolt and Mark D. Thompson, eds, *Donald Robinson: Selected Works, Volume 1: Assembling God's People* (Camperdown, N.S.W.: Australian Church Record, 2008), pp. 160-169; originally published in *Reformed Theological Review* 22/2(1963): 45-53.

[6] In the Greek one definite article ('the') governs the whole expression suggesting that one group of people is on view.

[7] The word translated 'saints' is a plural of the adjective meaning 'holy'.

who would rule the world (Dan. 7:22). Yet Paul calls this gathering of mainly non-Jewish Colossians 'holy'. It is not a description of their character or conduct. They are *holy* in the sense that Israel was *holy*: set apart by God and for God.

It is an astonishing privilege to be able to say that this is true of Christian believers today. The arrogance of the claim would be breathtaking were it not all of grace: *we* are *God's holy ones*. Is that how you see yourself, and your fellow believers? Later in the letter we will hear Paul draw out some of the consequences of this wonder: 'Put on then, as God's chosen ones, *holy* and beloved, compassion, kindness, humility, meekness, and patience …' (3:12).

b. Believing

Second, Paul calls them 'believing'. If that is the sense (rather than 'faithful') it demolishes any misunderstanding that 'holy' could be an arrogant claim. For 'believing' is not something you can boast about. He does not say 'circumcised', or 'baptized', but 'believing' or 'trusting'. Believing here means *dependence on another* (namely, Christ Jesus, as we will hear in 1:4). Such faith is not *impressive*, but it is all-important. In a few lines Paul will be saying how he *thanks God* because he had heard of the Colossians' *faith* in Christ Jesus (1:3, 4). A little later, he will underline the supreme importance of continuing in this trusting dependence (1:23). It is a theme that we will hear much more of as this letter unfolds (see 2:6, 7).

c. Brothers

Third, Paul calls these Colossian Gentiles he had never met 'brothers'. As truly as Timothy, Paul's close companion and trusted co-worker, who was with him as he penned this letter (Timothy may have been the scribe who took down the apostle's words, see 4:18), was a brother (1:1), so were they. Christ Jesus, you see, was drawing together a new family in which people – as different as Greek and Jew, barbarian, Scythian, slave and free (3:11) – love one another as brothers (3:14).

We have an awkward language problem here that I doubt we can solve. 'Brothers' in this context, of course, embraces 'brothers and sisters'.[8] The problem is that 'brothers and sisters' categorizes us into two groups at the very point where the biblical language wants us to see one group. We are to understand that we believers are *all* 'brothers'.[9]

d. In Christ

The fourth reality Paul points to is the Colossians' life 'in Christ'. He will say later 'your life is hidden *with Christ* in God' (3:3). The intimate, personal relationship they have come into with Christ Jesus accounts for everything that has been said so far. 'In Christ' they are the holy ones. 'In Christ' their faith rests. 'In Christ' they are brothers. These things, in other words, are only real because of Christ, and because of their relationship to him. We will hear more about this wonder in due course.

e. In Colossae

The fifth thing Paul says here about the Colossian believers is simply that they are 'at [literally "in"] Colossae'. The wonderful theological assertions that have been made (holy, believing, brothers, in Christ) apply to a particular group of real people in a specific location in this world. They are not abstract ideas. They are as real as the people gathered in Philemon's house in Colossae, listening to this letter being read.

3. How to think of life (1:2b)

The identification of the sender and the recipients of the letter is followed by a greeting: **Grace to you and peace from God our Father.** This is what I want you all to know in life, Paul seems to say: Grace and peace from God our Father.

a. Grace

Grace is what characterized the message about Christ Jesus that Epaphras had brought to Colossae some time earlier.

---

[8] Some English versions make this explicit by rendering the Greek word as 'brothers and sisters' (so NRSV and TNIV).

[9] The only way to capture this in contemporary English is with the rather uncommon word 'siblings'. I doubt that it will catch on as a translation!

Paul describes that day as 'the day you ... understood the *grace* of God in truth' (1:6). He will conclude this letter with the simple powerful words, '*Grace* be with you' (4:18).

Of all the forces and influences that surround you, does grace, the grace from God our Father, have its dominant place? Soon we will hear something of the transforming power of this divine kindness in the lives of those touched by it (see 1:3-14).

b. Peace

Peace here is not simply peace of mind, but the peace that the grace of God has established: the peace that has been made by the blood of Christ's cross (see 1:20). Later in the letter Paul will fill out this brief word: 'And let the peace of Christ *rule in your hearts*, to which indeed you were called in one body. And be thankful' (3:15).

'Grace and peace to you from God our Father' is what we know if we are 'in Christ Jesus'.

Conclusion

It would have been something, wouldn't it, to have been in Philemon's house in Colossae on the day Tychicus began to read Paul's letter?

In every way that matters, it is just as important for us today to hear these words from Christ's apostle. There is no good reason why their impact on us should be different from their impact on them. Think carefully, in the light of these opening words, about your own attitude to Christ's apostle Paul, your understanding of yourself as a Christian believer, and what matters to you in life.

Study Questions

1. What attitudes have you encountered, among contemporary Christians, towards Paul? Why is what we think about Paul important?
2. What do we learn about God's 'will' from the three mentions of it in this letter (1:1, 9; 4:12)?

3. Consider what it means to you to be a Christian. How would you describe your relationship to Jesus Christ? How does this compare to Paul's view that the Christians in Colossae are 'in Christ' and therefore
   a. holy,
   b. believing, and
   c. brothers?

4. How do Christians experience
   a. grace,
   b. peace, and
   c. God as 'our Father'?

2

'We always thank God'
(Colossians 1:3-8)

It is altogether too easy, even for Christian believers, to underestimate the significance of Christian faith. Indeed formidable pressures to do so surround us. There are the direct attacks on Christian faith from the angry atheists of our time, as well as the prevailing mood of secularism in the media and institutions of our society, demanding that 'religion' stay where it belongs, on the margins and out of the public discourse. There is the relatively recent distortion of the concept of tolerance, which pretends (and, of course, it can only ever be a pretence) to give equal honour to every belief and culture. There is also the close familiarity and contact that we now have with so many different, sincerely held, religious beliefs. Perhaps we should add the overwhelming problems of today's world, in the face of which *Christian faith* can seem insignificant, impotent and unimportant.

From these and many other directions there is pressure on Christian people to keep their Christian faith 'in its place'. This may mean to keep it to yourself, or to recognize that it is, after all, only a 'belief', or to acknowledge the irrelevance of your faith to the vast majority of people today, whatever it might mean to you personally.

I am sure you could expand this sketch of the pressures around us *to underestimate the significance of Christian faith.*

The form these pressures take may be new, but such powerful pressures are as old as Christian faith itself.

We have begun to listen to the remarkable letter that was brought from Rome to Colossae by Tychicus and Onesimus, and read out (as I imagine it happened) to a small gathering of relatively new Christian believers which met that day in the house of one of their number named Philemon.

The letter is remarkable in several respects. Some of them are hard for us to appreciate, since we are so far from the historical situation, and this letter has become so well known because it is now included in the pages of the Bible. But it is worth the effort to put ourselves in the place of those Colossians that day, gathered in Philemon's home to hear this letter from a Jewish man whom most of them had never met, who was in prison in Rome.[1] He was in prison very largely because he was out of favour with the Jewish authorities. The rather complicated story is told in Acts 21–28. The Colossians listening to Paul's letter were not Jewish (most of them at least), but Paul wrote to them about their faith in the one he called Christ (Messiah) Jesus. Every aspect of this situation was strange!

After the greetings in the first few lines of the letter (which, as we have seen, hint at the astonishing situation that occasioned this letter from the Jewish prisoner of the Roman authorities to this group of Gentiles in the distant town of Colossae), and before the actual purpose of the letter becomes clear (which does not really happen until 2:6), there is a long section that, in effect, presents the astonishing *significance* of what had happened: the significance of their faith in Christ Jesus. That, it seems to me, is the purpose of this introductory section of the letter (1:3– 2:5).

It is very important to notice that Paul chose to take them into that subject by telling them about his prayers. Paul's account of his prayers (1:3-14) has the effect of showing us the astonishing significance of Christian faith. It begins:

---

[1] Paul was, in fact, under house arrest (see Acts 28:16, 30), if we are correct in our assumptions about when he wrote to the Colossians (see the Introduction). Paul describes his circumstances as 'my chains' (Col. 4:18).

> We always thank God, the Father of our Lord Jesus Christ, when we pray for you, since we heard of your faith in Christ Jesus and of the love that you have for all the saints, because of the hope laid up for you in heaven. Of this you have heard before in the word of the truth, the gospel, which has come to you, as indeed in the whole world it is bearing fruit and growing—as it also does among you, since the day you heard it and understood the grace of God in truth, just as you learned it from Epaphras our beloved fellow servant. He is a faithful minister of Christ on your behalf and has made known to us your love in the Spirit (1:3-8).

1. Giving thanks to God (1:3)

We always thank God. Thankfulness to God is a distinctive characteristic of the Christian life. In the course of this letter the subject will be touched on repeatedly. In 1:12 we will hear Paul pray for the recipients of this letter that *they* will be 'giving thanks to the Father', echoing his own thanks expressed here in verse 3. In 2:7 we will hear him exhort his Colossian readers to 'abound in thanksgiving'. A little later in 3:15 he will say simply, 'And be thankful'. He will underline those simple words by speaking of 'thankfulness in your hearts to God' in 3:16, and then 'giving thanks to God the Father' in 3:17. In 4:2, as he urges them to continue in watchful prayer, he cannot help adding 'with thanksgiving'.

Indeed when, on another occasion, Paul set out to describe the plight of the human race from the perspective of the gospel he was proclaiming, he said: 'they did not honour [God] as God or *give thanks* to him' (Rom. 1:21). That is the expression of the futility of the human mind, the dark foolishness of the human heart: to fail to *give thanks* to God our maker.

Therefore it would be misleading to simply hear Paul's expression of his own thanksgiving to God at the beginning of this letter as no more than a formality, as though Paul was simply following the conventions of contemporary letter writing. This is thankfulness of a particular character: an expression of the very change that had taken place in the lives of this group of Colossians. They were now to be people who give thanks to God the Father (1:12). Here Paul expresses his (and Timothy's) thankfulness to God.

Any reader of Paul's letter should reflect on whether he or she shares with Paul this experience of thankfulness to God. Is it a reality (more than a formality) in your life?

What produces this thankfulness to God that should characterize the Christian life? Notice that what we hear from Paul in verse 3 is not of a *general* thankfulness to God for good health, family, friends and food. Indeed his *situation* at this time gave him plenty he could be reasonably *complaining* about. He was incarcerated, probably in Rome. A death sentence was a distinct possibility. We gather from the way he refers to his circumstances later in the letter that his Colossian hearers knew about them (see 4:18). Paul's thankfulness does not come simply from how well things were going for him!

The thankfulness that marks the Christian life (about which we will be hearing so much in this letter) is always much more than a response to happy days. So again I wonder how familiar we are with the kind of thankfulness expressed by Paul here. Perhaps the best test of this is how much we know of this thankfulness when our circumstances in life are not as happy as we might like.

The first striking thing about Paul's words of thankfulness in verse 3 is his description of the God he thanks: **the Father of our Lord Jesus Christ.** If we were not so familiar with such words, perhaps we would notice how remarkable they are. This Jewish monotheist, who knew God was the Father of *Israel*, and that *Israel* was his son (Exod. 4:22; Hosea 11:1), speaks of God as the Father of *Jesus Christ*, whom he also calls 'our Lord'! These expressions are all pointers to the message that Paul had been taking around the Mediterranean world. The message included the following truths about Jesus, the Jewish man who had lived, died and risen from the dead about 30 years earlier in Jerusalem, some 600 miles to the south-east of Colossae:

(1) He was *the Christ*, that is, the long-promised Messiah of Israel;
(2) He was *the Lord*, that is, the ruler of the world; and
(3) He was the Son of God, and that God is therefore called his *Father*.

We could say that one of the most astonishing early consequences of the Christian message was this man, Paul, expressing this thankfulness to the God he now calls 'the Father of our Lord Jesus Christ'.

The second thing to notice about Paul's thankfulness in verse 3 is that it is not about himself or his circumstances at all. It is about 'you' – you Colossians. The very Jewish Paul says 'we always thank God ... **when we pray for you**' – you very gentile Colossians. This is remarkable. In the history of the world, in particular the history of Israel, can you think of an occasion prior to this when a Jewish man spoke like this? This is not how David spoke of the Gentiles ('the nations'[2]) in some of the Psalms (see Ps. 2:1; 9:5, 15, 17, 19, 20). It is not how Isaiah (Isa. 17:13), Jeremiah (Jer. 1:10), or Ezekiel (Ezek. 28:7) spoke. This expression of *thankfulness* from Paul concerning these gentile Colossians is itself one of those wonders of history that calls for an explanation. What had happened to cause this Jewish man to write these words to the group that gathered to hear them in Philemon's house on the day this letter was first read?

2. What had happened? (1:4-5a)

The immediate cause of Paul's thanksgiving to God was something that had happened in the lives of these Gentiles.

Modern Christians can easily miss the fact that a major interest for first-century Christianity, reflected in much of the New Testament, was the relationship between Jew and Gentile, Israel and the nations. The issue is addressed explicitly often enough in the New Testament (e.g.

---

[2] It is important to be aware that the Greek term *ethne*, while often translated 'Gentiles' (e.g. Col. 1:27) is the normal word for 'nations' (e.g. Rom. 4:18). In some cases where 'Gentiles' occurs in English Bibles 'nations' may be a preferable translation.

Rom. 9–11; Gal. 3:28; Eph. 2:11-22). It is in the air, so to speak, almost everywhere in the New Testament.

This is hardly surprising, if we keep in mind the story that the whole Bible tells. Very early in that story we hear of the promise God made to Abraham that God would bless, not only Abraham's descendants, but through them also 'all the families of the earth' (Gen. 12:1-3). We then find that the Bible's climax (the New Testament) involves profoundly the matter of the blessing promised to Abraham reaching beyond Israel (Abraham's descendants) to the nations (or Gentiles). (See, for example, Gal. 3:7-9.)

It is also important to understand this in the light of the message of the Old Testament prophets, who reiterated the promise to Abraham in fresh terms appropriate to their historical context. If Israel's Messiah has now come, and we remember the message of, say, Isaiah, we will be asking: How will *the nations* come to 'the mountain of the house of the LORD' (Isa. 2:2)? How will God's servant bring forth justice to *the nations* (Isa. 42:1), and be a light for *the nations* (Isa. 42:6; 49:6)? How will *the nations* come to the light (Isa. 60:3)? How will the wealth of *the nations* come to Israel (Isa. 60:5, 11; 61:6)?

When Paul heard about what had happened to this group of Colossian Gentiles who had become believers, he understood that God's ancient promises concerning *the nations* were being realized. That is why he gave thanks!

a. Faith

Since we heard of your faith in Christ [Messiah] **Jesus.** It was wonderful enough for Paul and other *Jewish* believers to have recognized Israel's Messiah. That was no small thing, particularly in Paul's case (see his own reflection on this in 1 Timothy 1:12-15). But for these *Gentiles* (from 'the nations') to have been brought into the sphere of influence of Messiah Jesus, and there not to be hostile or afraid, but to believe, to trust, to have confidence – that was an *extraordinary* wonder! That is why we thank God, says Paul.

b. Love

... and of the love that you have for all the saints. We noticed previously that for Paul 'the saints' (or 'the holy ones') is often a reference specifically to Jewish believers in Jesus, the true 'descendants of Abraham'. This is probably the sense here. What he heard was that these Gentiles in Colossae who had come to faith in Messiah Jesus now had a love for those who were the first believers in Jesus, without whom, humanly speaking, they would never have heard of Jesus and to whom they have now been joined as God's people. What a wonder, that between these Gentiles and these Jews there should now be *love*! That is why we thank God, says Paul.

c. Hope

... because of the hope laid up for you in heaven. A little later we will hear more about this 'hope'. It is the privilege of these Gentiles to share in the inheritance of 'the saints' (see 1:12, 22; 3:4). That is why we thank God, says Paul.

The truly thrilling thing as far as we are concerned is that the experience of these Colossians described here by Paul is the experience of Christian people today. We may not be as aware as we should of the Jewish roots of our faith, but we have certainly come under the influence of Messiah Jesus, and in doing so we have come to *faith* in him, to a *love* that crosses boundaries, and to a *hope* that is beyond this world. In other words, what caused Paul's remarkable thanksgiving to God is a reality known to Christian believers today.

We will have the opportunity to think further about this faith and love, caused by hope, as these three themes reappear later in the letter. Here we will briefly notice *how* this wonder had happened in Colossae and *when* it had happened.

3. How had it happened? (1:5b-6a)

Of this [hope] **you have heard before in the word of the truth, the gospel, which has come to you.** The hope that gave rise to their love for all the saints and their faith in Christ Jesus came to them in a message. It was, of course, the very message that Paul himself had been proclaiming throughout the Mediterranean world. Paul's word for this message ('gospel' or 'good news') again provides a glimpse of Paul's understanding of what was happening. It was Isaiah who had used this vocabulary when he promised a day when *good news* would be proclaimed:

> How beautiful upon the mountains
> are the feet of him who brings good news,
> who publishes peace, who brings good news of happiness,
> who publishes salvation,
> who says to Zion, 'Your God reigns'.
> (Isa. 52:7; cf. 40:9; 41:27; 60:6; 61:1).

The message that had now come to Colossae and changed the lives of these Gentiles was the good news, the gospel, of which Isaiah had spoken!

Furthermore, Paul calls this gospel (literally) 'the word of the truth'. Here we should not overlook the verbal character. The gospel came (and comes) to people in words. It must be spoken (cf. Rom. 10:14). They are, of course, not just any words, but the words that tell us 'the truth' – the truth about God and his purposes.

... as indeed in the whole world it is bearing fruit and growing – as it also does among you. That way of putting it seems to reflect God's wonderful purpose from the beginning of creation. Then God said to mankind, 'Be fruitful and multiply and fill the earth' (Gen. 1:28). God's promise to Abraham and the patriarchs was expressed in similar terms (see Gen. 15:5; 22:17; 26:4; Exod. 1:7) which indicated that through Abraham's descendants God would bring his good creation purpose to pass: they would, so to speak, be fruitful and multiply and fill the earth, and thus bring blessing to the nations of the world. The prophets also spoke in language like this, echoing the promise to Abraham, and the word of blessing in Genesis 1:28 (see Jer. 33:22).

It does seem that Paul understood that God's purpose to bless the whole world and the human race he had created, the nations of the world, was now being realized as the gospel was *being fruitful* and *growing* there in Colossae and in the whole world.

'In the whole world' may seem to us a rather over-stated claim for the spread of the gospel at this time (cf. 1:23!). Yet the utter wonder that people were being brought into the kingdom of Jesus Christ (1:13), without ethnic distinctions (3:11) or geographical restriction, was evidenced by what had happened when the gospel had come to Colossae.

4. When had it happened? (1:6b-8)

... since the day you heard it and understood the grace of God in truth ... Do not overlook the fact that the Colossians had benefited from the gospel by *hearing* and *understanding*. It would be wrong to reduce Christian experience to the intellectual grasping of ideas, but it would be equally wrong to ignore the fundamental place of *hearing* the word of the truth and *understanding* it. This can never be a merely intellectual experience, for what is understood is 'the grace of God'. The message about Jesus Christ is the truth about God's grace.

... just as you learned it from Epaphras. The wonder of the gospel bearing fruit there in Colossae had come about by the faithful Epaphras who had told his fellow Colossians the news he had heard and learned, almost certainly from Paul, probably when Paul had been in Ephesus.

Paul's affection for Epaphras and his confidence in him are conveyed in the warm designation **our beloved fellow servant.** Epaphras shared with Paul the status of a slave (as the word can be translated) of Jesus Christ (cf. Rom. 1:1; Gal. 1:10; Phil. 1:1; Titus 1:1).

It is most important to underline the faithfulness of Epaphras. This implies Paul's full confidence in the gospel Epaphras had brought to Colossae. **He is a faithful minister** [or, servant[3]] **of Christ on your** [possibly, our[4]] **behalf ...** If

---

[3] Two different Greek words are used in verse 7, translated in the ESV by 'servant' and 'minister'. However both are close in meaning and refer to one who renders service.

[4] As the ESV footnote indicates, some Greek manuscripts have 'on your behalf', while others have 'on our behalf'.

the reading should be 'on your behalf' Paul is emphasizing that the Colossians were the beneficiaries of the labours of Epaphras (see 4:12). If Paul wrote 'on our behalf' he was underlining that Epaphras bringing the gospel to Colossae was an extension, so to speak, of Paul's own gospel work.

Epaphras had now brought news to Paul in his Roman prison of what had happened when he brought the gospel to Colossae. He **has made known to us your love in the Spirit.** Epaphras told Paul of the fruit of the Holy Spirit in the lives of these Colossians: their love. It was, as Paul has said in verse 4, 'for all the saints'.

Conclusion

Epaphras did what countless 'faithful ministers (servants) of Christ' have done since that day. The wonder that occurred in Colossae continues to happen as people in every place 'understand the grace of God in truth'. Who did for *you* what Epaphras did for the Colossians? For whom have you been an Epaphras? Can you therefore share in Paul's thrilled thankfulness to God?

Study Questions

1. Why is thanking God important for Christians? How can we learn to be thankful, as Paul was thankful? What might cause us to be less thankful than we ought?
2. Consider how knowing God as 'the Father of our Lord Jesus Christ' is the distinctive experience of Christianity.
3. How is Christian hope the cause of faith and love (see '*because of* the hope' in v. 5)?
4. Make a note of everything that we learn about 'the gospel' from Colossians 1:3-8. Are all these things true of the gospel as you have heard it?
5. What do we know about the Christian experience of the believers in Colossae from Colossians 1:3-8?

In your own words describe how your experience is like and/or unlike theirs.

6. How does Paul's view of *the gospel* shape his attitude towards *the nations*? How should our view of the gospel affect our attitude to so-called missionary work?
7. What is the importance of the relationship between Jewish and gentile Christians today?

3

'We have not Ceased to Pray for you'
(Colossians 1:9-14)

We return to the gathering in the home of Philemon in the Lycus Valley town of Colossae. Tychicus has begun to read the letter he and Onesimus had brought all the way from Paul in Rome. We have heard Paul begin to tell them of his prayers. It is our privilege to listen in as Tychicus continues to read:

> And so, from the day we heard, we have not ceased to pray for you, asking that you may be filled with the knowledge of his will in all spiritual wisdom and understanding, so as to walk in a manner worthy of the Lord, fully pleasing to him, bearing fruit in every good work and increasing in the knowledge of God. May you be strengthened with all power, according to his glorious might, for all endurance and patience with joy, giving thanks to the Father, who has qualified you to share in the inheritance of the saints in light. He has delivered us from the domain of darkness and transferred us to the kingdom of his beloved Son, in whom we have redemption, the forgiveness of sins (1:9-14).

1. Paul's praying (1:9a)

As Paul begins to speak about his praying in verse 9, he indicates something about *why* he prayed, and something about *how* he prayed.

a. Why he prayed

And so (literally, 'Because of this'; TNIV, 'For this reason') points us back to the preceding paragraph to indicate *why* Paul prayed in the way he is about to describe. The preceding paragraph (1:3-8) is Paul's report of how he was constantly *thanking* God. In other words, there is a connection between Paul's *thankfulness* and his *prayerfulness*. He always gives thanks to God (1:3) and *that is why* he does not cease to pray (1:9).

The connection was already there in verse 3: 'We always *thank God,* the Father of our Lord Jesus Christ, *when we pray for you* …' We will see shortly that Paul's report of his praying will end up taking us back to this subject of *giving thanks*. He will tell us in verse 12 that the culmination of his prayers is asking that the Colossians themselves will be joining him in giving thanks to God the Father.

This connection between thankfulness and prayerfulness is vital. On the one hand, we see that Paul's own praying for the Colossian believers was not just from a sense of duty. There is nothing wrong with a sense of duty, of course. I am not criticizing anyone who prays out of a sense of duty. Yet can you see that Paul's prayers were motivated by *more than* duty? Furthermore, it was not just that Paul was worried, anxious or fearful for these believers. He may have been, and there is nothing wrong with responding to our fears and anxieties by praying. Indeed, what better way is there to respond to concerns we feel? Again, do you see that there is *more than* anxiety behind Paul's prayers here?

Paul was constantly praying for these believers *because of what God had already done*. He was always thanking God for his actions (1:3), and *that is why* he was always praying for them (1:9). It was Paul's *thankfulness* to God that moved him to *pray*. We will come back to this in a moment, after we see something about *how* he prayed.

b. How he prayed

… from the day we heard, we have not ceased to pray for you, asking … Paul generally distinguishes *thanksgiving* and *prayer*. Giving thanks to God is one thing, and he was constantly doing that. But prayer was another thing, and he was constantly doing that as well. For Paul, prayer was asking. I cannot see any point in being overly fussy about the terms. We usually speak of 'praying' to cover all forms of speaking to our heavenly Father. But for Paul 'to pray' generally meant 'asking'.

There is, therefore, something of a puzzle here. The close connection between *thanking* and *asking* is strange. I suspect that in our own experience we find *thanking* and *asking* tend to be alternatives. I am full of thanks to God when all is well. The more *thankful* I am, the less there is to *ask* for. On the other hand, when I am desperate, when I am worried, and I am begging God to act, then I am least motivated by thankfulness. As I thank God for good health, I am not usually praying for healing. As I cry out for deliverance from some threat, you can be reasonably sure that at that moment thankfulness is not at the front of my consciousness.

What then (if I may put it like this) is the *logic* of Paul's praying? *Because* he was so overwhelmingly *thankful* to God (vv. 3-8), he did not stop *asking* (vv. 9-14). The answer to our question lies in the connection between *what he was thankful about* and *what he prayed for*.

So let us listen carefully to what he was constantly asking for, and notice the connections to what he was so thankful for.

2. What Paul prayed for (1:9b-12a)

What Paul asked for is the subject of one of his extraordinary long sentences, which in my edition of the Greek text runs from verse 9 all the way to verse 20![1]

a. Knowledge of his will

The fundamental request is indicated in verse 9b: **that you may be filled with the knowledge of his will.** This is what Paul *asked for* because of what he *thanked God for*. Let us begin to see the connection.

What Paul thanked God for in verses 3-8 was the astonishing fact that when his friend Epaphras had come

---

1. English translations break Paul's long sentence into shorter sentences to make it easier for English speakers (who are not used to such long sentences!) to read.

to Colossae some time earlier (v. 7) and told them 'the word of the truth, the gospel' (v. 5), these gentile Colossians had heard and understood the grace of God in truth (v. 6). Because of the hope laid up in heaven of which this gospel spoke (v. 5), they came to faith in Messiah Jesus and to love for God's people (v. 4), whom they had now joined. And more than that, this wonder in Colossae was but one local instance of a wonder that was taking place, Paul tells them, in the whole world, as this gospel was bearing fruit and growing (v. 6). *That* is why Paul was constantly thanking God.

And that is why Paul kept asking that they may be *filled with the knowledge of God's will*. 'God's will' is God's great and gracious purpose for his whole creation. Elsewhere Paul speaks of 'the mystery of *his will* according to his good pleasure, which he purposed in Christ, to be put into effect when the times reach their fulfilment – *to bring unity to all things in heaven and on earth under Christ*' (Eph. 1:9-10, emphasis added).

This *will of God* had been behind the Old Testament history of Israel. From the promise to Abraham (Gen. 12:1-3) to the words of the prophets (e.g. Isa. 2:2-5), there had been clear indications that God intended, from the beginning, to bless the nations of the whole world. How he would do so was certainly a mystery, but now the word of the truth, the gospel, was bearing fruit and growing *in the whole world* (Col. 1:6).

The gospel 'bearing fruit and growing' in the whole world (and what had happened in Colossae was one instance of this) was, as we have seen, a realization of *God's will* from the beginning of creation (cf. Gen 1:28). *Because* that was so (that is what Paul was so thankful to God about), he did not cease to pray for these Colossian believers asking 'that you may be *filled with the knowledge of his will*'.

The acquisition of knowledge is a common human pursuit. What you know can be that which distinguishes you from others. It may qualify you for certain work that others cannot do: they do not know what you know. Often knowledge is power. Ignorance is rarely bliss. But if God is blessing the whole world through the word of the truth, the gospel, then Paul says, I want you to *know* this reality, and know it fully. I am constantly asking that you will be filled with *that* knowledge.

On the one hand, we should notice that this is not esoteric knowledge, for the elite, the clever, or just the academics. This is knowledge with which Paul wants every believer to be filled. It is not a complex matter that only a few can grasp, nor an abstract matter that only some minds can manage. It is not knowledge that you have to go to a theological college to learn. Indeed, it is possible to gain a higher degree in theology, and still lack this knowledge. It is knowledge of God's will, of God's grace, of God's truth. To be *filled* with this knowledge will mean being deeply affected by the reality you know.

On the other hand, it is wrong to miss the importance of the human mind in this attaining of knowledge. Paul's thanks and prayer have an important emphasis on *understanding* and *knowledge*. The Colossians had 'heard and understood' what they had learnt from Epaphras (1:6). Now Paul tells them that he prays for them to be filled with *knowledge*. Hearing, learning, understanding, knowing – these are fundamentally spiritual activities, if what is learnt is *God's will – God's grace – God's truth*.

Therefore, do not underestimate the importance of the *study* of the things of God. It is worth noticing how the experience of *understanding* and *knowledge* will recur through this letter. In 2:2 Paul speaks of his struggle to see these Colossians and many others 'reach all the riches of full assurance of *understanding and the knowledge* of God's mystery'. In 2:3, that mystery is Christ 'in whom are hidden all the treasures of *wisdom and knowledge*'. In 3:10 the believers are told that they are 'being renewed in *knowledge*'.

Do not be deluded with the thought that there is some kind of tension or opposition between the intellectual and the spiritual. Such a thought creeps in under many guises: that you put the intellect to one side in order to be spiritual, that your *study* of God's Word and your *prayers* are unrelated, that preaching with spiritual power will be something other than teaching.

To be filled with the knowledge of God's will is the best possible equipment for life, for such knowledge brings us **all**

spiritual wisdom and understanding. The Old Testament prophets knew that the Messiah would be marked by the Spirit of wisdom and understanding (Isa. 11:2). In the Old Testament more generally *wisdom and understanding* are God's purpose for human life: humbly and sensibly living in God's world as God intends.

Here Paul draws a close link between Spirit-given wisdom and understanding on the one hand and being filled with the knowledge of God's will on the other. This is another way of saying (as he will say in 2:3) that in Christ (who is at the centre of God's will) are hidden all the treasures of wisdom and knowledge. To know Christ is to find the key to understanding all things.

b. The purpose of this knowledge

The purpose of this knowledge is its practical outcome: **so as to walk in a manner worthy of the Lord, fully pleasing to him.** Knowing God's will transforms how you live.

c. The character of this life

The next few lines sketch out what walking worthily of the Lord, fully pleasing him, means. They are not exhaustive, but they are very informative. The outcome of being filled with the knowledge of God's will is (1) bearing fruit, (2) growing, (3) being empowered, and (4) giving thanks.

(i) bearing fruit

... bearing fruit in every good work. How remarkable that Paul would expect these gentile Colossians to be pleasing the Lord with all kinds of good works. But that is precisely what was happening. As the gospel was bearing fruit in the whole world in the form of believers (1:6), they were to be bearing fruit in the form of good works (1:10)! That is what the knowledge that matters (knowledge of God's will) produces.

(ii) growing

... and increasing [or 'growing'[2]] **in the knowledge of God.** This is wonderfully circular. It is how the Christian life works. As we are filled with the knowledge of God's will,

[2] Exactly the same Greek word as the one translated 'growing' in 1:6.

we live more and more in the way that pleases God, bearing good fruit, and so we grow in the knowledge of God!

Notice again that as in verse 6 it was *the gospel* that was bearing fruit and growing in the whole world, so now it is *the believers* (the fruit of the gospel) whose lives are to be bearing fruit and growing there in Colossae. Still the vocabulary echoes Genesis 1:28 and the reverberations of that verse through the Old Testament. God's creation purpose of blessing the whole world is being realized as the knowledge of his will shapes the lives of those who come to faith in Christ Jesus.

(iii) being empowered

May you be strengthened with all power, according to his glorious might, for all endurance and patience … If being filled with the knowledge of God's will bears fruit in good works, it is also empowering. The might of God's glory is the source of this power. If those Colossian believers were becoming familiar with the Old Testament Scriptures – as I am sure that by now they were – they would be familiar with God's glory. It had accompanied Israel in the early days (Exod. 40:36-38) and had filled the tabernacle and the temple (Exod. 40:34, 35; 1 Kings 8:11). Ezekiel had seen the glory by the River Kebar (Ezek. 1:28).

I am praying, says Paul, that you will be so filled with the knowledge of God's will that the might of the glory of the Lord will fully empower you. Is that not an extraordinary thing to pray?

What will that mighty power enable me to do? Answer: It will be seen in 'all endurance and patience with joy'! This is not a common understanding of spiritual power: endurance in impossible situations; patience with impossible people.[3] But it is the power you will know when you are filled with the knowledge of God's will.

(iv) giving thanks

… giving thanks to the Father. We have come full circle. Paul's thankfulness in verses 3-8 led to his prayer in

---

[3] N.T. Wright, *The Epistles of Paul to the Colossians and to Philemon* (Leicester: Inter-Varsity Press, 1986), p. 60.

verses 9-12, which culminates in his asking that the Colossians will share in his thankfulness.

We have in these few lines a wonderful description of the Christian life: the fruit that the gospel was bearing in the whole world and which it continues to bear today. Reflect on the fact that this prayer for the Colossian believers would also be Paul's prayer for you: that you would be filled with the knowledge of God's will, so that your living would be transformed by this knowledge, actually doing good, and knowing God more and more, strengthened to endure and remain joyfully patient, and thanking God.

I have no doubt that Paul told the Colossians what he was constantly praying for *so that* they would be clear about what *they* should be longing for, and so that they would not make the mistake of underestimating the astonishing significance of this faith.

3. Again — Why? (1:12b-14)

Now that Paul has returned to the subject of giving thanks to God, he cannot stop himself from showing again why such thankfulness to God must happen. He takes us behind the account in verses 3-8 of the gospel doing its wonderful work through the world. He goes deeper into the work of God that has made possible the work of the gospel.

This is indicated simply in the wonderful words in verse 12, 'giving thanks to *the Father*.' In verse 3 Paul called God the 'Father of our Lord Jesus Christ.' In verse 2 he spoke of 'God *our* Father.' How is it that Paul, let alone these Colossian Gentiles, could know God as Father and thank him *as Father*? For that is exactly what God has made possible. Paul now gives a profound outline of what God has done.

a. What God has done for 'you'

... who has qualified you to share in the inheritance of the saints in light. 'The inheritance of the saints' is a reference to God's promised blessings to his people.[4] It was, in the

[4] We noted earlier (when discussing 1:2) that Paul often uses the word 'saints' in reference to Jewish believers in Jesus. See D.W.B. Robinson, 'Who were "The

Old Testament, especially the land God gave to his people Israel that was their 'inheritance' (Num. 26:53; Deut. 4:21; Josh. 11:23; 1 Kings 8:36; Ezra 9:12; Ps. 105:11; Ezek. 45:1; Acts 13:19). The inheritance was theirs by virtue of their being the people to whom God had promised it. Jewish people like Paul had now come to know the fulfilment of that inheritance, not now in the land of Canaan, but in heaven, 'in light'. But of course the gentile Colossians had no claim on the inheritance. They were not 'qualified' to have any claim on the inheritance promised to God's people. They were strangers to the covenants of promise (Eph. 2:12). But – wonder of wonders! – God has qualified *you* (yes, you *Gentiles*) to share in the inheritance of his people!

b. What God has done for 'us'

What is the 'inheritance' of God's people 'in light'? **He has delivered us from the domain of darkness and transferred us to the kingdom of his beloved Son, in whom we have redemption, the forgiveness of sins.** Jewish people, like Paul, who had received Jesus as Lord and Messiah had received the fulfilment of Israel's experience. The Old Testament experience of Israel was deliverance from the tyranny of Pharaoh and transference eventually to the kingdom of David. That redemption has now come to its fulfilment: a redemption on another level. Bondage to Pharaoh had been one historic expression of the deeper bondage into which the human race has fallen: the tyranny of sin and death, the dominion of darkness. The redemption of those who now have Jesus as their King is nothing less than the forgiveness of sins. And he has qualified *you* (gentile Colossians) to share in *our* inheritance in light, says the Jewish Paul.

How could that be? How has that happened? That will be explained by Paul in the verses that follow.

Saints"?', Chapter 10 in Peter G. Bolt and Mark D. Thompson, eds, *Donald Robinson: Selected Works, Volume 1: Assembling God's People* (Camperdown, N.S.W.: Australian Church Record, 2008), pages 160-169; originally published in *Reformed Theological Review* 22/2(1963): 45-53.

Conclusion

Let us return to the thoughts with which we began our previous chapter. It *is* altogether too easy to under-estimate the significance of the Christian faith. One way to beat such foolishness would be to make Paul's prayer in Colossians 1:9-14 our prayer – to make these things our longings. But we will only do that by being full of thankfulness at what God has done in Jesus Christ (1:3-8). One way to do that would be to read on to the end of Paul's long and astonishing sentence (1:9-20), which we will do in our next chapter.

Study Questions

1. Why does Paul's thankfulness to God lead him to be constantly praying (asking)?
2. What does it mean to be 'filled with the knowledge of God's will'? How can that happen?
3. Can you think of some practical examples of how being 'filled with the knowledge of God's will' could equip you with 'wisdom and understanding' for living, and lead to doing 'good works'?
4. From his prayer, how does Paul expect believers to experience God's power? What will be the effect of God's power in their lives? Have you known God's power in this way?
5. What makes Gentiles (like the Colossians, and like many readers of this commentary) unqualified to share in the inheritance Paul speaks of in verse 12? How has God 'qualified' them?
6. Look back over Colossians 1:3-14 and consider what made Paul so excited to hear of the faith of the believers in Colossae? Do you share his excitement?

4

Christ and All Things
(Colossians 1:15-20)

Today's atheistic secularists consistently assume that the future of the human race will be the complete triumph of secularism and the abolition of every kind of belief in God. 'Enlightened understanding' demands no less than the abolition of any belief not founded on the empirical methods of science. The arrogance of the secularist claim that their own understanding of reality is superior to all others is seldom noted. It is staggering nonetheless.

They are wrong. Just how wrong could be argued and illustrated from statistics and observations that show that the human race is becoming more, not less, 'religious'. However, we are about to see, from a remarkable section of Paul's letter to the early Christian believers in Colossae, that their error is deeper and far more serious.

When Paul wrote this short letter (in the early 60s of the first century), his first concern was to ensure that his readers grasped the full significance of what they had come to believe, and that they were not deceived by anything in the intellectual climate of their day that undermined their new faith. It is sometimes supposed that there was a specific false teaching being promoted in the Colossae region that was threatening the faith of these people. I think this is unlikely.[1] In contrast to Paul's letters to the believers in Galatia, or Corinth, or even Philippi, this letter does not seem to signal the presence of any particular threat.[2] Paul had heard of their faith and their love (1:4, 8; 2:5). He knew well that this faith is always under attack. He had a thorough knowledge of the world of alternative ideas in which he and the Colossians lived. Aware of these general and ever-present challenges to Christian faith, but not (in my opinion) of any particular crisis, he wrote this letter, which powerfully presents the reality of what God has done in Jesus Christ, what he is now doing in the whole world through the gospel, and where it will all end.[3]

The letter has now come down to us in the New Testament and continues to be a powerful message that stands against the challenging intellectual climate of every age, including today's atheistic secularists.

In verses 15 to 20 of the first chapter of this letter, we come to its heart, from which everything else will flow. If we hear carefully, understand clearly, and believe firmly what the apostle has written here, we will be equipped for every threat and challenge that life might bring. That is a bold claim. It is warranted by this remarkable portion of God's Word.

In the original (as we noted previously) 1:15-20 is the second half of one long sentence that began at 1:9. The

---

[1] See the Introduction. Many commentators argue that there was a particular false teaching that was threatening the faith of the believers in Colossae. A cogent argument against this hypothesis is presented by M.D. Hooker, 'Were there false teachers in Colossae?' *Christ and the Spirit in the New Testament: Studies in Honour of Charles Francis Digby Moule*, ed. B. Lindars and S.S. Smalley (Cambridge: Cambridge University Press, 1973), pp. 315-331.

[2] There is nothing in the letter to Colossae that corresponds, for example, to Galatians 1:9; 3:1; 2 Corinthians 11:4, 5; Philippians 3:2.

[3] Those who believe that Colossians was written to counter some particular false teaching(s) in Colossae tend to use this hypothesis to explain what Paul says at various points. Attempts are made to reconstruct at least some aspects of the false teaching by 'mirror-reading', that is by supposing that 'Paul said X because the false teachers were saying the opposite of X.' If (as I suppose) there were no particular false teaching in Colossae, but simply the general challenges to Christian faith that Paul's world presented we may propose that Paul said what he said simply because it was true and important!

connection with what precedes it should not be lost. Here Paul speaks of the one 'in whom we have redemption, the forgiveness of sins' (1:14), into whose kingdom the Father has transferred us, having delivered us from the domain of darkness (1:13). This is why Paul prayed that his readers would be joyfully giving thanks to the Father (1:12). This is God's will, which Paul was praying they would know fully (1:9). In this context he wrote verses 15-20.

Here I have set out these verses with some indication of their semi-poetic character. I have employed various forms of underlining to draw attention to repeated words and phrases (although sometimes this is obscured in the English translation).

He is
    the image of the invisible God,
    the firstborn of all creation.
        For by him all things were created,
            in heaven and on earth,
            visible and invisible,
            whether thrones or dominions or rulers or authorities
        – all things were created through him and for him.

And he is
    before all things,
    and in him all things hold together.

And he is
    the head of the body,
    the church.

He is
    the beginning,
    the firstborn from the dead,
        that in everything he might be pre-eminent.
            For in him all the fullness of God was pleased to dwell,
            and through him to reconcile to himself all things,
                whether on earth or in heaven,
            making peace by the blood of his cross (1:15-20).

I have often found the task of expounding God's Word overwhelming. What overwhelms me is a profound sense of inadequacy, not for the task of speaking or writing as such. It is the astonishing responsibility of having to say something remotely worthy of the words of Scripture that it is one's task to expound. Perhaps this is a small taste of what Paul meant when he said, 'Who is sufficient for these things?' (2 Cor. 2:16). I cannot remember being more deeply overwhelmed, in this way, than I am with the extraordinary words that are before us here in 1:15-20.

Let us spend a little time thinking in general terms about this amazing passage before we come to listen to what it says in detail.

The context of this passage

The very fact that these ideas were expressed as early as A.D. 60-something is astonishing. How was it that these extraordinary and extravagant things could be said about a man so soon after he had died in the most humiliating, shameful, indeed disgraceful, circumstances? The fact that these words were written within 30 years of Jesus' death by crucifixion 'fairly cries out for some explanation'.[4]

The resurrection of Jesus is the explanation, but even then the words are breathtaking. The words, if their claim is taken seriously, are overwhelming.

These lines of Paul's letter are so striking that they have often attracted the attention of biblical scholars, some of whom have (it seems to me) been so dazzled by the passage itself that they have lost sight of what it is here *for*. This is a little odd, because it is a safe assumption that the first half of the sentence, that runs from verse 9 to verse 20, has something to do with why the second half is there!

It is, therefore, worth noticing that 1:15-20 belongs to Paul's report of his praying for the Colossian believers that began in verse 9. What he says in verses 15-20, in other words, is related to what Paul was praying for in verses 9-12: in particular that his readers will be giving thanks to the

[4] C.F.D. Moule, *The Epistles of Paul the Apostle to the Colossians and to Philemon* (Cambridge: Cambridge University Press, 1968), p. 59.

Father (1:12), but also that they may be filled with the knowledge of God's will (1:9).

If we press the question, and ask what it was that called for *such* a big statement about Christ *here*, at *this* point in *this* letter to *these* believers in Colossae, I take it that the answer lies in Paul's purpose in the long introduction to his letter that runs from 1:3 to 2:5. I have suggested that there Paul was putting before those Colossian believers *the astonishing significance of their faith in Christ Jesus*. God has acted so that the nations (like these Gentiles in Colossae) were *qualified* to share in the inheritance of God's people (1:12b). How is it that Greeks and barbarians and Scythians (3:11), indeed people of every nation on earth, can be qualified to share in the inheritance of *God's people*? How is it, in other words, that the message Epaphras had brought to his friends and neighbours in Colossae was bearing fruit and growing *in the whole world* (1:6)?

After 2,000 years it is all too easy for us to take this marvel for granted, so that we do not easily see how utterly astonishing it is. We refer to Christianity as a 'world religion'. But that is not what we are talking about here. In this sense Christianity was no 'world religion' in A.D. 60. It was little more than a rather energetic Jewish sect, apparently attracting some interest from a number of non-Jewish people in some places around the Mediterranean world. That would have been a fair description of the phenomenon, as it seemed.

We need to recognize that the claim made by Paul in this letter is as astounding today as it was on that day when this letter was first read to the small gathering in Philemon's house, by Tychicus, who had brought the letter from Rome. The light has dawned, *for the whole world* (1:6). The news about Jesus Christ, the word of truth (1:5), the gospel, is now the most important force in world history! The Creator intended the human race to *be fruitful and multiply*. Now his purpose for the whole human race is being realized as the gospel of Christ *bears fruit and grows* throughout the world and in the lives of those who come to faith in our Lord Jesus Christ (1:6, 10). The time has come in the sorry history of the world for the darkness to give way to light (see 1:12, 13), for hostility to give way to peace (1:20), for ignorance to give way to knowledge (1:9), for evil to give way to good (1:10), for lies to give way to truth (1:5), for foolishness to give way to wisdom (1:28). Everywhere! In every nation, in every city, in every village – in the whole world. That is what is happening.

Do you believe that? Or do you feel just a little wobbly in the face of the attacks on Christian faith by the angry atheist secularists? Do you suspect, perhaps, that atheistic secularism may be a more powerful force than the Christian gospel in today's world?

It is (in my opinion) with such concerns (in a first-century form) that, at precisely *this* point of his letter, the apostle penned the astonishing words that are now before us in 1:15-20. The staggering significance of *this* group of people in Colossae coming to faith in Christ Jesus, the staggering significance of *every* group of people who come to faith in Christ Jesus, is because of who Christ Jesus is.

If today *we* are going to give thanks to the Father as we ought (1:12), if we are going to grasp at all the stunning importance of what has happened to *us* as we trust in Christ, bear fruit in good works, endure patiently, and as the gospel bears fruit in the whole world, we need to understand the profound dimensions of *who Jesus Christ is* as he is held out before us in these words.

The structure of this passage

Before we listen to *what* is said in Colossians 1:15-20, there is just one more thing to notice about the passage. It is difficult not to be also struck by the *way* in which it speaks. At the risk of oversimplifying the magnificence of the passage, I think it is helpful to see how it has two halves each with a similar three-part structure.

The first half (1:15-17) is about *Christ and the creation of all things*. The second half (1:18-20) is about *Christ and the reconciliation of all things*.

The first half (*Christ and the creation of all things*) has three parts:

A. A *concise statement of who Christ is* in relation to the creation of all things (v. 15), beginning with the words 'He is …'
B. An explanation (v. 16) of *why* he is who he is, beginning with the words 'For by [literally 'in'] him …'
C. A *summary* of all this (v. 17), beginning with the words 'And he is …'

The second half (*Christ and the reconciliation of all things*) has three corresponding parts, in a different order:

C. A *summary* of what is to follow (v. 18a), beginning again with the words 'and he is …'
A. A *concise statement of who he is* in relation to the reconciliation of all things (v. 18b), beginning as before with the words 'He is …'
B. Another explanation (vv. 19, 20) of *why* he is who he is, beginning again with the words 'For in him …'

The careful, almost poetic, structure of the passage has led to speculations that it might be an adaptation of an early Christian hymn. I find that suggestion thoroughly unpersuasive. Is it not inherently *probable* that one of the New Testament's most magnificent statements about Christ originated from the 'apostle of Christ Jesus by the will of God' (1:1), rather than an anonymous hymn writer (with all due respect to anonymous hymn writers!)? We have no reason to think that poetic writing was beyond Paul.

These preliminaries are no more than that. Aware of the context, and observing the structure, it is time to listen carefully to what is said in this extraordinary passage.

1. Christ and the creation of all things (1:15-17)

a. Who he is

He represents a relative pronoun in Greek ('who'). Remember that we are still reading the single long sentence that began in 1:9. The antecedent of 'who' is '[the Father's] beloved Son' (1:13b). This is the one 'in whom', says Paul, 'we have redemption, the forgiveness of sins' (1:14). This, of course, is none other than 'our Lord Jesus Christ' (see 1:3).

It is as though to reveal the astonishing significance of this redemption and forgiveness that Paul now starkly says that this Son **is the image of the invisible God.** On the one hand, this means that God, whom no one can see, was *visibly* represented in the person of Jesus Christ. It was not simply that Jesus *taught* about God. He was himself the 'image', the visible, tangible, representation of God himself. As Jesus said, 'Whoever has seen me has seen the Father' (John 14:9).

On the other hand, we must remember that 'the image of God' is what mankind was created to be. 'In the image of God he created him; male and female he created them' (Gen. 1:27). Human beings have had a long history of falling short of what we were intended to be, but without qualification, without any exaggeration whatsoever, Paul can say of Jesus that he *is* 'the image of God'. He is the exact representation of God *and* the perfect realization of humanity: 'the image of the invisible God.'

More than that, he is **the firstborn of all creation.** It would not have been inappropriate to describe Adam as 'the firstborn of all creation', not of course in the sense that he was the first created thing. He was not. According to Genesis 1 he was the *culmination* of creation. Genesis 1 emphasizes the priority of mankind (Hebrew *adam*) in that they were to have dominion over all things. All things were created, in an important sense, for the benefit of mankind. We might say that all creation was given to mankind as his inheritance. The word 'firstborn' has this sense of priority, not necessarily referring to time, but more specifically to status and rank, perhaps with connotations to do with inheritance.

In due course God's chosen people Israel were called God's 'firstborn' (Exod. 4:22; Jer. 31:9). Again this spoke of Israel's privileged position among all the nations. It had to do with Israel's priority, not so much in time as in status. It implied an inheritance. In Psalm 89 God's promise to Israel's king was expressed like this: 'I will make him the firstborn, the highest of the kings of the earth' (Ps. 89:27). The Arians of the fourth century, like the Jehovah's Witnesses today, took Colossians 1:15 to indicate that the Son of God was a created being. They are guilty of ignoring the context, as we will see.

b. Why

Verse 15 (who Christ is: 'the image of the invisible God, the firstborn of all creation') is supported by verse 16: an explanation *why* he is properly so described, beginning with the words 'For in [ESV by] him.'

For by him all things were created. All creation is profoundly related to Christ. Christ is clearly distinguished from 'all (created) things'. This is the part of the context the Arians most obviously overlooked. If 'all things' were created by him, then he is clearly not included in the 'all things' that have been created. There is nothing in all creation that is independent of him.

As though to make sure that we understand the phrase 'all things' Paul emphasizes that there are no limits to what is included: **in heaven and on earth** (it does not matter where), **visible and invisible** (not just the things we are aware of but the things beyond our senses and knowledge). And 'all things' includes all the powers that exercise any influence anywhere: **whether thrones or dominions or rulers or authorities.** It is not important to precisely define each of these terms. Paul's purpose is to make sure we understand that by 'all things' he means *all things*: **all things were created through him and for him.**

Three prepositions in verse 16 indicate the comprehensiveness of Christ's supremacy over all creation, but also his deep involvement with all creation. All things were created by God[5] '*in* him', '*through* him' and '*for* him'. 'In him' indicates that all things were created within Christ's sphere of influence, so to speak. 'Through him' means that he was God's powerful agent in creation: he was the word by which God created all things (cf. Ps. 33:6 and John 1:3); he was the wisdom of God that accomplished the creation of all things (cf. Prov. 8:27-31 and 1 Cor. 1:24). 'For him' says that the purpose and goal of all things lies in their relation to him.

Here is the ultimate unity of *everything*. This is not a piece of abstract philosophy. Paul is speaking, astonishingly, of

---

[5] The passive verb 'were created' implies God is the subject. 'In him' is therefore a better translation than the ESV 'by him'.

the one who had recently been executed in Jerusalem, and who had risen from the dead, and appeared to Paul on the road to Damascus. This is what he is saying about him: *All things* have their origin, existence and purpose *in him*!

c. Summary

In verse 17 there is a summary of this first half of our passage, beginning 'And he is'. **And he is before all things, and in him all things hold together.** There is something radically bigger here than any theory of 'intelligent design'! The man who was crucified about thirty years before these words were written is said to be prior to all created existence, both in the temporal sense, but more importantly in his supremacy. The universe, and whatever else exists, owes its being, continuation and coherence to him!

Do you begin to see that coming to trust *him* is highly significant? Do you see why the message about him is 'the word of the truth' (1:5) and that it is a word that must impact the whole world (1:6), indeed all creation under heaven (1:23)?

2. Christ and the reconciliation of all things (1:18-20)

The second half of our passage has three sections corresponding in form to the three in the first half, but going beyond them to speak of *Christ and the reconciliation of all things*.

a. Summary

This time we begin with the summary of what is about to be said, introduced again by 'And he is' (compare 1:17).

And he is the head of the body, the church. Do you sense the shock of the shift of focus? From his eternal priority to *all things*, his unique role in the *origin* of all things, and his supreme position in the *integration* of all things and their final *destiny*, we turn to the fact that he is 'the head' of something called 'the church'. The word usually translated 'church' in English Bibles means, quite simply, an 'assembly' or 'gathering' of people. What is this 'assembly' of which Christ is the 'head'?

The first half of the passage (1:15-17) could have led us to expect something like, 'he is the head of the universe', or 'he is the head of the totality of all things'. 'Head' would be a very fitting metaphor for what has been said of Christ's relation to 'all things' in verses 15-17. But that is not what is now said. 'The body' of which he is 'the head' is 'the assembly'! What assembly?

As we imagine the group of believers gathered in Philemon's house listening to this letter read to them by Tychicus, we should recognize that this gathering was referred to as 'the assembly [ESV 'church'] in [Philemon's] house' (Philem. 2).

Are we to understand that Paul has changed his subject as dramatically as this? Is he drawing some kind of connection between Christ's relation to the whole universe and beyond (1:15-17), and his relation to this small gathering of people who have come to faith in him in Colossae (1:18a)?

b. Who he is

The answer is, Yes, that is precisely what Paul is doing! This answer will only make sense if we grasp what is now said about *who he is*, beginning again with the words 'He is' (compare 1:15).

He is the beginning. He is not only the beginning of all things (1:16), he is the new beginning. The one who is the firstborn of all creation (v. 15), we are now told, is **the firstborn from the dead.** Not only is he prior to all things in every sense (1:17), he has been raised from the dead *in order* **that in everything he might be pre-eminent.**

There is clearly something unsaid here. The second half of our passage presupposes a problem: a disruption in the totality of all things. A few lines before this passage, Paul spoke of 'the domain of *darkness*' (1:13). In verse 14 he spoke of 'the forgiveness of *sins*'. In other words, while Christ *is* the supreme one, in whom all things have their origin, on whom all things depend for their very existence, and to whom all things move (1:15-17), he is *not* now the 'head' of all things, as he ought to be. All powers do not presently recognize his pre-eminence. There is sin, darkness and death.

But that will change. By his resurrection from the dead, he is the *new* beginning. And the purpose of this new beginning is that he will *become* what he in fact *is*: first, in every sense.

c. Why

And why is it possible to say something as extraordinary as this about him? Verse 19, like verse 16, begins with the words 'For in him'.

For in him all the fullness of God was pleased to dwell, and through him to reconcile to himself all things. We come to the climax of this astonishing passage. Why it is that Jesus' resurrection from the dead makes him the new beginning is explained by reference to the purpose of his *death*. Indeed the purpose of the creation of all things comes together in the death of Jesus of Nazareth.

The three prepositions we saw in verse 16 appear again. '*In* him' all the fullness of God was pleased to dwell (1:19). '*Through* him' all things were reconciled '*to* him'[6] (v. 20). In the death of Jesus, God was doing something fully comparable to the creation of all things. It was as big as that, as important as that, and as purposeful as that.

Verse 19 is not easy: (literally) 'in him all the fullness was pleased to dwell'. From verse 16 we might remember that all things were created(literally) 'in him'. Since Psalm 24:1 says, 'The earth is the LORD's and the *fullness* thereof,' perhaps verse 19 is reiterating verse 16: the fullness of all things is 'in him'. But verse 19 seems to go further. It seems to reflect other Old Testament language:

> *God* was *pleased* to *dwell* in [Mount Zion].[7] (Ps. 68:16)
>
> 'Do I not *fill* heaven and earth?' declares the LORD. (Jer. 23:24)
>
> May the whole earth be *filled* with his glory. (Ps. 72:19)
>
> The whole earth is *full* of his glory. (Isa. 6:3)
>
> The glory of the LORD *filled* the temple. (Ezek. 43:5)

Colossians 1:19 says that all the fullness (all the fullness *of God* we are to understand, all the fullness of God's glory and wisdom and goodness, all the fullness of God's grace, all the

---

[6] 'To himself' in 1:20 and 'for him' in 1:16 represent exactly the same Greek phrase. I understand the reference in verse 20 to be to God reconciling all things to *Christ* rather than to *himself*. Of course the difference is not substantial.

[7] Translation of the Septuagint.

fullness of God's power, all the fullness of God's purposes) was pleased to dwell in Jesus. It was God's pleasure and delight that this should be so.

To what end? That 'all things' (again filled out as in verse 16: **whether on earth or in heaven**) might be *reconciled* through him and to him. The great rupture in the unity and harmony of all things has been mended through Christ's sacrificial death: **making peace by the blood of his cross.** The rebellion has been put down, the hostilities have been brought to an end, peace has been made.

The message of Christianity is nowhere more remarkable than in what is claimed for the death of Jesus. The claim here is that the fundamental disharmony in the universe, the dissonance in the totality of all things, the discord in the whole of created existence, has been put right 'by the blood of his cross'. It is an astonishing thing to say. The word 'blood' in verse 20 suggests that the death of Jesus was a sacrifice ('blood' was important in the Old Testament sacrificial system, see Lev. 17:11). However, this sacrifice did not just have consequences for Israel and Israelites (like the sacrifices of the book of Leviticus) but for *all things* 'whether on earth or in heaven'. How could this be? That his death could have such cosmic consequences is accounted for by who this person is (1:15).

We must wait until later in the letter to learn more about how the death of Jesus could possibly have had such an astounding effect (see especially 2:11-15). Here we are simply told that it has because of who he is.

The breathtaking significance of the death of Jesus Christ accounts for why he is the new beginning and in his resurrection he is the firstborn from the dead (1:18b). It is why the body of which he is now the head is not yet the totality of all things, but the assembly of those who have now been reconciled to him – no matter how small and insignificant such an assembly might for now appear to be. The assembly that had gathered that day in Philemon's house was *that assembly* in that place – the assembly of which HE is the head.

The same is true of each assembly of Christian believers today. It is something of extraordinary importance, no matter how unimpressive it might seem. The assembly of believers in any place is the body of which this Lord Jesus

Christ is the head.

My hope for this chapter is that it will have helped you to hear these grand words of the apostle about our Lord Jesus Christ. May the hearing of these words be the means by which you are filled with the knowledge of God's will in all spiritual wisdom and understanding, to walk worthily of the Lord, with a view to fully pleasing him, in every good work bearing fruit and growing in the knowledge of God, in all power being empowered, according to the might of his glory, for all endurance and patience, with joy giving thanks to the Father (1:9-12).

Then you will understand how the atheistic secularist could not be more wrong!

Study Questions

1. What do you see as the major challenges to the Christian faith in today's world? Consider how the teaching of Colossians 1:15-20 equips Christian believers to see these challenges in a true light.

2. What is the connection between Paul's understanding of Jesus Christ and his conviction that the gospel is for the whole world? How should our view of Christ affect our attitude to missionary work?

3. How would you respond to the claim that verse 15 shows that Jesus Christ is less than divine because he is 'the firstborn of all *creation*'?

4. Think about some of the consequences of really believing that *everything* was created through and for Jesus Christ.

5. If 'the church' refers to the assembly of believers (there in Philemon's house in Colossae, or in any other place), how should Colossians 1:15-20 transform your appreciation of the group of believers to which you belong?

6. Summarize (in your own words) what you have learnt about the death of Jesus from Colossians 1:15-20.

5

'And you ...'
(Colossians 1:21-23)

Have you heard, as I have, sharp criticism of those who present the Christian faith in terms of an answer to the human search for meaning in life? Indeed I have made such criticisms myself. I am sure I will continue to do so. The idea that the Christian faith is a kind of *self-help technique,* designed to add some sense of importance to our boring, empty, sad lives, is a pathetic caricature.

As we have been listening to Paul's letter to the believers in Colossae we have heard the most astonishing assertions about Jesus Christ. 'He is the image of the invisible God'. 'All things were created through him and for him'. 'He is the beginning'. 'In him all the fullness of God was pleased to dwell' (1:15-20).

It is missing something (don't you agree?) to suggest that faith in Jesus Christ (*this* Jesus Christ!) is about my finding meaning and purpose in my little life! And yet in reacting to that domestication of the gospel, which turns Christianity into something that is all about *me,* it would be a mistake to miss the fact that there is *nothing* that gives meaning and purpose to life *remotely comparable* to faith in Jesus Christ. It sounds as though I want to have my cake and eat it, doesn't it?

What I am trying to say is that if you start with *my need* for meaning and purpose in life, and the gospel you believe or preach is shaped to meet that need, it will be a pathetic caricature of the truth. But if we start with Jesus Christ, make no mistake: the truth about Jesus Christ brings to our lives the most *profound* meaning and purpose.

As we continue listening to Paul's letter to the Colossians we now reach the point where the consequences of the truth about Christ we heard in 1:15-20 are spelled out for the believers in Colossae who first heard this letter as they were gathered in Philemon's house for that very purpose. What we are about to hear will show very clearly the consequences of who Jesus Christ is and what he has done for believers today.

> And you, who once were alienated and hostile in mind, doing evil deeds, he has now reconciled in his body of flesh by his death, in order to present you holy and blameless and above reproach before him, if indeed you continue in the faith, stable and steadfast, not shifting from the hope of the gospel that you heard, which has been proclaimed in all creation under heaven, and of which I, Paul, became a minister (1:21-23).

With the simple but emphatic words **And you,** Paul moves from the subject of Christ and all things in the heavens and on the earth, his pre-eminent role in the creation of all things, and his decisive role in the reconciliation of all things (1:15-20). He now turns to the small group of believers (the 'church', that is, the 'assembly') who had gathered in Philemon's house to hear this letter. 'And you,' he says, 'let us see *your lives* in the light of the Christ you have come to trust (1:4), and about whom we have now heard so much (1:15-20).'

With brilliant brevity Paul proceeds to show them (and us!) our past lives, our present circumstances, and our future, in the brilliant light of Christ and his work.

1. Your past: What you once were (1:21)

In verse 21 Paul provides a diagnosis of our former condition in the light of the gospel. It is not necessarily that we were ever remotely conscious that this was our state.

Now, however, we can see that this is precisely how we were. Just as the medical examination and pathology can reveal a deadly disease in a person who insists that he is 'just fine', so the gospel reveals the true state of affairs for those who are still apart from Christ, as we all once were. Three elements of our past life are highlighted.

a. alienated

who once were alienated. 'Alienated': being in the situation of an alien, a stranger, one who does not fit in. It is not a positive experience. Perhaps you have known the experience of *alienation* in some context.

The alienation of which Paul speaks is deep and terrible. It was clearly implied, though not explicitly stated, a few lines earlier (1:18-20). The whole creation, the totality of all things, has become alienated *from Christ* – the one in whom, through whom and for whom all things have been created, and hold together.

You also, Paul now says, were once *alienated* from the one on whom you depend for your very existence, in whom is the meaning and purpose of your life. There could be no deeper alienation than this.

Of course, those who are so alienated from Christ may well experience alienation in many other ways. After all, the intended harmony and unity of the totality of creation lies *in Christ,* as we saw in verse 17: all things actually hold together *in him*. Alienated *from him,* it is no wonder that we find only the most fragile and superficial unity and harmony with other people and with all things around us. Conflict and tension, hostility and division, are *normal* for those alienated from Christ. You do not have to be a genius to see that!

This deep alienation from the source and sustainer of all things was expressed in the world of the believers in Colossae who first heard this letter in a particular way. In a similar context in another letter that Paul wrote about the same time to another group of gentile believers, not far from Colossae, he filled out the 'alienated' of 1:21:

> '... remember that you were at that time separated from Christ, alienated from the commonwealth of Israel and

strangers to the covenants of promise, having no hope and without God in the world' (Eph. 2:12).

In Israel, there were at least God's promises, there was God's Word and the history of God's grace towards them. There was, in Israel, at least *in principle*, knowledge of God. This was not true of the nations. There was a time when Gentiles knew nothing of these things. 'Once you were alienated.'

It is very important for us to see the reality of this condition. How do you see those we encounter every day who are as yet unconverted? So often they seem to be very comfortable with themselves, very much at home in the world, often secure and happy. Not always, of course, but it can seem like that. Yet it is *not* like that. The totality of all things, and therefore every single person, must be seen in their relation to Christ. We must learn to see the unbelievers as they are, and as we once were: 'alienated'.

b. hostile in mind

and hostile in mind. That is, enemies in your thoughts, attitudes, intentions. The alienation that characterized our past life was not just external to us as persons. It was not that we were passively caught up in a cosmic situation beyond our control. That was true, but in that condition our own attitudes and thinking were hostile to Christ, and therefore to God.

There is a great contrast between what we *once* were and what Paul prayed for in 1:9: 'that you may be filled with the knowledge of [God's] will in all spiritual wisdom and understanding'. By contrast, *once* we were 'hostile of mind'. This is the attitude of those who have repudiated their true place as creatures, dependent on God, and owing him thanks for everything. It is that futility of thinking and foolish darkness of heart that does not honour God as God, or give him thanks, famously described by Paul in Romans 1 (see Rom. 1:21).

I used to think that many of my fellow Australians were not *hostile* to God. They were just apathetic (I thought). They simply did not care. But apparent apathy is only a cover for this deep antagonism. It comes to the surface readily enough. We see it again and again these days. In recent times the hostility has been sharply expressed in the popular publications of the angry atheists. 'Hostile of mind' is a precisely accurate description, don't you think? This hostility should be seen in its true light: it is hostility to the one who is the firstborn of all creation, in whom all things were created and all things hold together. What utter foolishness to have such antagonism to him!

Paul is reminding his readers that this is what *you* once were.

c. evil deeds

The third element in Paul's description of our past life is how this alienation and hostility of mind was expressed: **doing evil deeds**. Again there is a stark contrast between what we were and the Christian life for which Paul prayed earlier. In 1:10 we heard that Paul prayed that the Colossian believers would bear 'fruit in every *good* work'. They *once* lived 'doing *evil* deeds [works].'[1] The *alienation* and the *hostility of mind* was naturally expressed in *behaviour*. It always is. 'Evil deeds' would include idolatry and immorality. An elaboration of such works can be seen in Romans 1:18-32. Again, Paul's point is that this is what you *were*.

I am conscious that at least some reading these words from Paul today do not easily relate to them. Our lives have never been as degenerate as this sounds. Some of us were brought up in very good families, sometimes Christian families. We might even find it difficult to remember *anything* particularly shameful in our past. We find it hard seriously to think that we have ever been 'alienated', 'hostile in mind', 'doing evil deeds'. It sounds like a grotesque overstatement. People who have grown up under good influences sometimes find that words like these send their consciences searching for something that might fit. They light on some relatively small thing they have done which was an aberration of their normally good behaviour, and exaggerate it in their minds. They then feel terribly guilty about their 'evil deed'.

That is not what these words from Paul are meant to do. They are meant to help us to see that *apart from Christ* we

---

[1] 'Work' in 1:10 and 'deeds' in 1:21 represent the same Greek word.

were *utterly lost*. If you cannot remember a time when you were apart from Christ, that is beside the point. Can you see what life apart from Christ really is like?

2. Your present: What Christ has now done (1:22a)

The whole point of appreciating how lost I once was is to realize the wonder of being found. In verse 22 Paul moves from the past to the present.

a. 'But now'

Corresponding to the 'once' of verse 21, verse 22 begins (literally) 'but *now*'. This is a strikingly distinctive New Testament way of speaking. What has happened in Jesus Christ means that there is a dramatic contrast between 'once' and 'now'. There really is no need to dwell on the 'once', except to appreciate what has happened to change everything, and how much everything has been changed.

b. reconciled

he has now reconciled. What has happened is captured in one word. Corresponding to and in contrast with the 'alienated' of our past (1:21), in the present we are 'reconciled'. Paul is picking up the very word he used in verse 20. In Christ all the fullness of God was pleased to dwell (1:19) and through him to *reconcile* all things to him (1:20). God has acted in Jesus Christ to put the universe back together, to overcome the alienation, to bring peace where hostility had arisen, good where evil had taken hold. In other words, God has acted to bring all things back to Christ, to submission to him, to honour him, to peace with him.

And you (1:21): what matters for you in the present is that the past is past. Your present life is now determined by this *reconciliation*. No longer *alienated*, but *reconciled*.

c. in his body of flesh through his death

If we follow through on the parallels between verses 21 and 22 ('once'/'now'; 'alienated'/'reconciled') we might notice that the *once alienated* life was lived 'in evil works' (literal translation of the phrase in 1:21), while our *now reconciled* life is **in his body of flesh by his death.**

According to 1:20, the reconciliation of the universe, the pacification of all things, was accomplished 'by the blood of his cross'. Now we are to understand that the sacrifice that put the universe back together has also been *for us*. He has reconciled *us*! Here are the *personal* consequences of this cosmic event for the group of believers in Colossae, the assembly there in Philemon's house that day. In 1:18 they have already been called 'the body' of which he is 'the head'.

It is not clear if Paul meant a play on the word 'body', but he may have. 'His body of flesh' died on the cross. The effect was to create a new 'body', not now of flesh, but the assembly ('church') of those who have been reconciled to him as their head: specifically those gathered that day in Philemon's house. The same is true of every gathering of those who have faith in Christ Jesus.

The remarkable thing that is being said about Jesus' death is now emphasized by the real, this world, physical, human death that it was: 'in his body of flesh by his [or its] death'.

At this point no more is said about *how* the death of Jesus has accomplished the reconciliation of all things and our reconciliation. The idea of sacrifice we noted in 1:20 should not be forgotten. This death that cleansed (to extend the sacrifice language) *the universe*, has cleansed *you* also. As his death has reconciled *all things*, so he has reconciled *you*.

Do take careful notice that our reconciliation was accomplished *in Jesus' body of flesh, by his death*. He accomplished this *for us*, without our assistance or even cooperation. It was *his* doing, not *ours*. We are going to hear in a moment about what we must do, but we must realize first that this reconciliation was not *our* doing at all. Our present reconciliation to Christ, and therefore to God, was accomplished for us on the cross in A.D. 30 (or thereabouts), outside the city of Jerusalem.

3. Your future: The purpose of what Christ has done (1:22b)

Nevertheless, our reconciliation (accomplished then) is not the end of the story. In addition, it has a purpose, yet to be realized. Paul now points to a future occasion when those who have been reconciled in the body of Christ's flesh are to be presented before him.

a. to present you before him

in order to present you ... before him. There is a small ambiguity in Paul's words in this context. Whether 'he' and 'him' in these verses refer to Christ or God (the Father) is not always clear. That is not a great problem since all the fullness of God was pleased to dwell in Christ (1:19)! To stand before Christ is to stand before God; to be reconciled to Christ is to be reconciled to God. I am not sure that Paul was always concerned to make the distinction clear.

The future occasion envisaged here is judgment – the divine court when each of us will be brought ('presented') before the judge. Here is the astonishing truth: the death of Jesus on the cross had in view *that day*. What Jesus accomplished for us in his death was in order to determine what will happen on the day of judgment.

b. holy, blameless, above reproach

What will happen on that day because of Jesus' death is that you will be presented before him **holy and blameless and above reproach.** There is a hint here of the world of sacrifices again. When sacrifices were 'presented before' the Lord, they were required to be 'without blemish' (Exod. 12:5; Lev. 22:17-25). But the key wording here seems to be 'above reproach'. It means *free from accusation*. In other words, innocent. Another word would be 'justified'.

The wording is peculiar to this passage, but the truth should be wonderfully familiar to each one of us who belongs to Jesus Christ. Christ's death was the death of the holy and blameless one who was above reproach (cf. 1 Pet. 1:19). Those words perfectly describe *him*. Because of his death we, who were *once* alienated, hostile in mind and doing evil deeds, are *now* reconciled, so that we *will be* presented before him holy and blameless and above reproach.

4. What you must now do (1:23)

What God was pleased to do in Christ's body of flesh, by his death, has consequences for the whole universe. It is the meaning and purpose of life for us. Once we were *alienated*.

Now we are *reconciled*. Then we will be *presented before him blameless*. This has consequences for us here and now. These consequences will be spelled out more fully as the letter unfolds, but here they are put sharply, first positively, then negatively.

a. Established stability

if indeed you continue in the faith, stable and steadfast. The sovereign grace of God on which everything depends does not obliterate human responsibility. We could translate the words in verse 23, '*since* indeed you *are* continuing in the faith, stable and steadfast', but that would not take away from the fact that persisting in the faith and being established and firm are *essential* if the purpose of our reconciliation is to be realized.

Do not imagine that a person who abandons the faith will be presented blameless before Christ. A person whose confidence in Christ has collapsed can have no such hope. There is therefore nothing more important for you in life than persisting in your dependence on Christ, firmly established in your faith in him.

What do you think has the potential to undermine that faith? A major concern of this letter will be to address that question for the believers in Colossae.

b. Not shifting

The same point is now put negatively: **not shifting from the hope of the gospel.** Paul has already emphasized that the gospel they had believed is the truth – the word of the truth, he called it in 1:5. In this gospel they had heard of the hope laid up for them in heaven (1:5). That hope included the prospect of being presented before the heavenly judge holy and blameless and above reproach. There is nothing more important in life for you than *not shifting* from the hope of the gospel.

This verse (1:23) is the first clear indication of the specific purpose of Paul's letter. I have mentioned earlier that I am not persuaded there was a particular false teaching that had emerged in Colossae, which stirred Paul to write this letter. He tells them he had heard of their faith and love (1:8). He does not say that he had heard of any particular problem. Nonetheless, there are always forces, pressures, influences that fight against faith in Christ Jesus, that undermine the hope of the gospel. Without knowledge of any particular threats the Colossian believers were facing, Paul knew well the danger of moving away from the hope of the gospel.

c. The gospel that will establish you

Paul's letter will have much more to say about this. The key is here in 1:23. It is *the gospel* that will establish you in the faith, stable and steadfast, and keep you from shifting from the hope. At the end of verse 23 Paul says three vitally important things about this gospel.

i. heard

First, it is the gospel **that you heard.** It is the message that was spoken to you by Epaphras, an ordinary man, a man of Colossae, like you (see 4:12). The gospel was expressed in words you could understand. It has come to you by the ordinary means of human speech. It is very important to understand that the gospel we are speaking about is that gospel. It is not a mystical experience. It is not an unknowable idea. It is the gospel *that you heard.*

ii. all creation

Second, we should nonetheless understand by now that it is *utterly extra*ordinary. Indeed, says Paul, it is the gospel **which has been proclaimed in all creation under heaven.** This is what Paul had said earlier in 1:6, where he spoke of the gospel 'which has come to you, as indeed in *the whole world* it is bearing fruit and growing'. This gospel *that you heard* is God's word to the whole world, indeed the whole creation. The one in whom you have come to believe when you heard this gospel is, remember, the one in whom, through whom and for whom *all things* have been created and have their existence (1:16,17). The one in whose death you have been reconciled is the one who has reconciled *all things* to himself through the blood of his cross (1:20). The gospel message of what he has done is the message that does not just give meaning and purpose to our little lives. It is the meaning of the universe!

Paul is saying that as this gospel has been proclaimed by him, Epaphras and others around the Mediterranean world, do not just think of the towns and cities they have visited as the context of this preaching. Think of the whole creation under heaven. That is the audience for this message!

Nothing comes close to the importance and significance of this gospel! Stick with it! Do not allow some other way of seeing life and the world turn you from it. Do not move from the hope that this gospel has given you. It is the hope of all creation!

iii. Paul

and of which I, Paul, became a minister [or servant]**.** The first words of this letter introduced Paul 'an apostle of Christ Jesus by the will of God'. The significance of that self-designation now begins to unfold. The gospel you heard from Epaphras, he says, is the gospel for the whole of creation and it is the gospel that I, Paul, serve. Of course he is not alone in being a servant of this gospel. He has already described Epaphras as 'a faithful servant (ESV, minister)' (1:7).

In the next instalment of our journey through this letter we will see how and why it is important to appreciate Paul's servant role with the gospel. Meanwhile, the point to be clear about *here* is that the gospel of which Paul has said such extraordinary things is the gospel of which Paul became a servant. It is *this* gospel that will establish you. This gospel will make your faith stable and steadfast. This gospel will give you unfailing hope. This gospel will therefore bring you to that day when you will be presented before him, holy and spotless and blameless.

Study Questions

1. Carefully note all the connections you can find between Colossians 1:15-20 and Colossians 1:21-23.
2. Why do Christian believers see their past (pre-Christian) lives in such dark terms ('alienated and hostile in mind, doing evil deeds')? What value is there in being so negative about the past?
3. Using Colossians 1:15-23 explain the difference Jesus Christ has made to your life.

4. How can Christian people possibly claim that they will be presented to God 'holy and blameless and above reproach'? Is this your sincere expectation?
5. What are the major threats that you see to your continuing in the faith? What is your responsibility in the face of these things?
6. Earlier (in the Study Questions for Col. 1:1, 2) we considered the question, 'Why is what we think about Paul important?' Does Colossians 1:23 cast any more light on this question?

6

The Servant of the Gospel
(Colossians 1:24-29)

There is a force at work in the world today that is more powerful and more significant than any other in the history of the world. It is not the spread of democracy, nor is it any of the anti-democratic movements that are currently active and threatening. It is not capitalism, nor socialism. It is not civil rights, gay rights or feminism. It is certainly not atheistic secularism. The force that is more powerful and more significant than any other in the history of the world is *the gospel of Jesus Christ,* the gospel you who have come to faith in Jesus Christ have heard, understood and believed, which we have been learning from the apostle Paul is bearing fruit and growing in the whole world (1:6). Indeed it is reverberating in all creation under heaven (1:23).

We have been listening to Paul's letter to the believers in Colossae in which he has been explaining and confirming this extraordinary understanding of the times in which they lived – which in all relevant respects is precisely the same as the world in which we live. First, he expressed this in terms of how he was constantly thanking God and praying for them there in Colossae, because the gospel they had heard was bearing fruit and growing in the whole world, as well as in their lives (1:3-14). Then he showed that the universal significance of this gospel is because of who Christ is: the one *on whom all things depend* and *through whose death all things are reconciled* (1:15-20). Then he focused on what had happened to the Colossians themselves because of Christ and his death: once *alienated*, now *reconciled*, one day *to be presented blameless* (1:21-23). He then returned to the fact that the gospel they had heard, that was achieving all this, was for *all creation under heaven* (1:23).

The trouble (and it was the trouble then for those who *first* heard this letter just as much as it is for us today) is, it does not always look like that, does it? Indeed, let's be frank. It *rarely* looks as though the gospel of our Lord Jesus Christ is the most powerful and significant force in the history of the world.

As a Christian believer it is more than likely that you have faced and will face many discouragements. It is not easy to see that the gospel you believe is really so powerful when you find few persuaded by it, or even interested in it. The society around us is moving further and further away from any positive recognition of the truth of this gospel. Indeed, many of those who take any notice at all of Christianity grow more and more disdainful of this gospel. It is very easy to think that this gospel is, perhaps, not quite as significant as is being claimed.

If this is *our* experience, try to appreciate how hard it would have been for the *first Christians* to see that the gospel they had believed was the most powerful force in the history of the whole world.

I take it that this is why, at the point we have reached in the brilliant (and rather lengthy) introduction to Paul's letter (1:3–2:5), he now turns to speak about God's strange ways with this gospel. It is not working as you or I would do it, if we were in charge! Indeed the way the gospel is working is as distinctive as the gospel itself.

In 1:23 we heard Paul introduce the fact that he, Paul, had become a *servant of this gospel*. If we are to understand *how* the gospel is working so very powerfully in the whole world, then we must look at Paul, the servant of this gospel. The gospel is having its impact through *servants of the gospel* – like Paul.

That, of course, heightens the problem. The Colossians had heard the news. Paul, the leader of this allegedly powerful movement, was incarcerated in Rome, subject to the power of the Roman Empire, victim of the Jewish authorities. Just how powerful is this movement, really? It would appear to be considerably less powerful than the forces of Rome, or even the wiles of the Jewish opponents of the gospel!

Let us then hear what Paul has to say about this servant of the gospel, who may *appear* to be weak and ineffective:

> Now I rejoice in my sufferings for your sake, and in my flesh I am filling up what is lacking in Christ's afflictions for the sake of his body, that is, the church, of which I became a minister according to the stewardship from God that was given to me for you, to make the word of God fully known, the mystery hidden for ages and generations but now revealed to his saints. To them God chose to make known how great among the Gentiles are the riches of the glory of this mystery, which is Christ in you, the hope of glory. Him we proclaim, warning everyone and teaching everyone with all wisdom, that we may present everyone mature in Christ. For this I toil, struggling with all his energy that he powerfully works within me (1:24-29).

Paul's purpose in speaking of his own role as a servant of the gospel is to show *the manner in which God has chosen to have the gospel work*. Paul is not the only servant of the gospel. He moves easily in this passage from the singular 'I' to the plural 'we' (see 1:28). Epaphras was also a servant (1:7). As, of course, were many others, such as Timothy who joined Paul in the writing of this letter (1:1), and Tychicus who brought the letter to the Colossians from Rome (4:7). There have been many other servants of the gospel through the centuries that separate us who are now reading this letter and those who first heard it. Indeed, if you, like these Colossians, have heard the gospel, it will have been through a servant of the gospel. That is how God is doing it.

Therefore it is very important to understand the role of *the gospel servant* in God's plans. Otherwise, as we will see, you might easily miss the great thing that God is doing.

There are three main things for us to learn here about the servant of the gospel.

1. The servant suffers (1:24-25a)

In its details, 1:24 is the most difficult verse in the letter, and one of the most difficult in the New Testament. The important principle with any difficult part of the Bible is to focus on what is clear before worrying about what is more tricky. Often what remains unclear is less important than what is clear and indeed illuminated by what is clear. Three things are clear here: (1) the gospel servant *rejoices*, (2) he *suffers*, and (3) in this way he *serves the assembly*.

a. He rejoices

Before we get to the suffering, notice that for Paul there is *joy* in being a gospel servant. **Now I rejoice**, he says. This follows from the end of verse 23, where he said, 'I, Paul, became a servant[1] [of the gospel]. *Now* I rejoice.' That is, *now* that I have become a servant of the gospel.

I do not want us to slip over this. It *is* a joy to serve this gospel. Paul indicates a sense of the privilege. What better way to spend one's life? How marvellous that I should be involved with this gospel! This is the joy of the gospel itself. Remember 1:11: the *joyful* endurance and patience that every believer should know *because of what God has done in Christ*. Of course, it is a joy to be a servant of this gospel! The joy of serving the gospel is an expression of the joy of believing the gospel. I do hope that you know this joy.

b. He suffers

However, the joy is not the *focus* of Paul's words in verse 24. He speaks, paradoxically, of joy **in my sufferings.** The gospel servant suffers.

The sufferings of Paul are well documented in the New Testament. As he wrote this letter the distinct possibility of execution was before him. His life as a servant of the gospel had involved much suffering. There had been rejection, hardship, misrepresentation, slander, loss and conflict (see 2 Cor. 11:23-33, also 2 Tim. 1:8, 12; 2:3, 9; 3:11; 4:5).

It is striking to notice that Paul does *not* say, 'Now I have become a gospel servant, I rejoice in the status that has been

[1] The word translated 'minister' means 'servant'. The latter is preferable as a translation in modern English because 'minister' has largely lost the sense of serving that is basic to the word's meaning.

conferred on me, the authority that has been given to me, the reputation I expect to win, the impact that I will make, or the financial security that ordination will bring!' The ways of this gospel are very strange. The servant of this gospel says, 'I now rejoice in my *sufferings*.'

Paul is no masochist. Just as the joy is *gospel joy*, the suffering is *gospel suffering*. The part of this verse that is *really* difficult is where Paul explains what his sufferings mean: **and in my flesh I am filling up what is lacking in Christ's afflictions.**

Paul quite often spoke of suffering with Christ, or sharing in Christ's sufferings (see Rom. 8:17; 2 Cor. 1:5; Phil. 1:29; 3:8; 2 Tim. 2:3). The difficulty in 1:24 is the reference to 'what is lacking in Christ's afflictions'.

If we know anything of Paul's teaching we will know that he could not possibly mean that Christ's afflictions (what he called in 1:20, 'the blood of his cross'; in 1:22, simply, 'his death'[2]) were somehow *inadequate*. Paul cannot be saying that it was now up to him to *complete* what Christ had only *partly* done. That cannot be his meaning. By the blood of his cross, Paul said in 1:20, Christ has made peace, he has reconciled all things to himself. In his body of flesh through his death he has reconciled you (1:22).

The sense in which Christ's afflictions are 'lacking' should be seen in this context. For there is a very obvious sense in which all things are *not yet* reconciled and at peace. Anyone can see that! The hostilities are *not yet* ended. We have *yet to be* presented blameless before him (1:22). The death of Christ was everything that was needed to achieve these things. These things *will happen* because of Christ's death. But the effects of Christ's death have not yet been fully realized. His afflictions are not 'lacking' in the sense of

---

[2] Here I am differing from a number of commentators who insist that the 'afflictions' of Christ should not be referred to his death, but to the concept of the 'Messianic woes', the suffering that was thought would take place in the movement from the old age to the new (e.g. N.T. Wright, *The Epistles of Paul to the Colossians and to Philemon* (Leicester: Inter-Varsity Press, 1986), pp. 87-89). In the context of this letter, with its repeated references and allusions to the cross (see 1:20, 22; 2:11-15, 20; 3:3), but no clear expression of this other idea, I find the argument unpersuasive.

being 'not enough', but in the sense that they have not yet had their full effect.

The work of Christ on the cross (Christ's 'afflictions') is now having its effects on the whole world (1:6), indeed on all creation under heaven (1:23), through servants of the gospel. This involves the servants suffering. It is not that Paul's sufferings and Christ's afflictions are added together to make some quantitative whole that is greater than the parts. Rather we must understand that this work of God is of the same character from beginning to end. As the Lord Jesus suffered to reconcile all things, so there is suffering for those who serve the gospel by which the suffering-won reconciliation reaches into the whole world.

c. And so he serves the assembly

The suffering of Paul, the gospel servant, was for the sake of others: **for your sake** (1:24a). In other words it was **for the sake of** [Christ's] **body, that is, the church, of which I became a minister** [servant] (1:24b). In becoming a servant of the gospel, Paul became a servant of 'the church', or, better, 'the assembly'.

I am sure that Paul had in mind the particular assembly there in Philemon's house in Colossae (see Philem. 2). In verse 24, 'for the sake of ... *the assembly*' is parallel to and echoes 'for *your* sake'. There were many other similar assemblies of which Paul was equally and in the same way a servant. It therefore seems likely that he was also thinking of the 'assembly' of all those who were coming under Christ's headship through the gospel he was serving. As he said in 1:18: 'He is the head of the body, the assembly.'

That should not take away from the fact that he *was* serving the assembly ('church') in Colossae, a group of people he had never met, but who had nonetheless come to faith in Christ Jesus. 'A servant of the assembly' is an interesting expression (and it captures the meaning far better than 'a minister of the church'!). It is *the servant of the gospel* (1:23) who is *the servant of the assembly* (1:24), and in the process he will suffer.

Paul, therefore, presents the very thing that must have raised questions about the wisdom of the Colossians' faith in

Jesus, namely, the news that the leading missionary of this message was suffering in chains in Rome, as the essential character of this new movement. The servant of this gospel, like the one of whom the gospel speaks, suffers.

In this context it may be instructive to reflect on what threatens to unnerve you about the supreme importance and power of the gospel of Jesus Christ. Is it the discouragements, the setbacks, the unimpressiveness, the unpopularity? It is important for us to see that such things are actually the character of this movement. The servant of this gospel suffers.

2. The servant and the sufferings are part of God's plan (1:25b-27)

It is very important, therefore, to see clearly the second main point made by Paul here. Paul's imprisonment did not mean that the might of the Roman Empire or the schemes of the Jewish authorities were mightier than the gospel of Jesus Christ. Far from it. The suffering of Paul, the servant of the gospel, the servant of the assembly, was according to God's plan.

a. God's plan and Paul's role

It was, he says, **according to the stewardship from God that was given to me for you.** The word translated 'stewardship' has two meanings in Paul's letters. One refers to his own administration of his God-given responsibilities as an apostle (see for example 1 Cor. 4:1; 9:17; Eph. 3:2). The other refers to God's administration of the world, his plan of salvation and its outworking (for example Eph. 1:10; 3:9, where the ESV has 'plan'). In 1:25 the word seems to have both senses. Paul is speaking about 'the plan of God' and the responsibility for that plan 'that was given to me for you'.[3] In context, 'you' almost certainly means 'you Gentiles'. Paul had been commissioned by God to take the gospel of Christ Jesus to the nations (Acts 9:15; cf. Rom. 11:13; 1 Tim. 2:7). This is Paul's astonishing claim: as a divinely appointed servant of the gospel he was playing a particular part in

[3] See Peter T. O'Brien, *Colossians, Philemon* (Waco, Texas: Word Books, 1982), p. 81.

the realization of God's plan for the world. He meant no less than this when he introduced himself to the Colossians as 'an apostle of Christ Jesus *by the will of God'* (1:1).

b. God's plan to fulfil his word

The plan, of which Paul was a steward, was **to make the word of God fully known.** The translation is not quite adequate. More literally, it is 'to fulfil the word of God', to bring the word of God to its fulfilment. 'The word of God' is the promise of God, the purpose or plan of God made known through the Old Testament prophets. Paul was a servant of the gospel in accordance with God's plan to *fulfil* all that he had promised and purposed.[4] Paul was making a remarkable claim for his role as a servant of this gospel!

c. God's plan is 'the mystery'

God's plan is called **the mystery** or 'the secret'. Paul is once again taking up an important Old Testament idea. It is found, for example, in the story of Daniel and King Nebuchadnezzar's dream in Daniel 2. '*The mystery* was revealed to Daniel' (Dan. 2:19), who then praised God as the one who 'gives wisdom to the wise and knowledge to those who have understanding. He reveals deep and hidden things' (Dan. 2:21, 22). Daniel informed Nebuchadnezzar that 'there is a God in heaven who reveals mysteries' (Dan. 2:28), and that he had done just that for Daniel ('this mystery has been revealed to me,' Dan. 2:30). Great King Nebuchadnezzar, for all his excessive wealth, glory and power, had no idea of God's secret plan. It was a complete 'mystery' to him. Even when God gave Nebuchadnezzar a dream that contained the plan, it remained a mystery to Nebuchadnezzar. Only when God revealed the mystery to a Jewish youth named Daniel, who explained it to Nebuchadnezzar, could he know anything of it.

The 'mystery' or 'secret' that was made known in Daniel 2 was God's plan for world history, dominated (as it appeared to be) by powerful pagan kingdoms. One

---

[4] C.F.D. Moule, *The Epistles of Paul the Apostle to the Colossians and to Philemon* (Cambridge: Cambridge University Press, 1968), p. 80. Cf. Eduard Lohse, *Colossians and Philemon* (Philadelphia: Fortress Press, 1971), p. 73.

day a kingdom would come that would do away with all kingdoms: 'the God of heaven will set up a kingdom that shall never be destroyed ... It shall break in pieces all these kingdoms and bring them to an end, and it shall stand forever' (Dan. 2:44). That was the 'mystery' or 'secret' revealed to Daniel. No one could ever have guessed that such a plan existed by simply looking at the state of world politics. Nebuchadnezzar, the pagan king, had destroyed Jerusalem, the city of God, and his temple there. He had taken captive Israel's king, Jehoiakim (see Dan. 1:1, 2). But there was a secret plan, known only to those to whom God revealed the mystery.

This is the idea taken up by Paul in Colossians 1:26. The big difference between Daniel and Paul is this: The plan now was not just to *make known* the plan (that is what happened with Daniel), but to *fulfil* the plan (1:25), to bring to fulfilment God's promises, God's purposes among the nations.

d. The mystery was hidden for ages

This secret plan, or 'mystery'' had been **hidden for ages and generations.** Paul is referring to the whole period of the Old Testament. Through those centuries much, of course, had been made known. God's promises to Abraham (Gen. 12:1-3), to Israel (Exod. 19:6), to David (2 Sam. 7:12-16) were known in Israel. Indeed we have just seen that the 'mystery' was made known to Daniel. And yet even then it remained a mystery. How, when, where would God's promises be realized? This remained 'hidden for ages'.

e. The mystery has now been revealed

But now the mystery has been **revealed to his saints.** Things have 'now' changed. The secret is out. God has chosen to make known his secret plan to certain of his people, that is, certain Jewish people.[5] Paul was referring to the apostles. He was one of them.

f. What is the plan?

Reaching for adequate words, in verse 27 Paul describes the secret that has now been revealed: **To them God chose**

---

[5] We noted at Colossians 1:2, 4 and especially 12 that by 'the saints' Paul often means Jewish Christians.

to make known how great among the Gentiles [better, the nations] **are the riches of the glory of this mystery.** He hasn't told us what the secret is yet. But it is wonderful! Richly glorious! And it has to do with *the nations*!

At the end of verse 27 the secret is at last revealed. The mystery is disclosed in these wonderful words: **which is Christ in you.**

The mystery is 'Christ', the one of whom Paul has said so much in this introduction to his letter (just glance back at verses 15-20!), the one on whom the creation of all things and the reconciliation of all things depend. *Christ* is the secret now revealed.

But more: 'Christ *in you*.' Israel's Messiah is now known and acknowledged not just in Israel, but in you Colossians. Christ *in you* Gentiles: that is how the secret plan of God is being worked out. The alienated and hostile Gentiles have been reconciled in Christ (1:21, 22).

The secret plan of God is to establish his kingdom, and overthrow all other kingdoms (Dan. 2), and this is how he is doing it. The gospel is bearing fruit and growing in the whole world (1:6). Christ is therefore in the nations, and people from every nation are being brought to Christ (cf. Rom. 1:5; 16:26).

The hope of glory. Paul has already emphasized that the gospel brings hope (1:5, 23). The hope of the gospel includes being presented before Christ 'holy and blameless and above reproach' (1:22). This is now called 'the hope of *glory*'. 'Glory' is a brilliant word to sum up the wonder, splendour and magnificence of God himself, and the consummation of his grand purposes. Christ now in you gentile believers in Colossae is the beginning of something so big the only single word for it is 'glory'.

Therefore, as Paul suffered, and as we witness and perhaps experience the suffering of various kinds that accompanies serving the gospel, we (like the first hearers of Paul's letter) must understand that the serving and the suffering are part of this remarkable plan of God for the nations: Christ in you, the hope of glory.

3. The servant proclaims Christ (1:28, 29)

One question remains. What does the servant of the gospel do? How does the servant play his role in bringing God's plan to fulfilment? What is it about serving the gospel that brings the sufferings?

Him we proclaim. The time has come for God's king to be known in the whole world. Therefore the servant of the gospel (who is therefore the servant of the assembly) proclaims Christ. It is what the servant does in public and in private. Formally and informally. Before a court, in a synagogue, in the marketplace, in private conversation, in the writing of letters. 'We proclaim *him*' – the Lord Jesus Christ.

Notice the 'everyone' three times in verse 28. In the original there are echoes of the 'all things' in 1:15-20. *All people* are now to hear of Christ in whom *all things* have their origin, existence and reconciliation.

a. Warning everyone

Proclaiming Christ means **warning everyone.** People's lives cannot be the same once Christ is known. They must change, and they must not drift back to old ways. The Greek word behind 'warning' is translated in 3:16 by 'admonishing'.

b. Teaching everyone

Proclaiming Christ means **teaching everyone**. People's thinking and understanding of life and the world cannot remain the same once Christ is known. There is much to learn.

On the one hand, this is a task that can only be done **with** [literally, in] **all wisdom**, in the sense that it will take wisdom to know how Christ is to be proclaimed in various situations and to different people. On the other hand, the message itself is the ultimate wisdom, for (as Paul will say shortly) 'all the treasures of wisdom and knowledge' are hidden in Christ (2:3). Paul prayed that the believers would 'be filled ... in all spiritual wisdom and understanding' (1:9). To proclaim Christ *is* therefore to convey wisdom.

c. With a purpose

Proclaiming Christ has this purpose: **that we may present everyone mature** [or, perfect] **in Christ.**That, you remember, is what Paul spoke of as the purpose of what Christ has done for you in 1:22: 'in order to present you holy and blameless and above reproach before him' at the final judgment. Paul, the servant of the gospel, proclaims Christ (1:28) in order that the purpose of Christ's death (1:22) might be fulfilled!

d. With pain

Paul wants his readers to understand that this proclaiming Christ is hard and painful work. **For this I toil, struggling.** It is work in which you do grow weary. It is work that leads to exhaustion. It can land you in a Roman prison cell (or several years under house arrest – the situation in which we believe Paul wrote this letter, Acts 28:30; see the Introduction).

e. With power

Finally, proclaiming Christ is nonetheless, despite all appearances to the contrary, despite all feelings to the contrary, very powerful. God is at work: **with all his energy that he powerfully works within me.** God is powerfully at work in the exhausted servant of the gospel. The effectiveness of the servant's hard work does not, after all, depend on him, but on God.

We began this chapter thinking about the force at work in the world today that is more powerful and more significant than any other in the history of the world. Paul has shown us how this work of God is taking place: through servants, like Paul himself, who proclaim Christ and suffer in the process. This work is not seen or recognized or understood by many people. It is taking place, nonetheless, and powerfully accomplishing God's great plan. We should not now be among those who are ignorant of the greatest force in the history of the world!

Study Questions

1. In your experience and observation what are some of the things that make the claim that the gospel of Jesus Christ is very powerful and important seem extraordinary?
2. Why does a servant of the gospel like Paul suffer? Why does he *rejoice* in his sufferings?

3. Explain God's plan for world history that was 'hidden for ages', but is now revealed.

4. Based on what you have learnt from Colossians 1:24-29, describe the work of a servant of the gospel. What is the purpose of this work?

5. Why does proclaiming Christ involve:
   a. warning; and
   b. teaching?

6. Why is the work of proclaiming Christ so hard?

7

The Great Struggle
(Colossians 2:1-5)

What do you think of Christian preaching? In many circles, of course, it is despised and ridiculed. To be 'preached at' means being berated and scolded. Who wants that? In some other circles today preaching – rather, *some* preaching – is remarkably popular. So much so, I have found myself wondering whether preaching might be almost trivialized by its popularity. Sermons are downloaded (by the hundreds sometimes) and played like pop music on the iPod as you jog! If you have not encountered this phenomenon, bear with me. I assure you that it is happening! But, I hear you ask, what's your problem? What better thing to do as you jog than listen to the Word of God? You may have a point. But I am still wondering. I want to reflect on the phenomenon that today's technology has created of literally thousands of sermons from the latest popular preacher being available in an instant anywhere in the world. What *is* the attraction? A preacher can buy into this phenomenon, and think of his weekly sermon as a *performance* – prepared for all week – delivered with polish and showmanship – and received by admiring fans. Again, you may fairly press me: Am I saying that it is wrong to appreciate good preaching? Is it wrong to want to preach well? And to work hard at it? Again, you may have a point. You may see that I am struggling to put my finger on the concern I am feeling, but I do want preachers to reflect on what is the driving force behind their preaching. For *if it is* to gain a following (to have lots of *your* sermons downloaded by joggers!) you know very well that there is something wrong. I want Christian people to think about this phenomenon, sometimes rather unkindly referred to as 'celebrity preachers'.

This is not an easy subject to address, partly because discussing it can very easily seem to be an attack on particular personalities. It seems to me, however, that the problem is not necessarily of the preacher's making, but it may lie with the way in which we Christian people treat particular preachers and their preaching. Furthermore, this is not a simple subject to analyse, because it has emerged with the rapid advances in technology, which themselves are not always simple to evaluate.

Of course it is wonderful that people in all kinds of remote places now have access to excellent Bible teaching through the internet. I also know that the wonders of modern technology should be harnessed for gospel purposes. Yet we should also recognize the problems caused by technology. What is my attitude to the preaching in my local church, which is very likely to be less remarkable than the most popular preachers I can now listen to daily? I do not claim to have all the answers here, and I readily confess that I have some trouble putting my concerns into words.

I have found myself thinking about this because of what we are learning from the apostle Paul at the point in his letter to the Colossians that we have reached. We must consider carefully the way in which God works at growing mature Christians.

Paul has drawn our attention to the way in which the gospel is doing its remarkable work throughout the whole world. God's secret plan for world history (the 'mystery' in 1:26) is being made known in the nations of the world *through servants of the gospel* (like Paul, 1:23). These servants (or 'ministers') proclaim Christ (1:28), and Christ in the nations is the hope of the world, the hope of glory (1:27).

In 2:1-5 Paul takes the general truth about the servant of the gospel that he outlined in 1:24-29 and applies it to the particular hearers of this letter gathered, as we have supposed they were, in Philemon's house in Colossae, listening to Tychicus reading the letter he had brought them from Rome. Tychicus' reading continued:

> For I want you to know how great a struggle I have for you and for those at Laodicea and for all who have not seen me face to face, that their hearts may be encouraged, being knit together in love, to reach all the riches of full assurance of understanding and the knowledge of God's mystery, which is Christ, in whom are hidden all the treasures of wisdom and knowledge. I say this in order that no one may delude you with plausible arguments. For though I am absent in body, yet I am with you in spirit, rejoicing to see your good order and the firmness of your faith in Christ (2:1-5).

'I want you to know'

It seems to me that the earnestness of Paul's letter becomes more intense at this point. **For I want you to know**, he says. I have no doubt he wanted them to know everything he had written. That's why he wrote it! But perhaps because the importance of what he says now could easily be missed, he underlines the point. I really do want you to know this! What he wants them to know is his great struggle in serving the gospel, and who it has all been for. It's worth asking *why* he so earnestly wants them to know this.

It is easy to think of situations in which such a desire would be far from worthy. Have you noticed how many of us these days – perhaps especially Christians in some kind of ministry – want everyone to know how hard we are working? There are some people you never meet without them telling you how tired they are! If you or I were saying, 'I want you to know how great a struggle I have,' what would *our* motive be?

Is Paul's motive here to attract sympathy, or admiration that he works so hard? Or does he want to appear more committed than others by talking about how hard he works? I don't think so. Neither is he trying to provide a model for Christian ministry for other servants of the gospel to aspire to. That's not his point here either.

It is actually much more important. Paul wants his readers to appreciate *the way in which God is in fact working to bring them to maturity in their Christian faith.* 'I want you to know', he says, *for your good.*

We have been breaking up Paul's letter into rather small sections in the chapters of this commentary. The advantage of this is that it allows us to think carefully about the details of what Paul has written. That is always worthwhile in studying the Bible. 'Big picture' is important, but much of the richness of the Scriptures is in the details. The disadvantage of what I have been doing is that we can lose sight of the flow of thought. It's 'the wood for the trees' kind of problem.

Here we need to see that the purpose of what Paul wants his readers to know has already been hinted at in 1:23, where Paul spoke of the absolute necessity for them to *continue in the faith, stable and steadfast, not shifting from the gospel that you heard.* That is where he said about this gospel, 'of which I, Paul, became a servant'. Since then he has been explaining his role as a servant of the gospel.

In 1:23 he was hinting at a danger. The danger will be made very clear as we move through chapter 2. It is the danger of *not* persisting in the faith, *not* being established and firm, but in fact *shifting* from the gospel that you heard.

It is *in order to prevent that happening* that our attention has been drawn so carefully and fully to the work of Paul, the servant of the gospel. This is the context of 'For I want you to know' in 2:1. A great deal is at stake. He wants the Christian believers in Colossae (and elsewhere) to know and understand *God's ways with the gospel* – how God works through servants of the gospel – so that they will not shift from the gospel. Failure to understand God's unexpected ways can make a believer vulnerable to being seduced by alternative messages which may come in more impressive ways (about which more will be said in 2:8-23).

The brief paragraph before us, therefore, speaks first of *the work* Paul wants them to understand (vv. 1-3), then *the danger* this should help them avoid (v. 4), and thirdly *the joy* he has that all this is already working (v. 5).

1. The work (2:1-3)

We look first at the work Paul is so determined that we should know about.

a. The great struggle

Paul's description of the work here begins by underlining again his own exhausting labour as a servant of the gospel: **how great a struggle I have.** How much I agonize! He is picking up what he has just said in 1:29: 'I toil, *struggling* with all his energy that he powerfully works within me.'

What exactly do you think Paul was talking about? What did he actually *do* that was *such* a struggle, such 'toil'? There were at least two strenuous activities to which I am sure he was referring.

The first was his *praying*. The language of toil and struggle may not be the way in which we usually think about something as simple as praying. However, Paul saw prayer as very hard work! Near the end of this letter, he will describe the praying of Epaphras for the Colossians in similar terms. He was 'always *struggling*[1] on your behalf in his prayers' (4:12).

Paul has already told us that (like Epaphras) he too did not cease praying for the Colossian believers (1:9). Part of the *struggle* that he wants them to know is his prayers for them. He has already gone to the trouble of telling them specifically what he was praying for: 'that you may be filled with the knowledge of his will in all spiritual wisdom and understanding' (1:9). Now he says, 'I want you to know how great a struggle I have.' This is what the gospel servant does. Praying is a struggle. It takes effort and discipline. 'I want you to know that,' says Paul. And I want you to know that that struggle is happening.

The second strenuous activity that Paul certainly has in mind here was mentioned in 1:28. He *proclaims Christ*, warning every person and teaching every person in all wisdom. That, too, is very hard work. It brought Paul the suffering he spoke of in 1:24. Everywhere the proclamation

---

[1]The same word as in 1:29 and 2:1.

of Christ is opposed with hostility, open or covert. More than that, to work hard at persuasion, at urgent warning, at careful instruction of every possible person was (and is) hard, hard work. This is what he means when he says, 'I want you to know how great a struggle I have.'

He continues: **for you and for those at Laodicea** [located not far down the Lycus Valley from Colossae] **and for all who have not seen me face to face.** This arduous work, in prayer and in proclamation, has been *for you* – and others like you, of course, says Paul.

b. The bold purpose

How was it that Paul's labours were for the benefit of these people whom he had never met? How was Paul, whom they had never met, working so hard *for them*? Look now at the bold purpose of his toil.

I am proclaiming Christ, he says (no matter how much effort it takes), and I am praying (with all the energy God gives me) to see a deep and profound outcome in your lives, described here in three dimensions.

First, in their hearts: **that their hearts may be encouraged**. At the centre of their personal life, Paul tells his readers, he was struggling that they would know the comfort and courage that knowing Christ brings.

Second, Paul was struggling that believers would know the powerful bond of love that knowing Christ gives: **being knit together in love**.

Third, he worked that they might know rich and full assurance: **to reach all the riches of full assurance of understanding and the knowledge of God's mystery.** How precious it is to *understand* and *know* God's glorious purpose for the nations of the whole world! What deep *confidence* understanding Christ confers. One translation puts it very well: 'the full wealth of conviction that understanding brings' (REB). Paul was struggling *so that believers would know that.*

In 1:28 Paul had described the purpose of his labour in terms of its final goal: 'that we may present every person mature [or perfect] in Christ'. Now he wants his hearers to know his strenuous work towards that end *for you.*

c. The clear focus

Just in case any of us is particularly dull, and not yet completely clear (and we all have a tendency to be a bit like that in these things), he tells us again that the secret ('God's mystery', see 1:26) he is working so hard for them to know and understand and be impacted by **is Christ, in whom are hidden all the treasures of wisdom and knowledge.** He is, after all, the one on whom all things depend (1:15-20). As we saw in 1:27, 'Christ in you [Gentiles] [is] the hope of glory.'

Certain Old Testament books, like Proverbs, Job and Ecclesiastes, speak about the wisdom human beings need to live in God's world, how difficult it is to find, and yet how precious. 'From where, then, does wisdom come? And where is the place of understanding? It is hidden from the eyes of all living and concealed from the birds of the air' (Job 28:20, 21). But now, Paul says, the secret is out! All the treasures of wisdom and knowledge and understanding are *in Christ*.

You can be perfectly sure that Paul never taught the Old Testament without proclaiming Christ! Paul never taught about the Christian life without the centrality of Christ. Paul never taught an understanding of anything without Christ. All the treasures of wisdom and knowledge and understanding are hidden in him!

The claim, of course, is astonishing. As we follow the rest of Paul's letter we will learn more of what this means. We may reasonably suppose that he does not mean that once you know Christ you automatically have all the answers to all of life's questions and challenges. If that were the case, then there would have been no need for this letter! On the contrary, the wealth of wisdom and knowledge and understanding found in Christ is so vast that we can expect to be exploring it all of our days. So we must realize that the claim of the gospel of Christ is immense. What the philosophers have sought down the centuries, what ordinary people have longed for – wisdom to live well – is all to be found in Christ.

Some commentators suggest that the last phrase of verse 1 ('and for all who have not seen me face to face') just means the other believers in the Lycus Valley, where

Paul had not visited. I suspect that Paul had much more in mind. He was the apostle to the nations (see Acts 9:15; Rom. 1:5). He saw his work in the context of the whole world (Col. 1:6), indeed of all creation under heaven (1:23). There is no good reason to restrict the phrase at the end of verse 1. It is right to understand that it includes *us*. We are the beneficiaries of the struggle Paul speaks of here. As we read his letter we are the very direct beneficiaries of his strenuous efforts to see Christ known in the nations. We – just like that gathering of Colossian believers in Philemon's house – need to know that.

2. The danger (2:4)

There was a specific reason that Paul wrote in this way: **I say this in order that no one may delude you with plausible arguments** [or persuasive speech]. This is the danger, already alluded to in 1:23, which led into the long discussion of his role as a servant of the gospel that began in 1:24. Now we should be quite clear why we need to appreciate the role of the gospel servant. It is because of the very real danger of being deluded, that is, deceived.

a. Deception

The seriousness of the danger of being deceived is the corollary of the wonder of the truth. The gospel is 'the word of the truth' (1:5). The truth is that Christ is the one on whom all things (including us) depend for our existence and our reconciliation (1:15-23), the blood of his cross is the power to heal creation (1:20), and Christ is the hope of the whole world (1:27). To be turned away from the truth (*this* truth) is a massively serious danger.

It is those who believe this gospel who tend to care most about the truth, and take the danger of deception most seriously –precisely because the truth is so good and important! To be deeply concerned about theological truth is not pedantic, it is wisdom and goodness.

b. Persuasive speech

What would it take to deceive us? What do we need to be aware has the power to deceive? Plausible arguments, or perhaps a better translation, persuasive speech.[2]

As we have previously noted, it is often thought that there was a specific erroneous teaching Paul knew was being promoted in Colossae. On this assumption, he is referring to that teaching as 'persuasive (but, by implication, misleading) speech'. While this is possible, it seems to me that his language here is general. I doubt that Paul had any *particular* deceptive ideas in mind. What he says is the kind of thing that needs to be said to Christian believers everywhere. Believers are not likely to be deceived by unimpressive arguments. It will take persuasive speech to deceive them, and so it is persuasive speech they must beware of. Persuasive speech will sound as though it is right. That's what makes it persuasive! The more right it sounds, the more dangerous it is (if it is not right).

Persuasive speech is itself neutral. It can be used to persuade of the truth, or it can be used to deceive. The point is that it should not be admired simply for that quality. Persuasiveness and plausibility can be deceptive.

That is why we need to recognize the true servant of the gospel, who very often will not be impressive. Remember, he suffers (1:24). The readers of this letter need to know and appreciate the labours of *Paul* for them so that no one will deceive them with persuasive speech. Today we need to know and appreciate the labours of those servants of the gospel who labour for us (as Paul did) and so not be deceived by other persuasive speech.

3. The joy (2:5)

Are we to understand from all this (the argument from 1:24 to 2:4) that God's great purposes for the whole world, the hope of the nations of the world, rests on the labours of the likes of Paul? Could it be undone by something as simple as the 'persuasive speech' of others? Does the plan of God really hang by such a thin thread? Yes, it does.

---

[2]The Greek term is a compound noun with elements suggesting the ideas of persuasion and utterance. It is variously rendered: 'plausible arguments' (ESV); 'persuasive arguments' (HSCB); 'fine-sounding arguments' (TNIV); 'specious arguments' (REB); 'beguiling speech' (RSV); 'enticing words' (AV).

That is why for every advance of the gospel, for every time we hear of faith in Christ Jesus among the nations (1:4), and for every person who continues in the faith, stable and steadfast, not shifting from the hope of the gospel (1:23), we thank God (1:3)! This is *his* work. *He* is doing it. The struggles of Paul, the difficult toil of gospel servants, are achieving their purpose because it is *God's* purpose, and it is God's purpose to do it in this way. Therefore Paul is writing this letter, not full of anxiety or distress, but joy.

a. Absent, but present

For though I am absent in body [literally, 'in the flesh']**, yet I am with you in spirit** [literally, 'in the spirit (or, Spirit)'] means much more than that he is with them in his thoughts. He is with them 'in the Spirit'. He has heard of their love 'in the Spirit' for all the saints (1:4, 8). There is a bond that the Spirit creates between all who are in Christ, all who have joined the assembly of which Christ is the head (1:18). It is a bond that the distance between Colossae and Rome does not weaken.

b. Rejoicing

Being *with them* in that very real sense, he is **rejoicing**! Paul began this discussion of his role as a servant of the gospel in 1:24 by saying that, now he has become a servant of the gospel, he rejoices. He rounds off this section of the letter (indeed this is the close of the magnificent introduction to his letter that began in 1:3) by returning to this note of joy (see also 1:11). In 1:24 he told us that he rejoices in the sufferings involved in serving the gospel. Now he tells us that he rejoices in the outcome of the struggles, namely, the stable believers there in Colossae.

c. Order and firmness

Presumably with reference to what Epaphras has reported to him (1:8) the cause of Paul's joy is **to see your good order and the firmness of your faith in Christ.**

With Christ as our head (1:18), reconciled to him by his death (1:22), life is put back in *order*. Later in the letter we will learn more about the order of life in Christ (see especially 3:5–4:6). Here Paul tells us that it is something to be delighted about. Ordered lives come from firm *faith in*

Christ. Since all the treasures of wisdom and knowledge are to be found in him (2:3), firm faith in him is the best basis there is for ordering our lives. Beware, then, of the danger of being deceived. Rejoice in the spectacular work that God is doing through the servants of the gospel, establishing firm faith in Christ and reordered lives.

What, then, do you think of Christian preaching and Christian preachers? What are we to say about listening to sermons on your iPod as you jog? Does the way in which God is actually working, as Paul has explained it here, have anything to say to my concerns with which I began this chapter?

At least three things should be learnt.

(1) Let us not get too excited about persuasive speech, as such. Part of the problem with the 'celebrity preacher' phenomenon is that what attracts so many to certain preachers is the quality of the oratory and rhetoric. We have noted that there is nothing wrong with persuasive speech. Yet it is quite likely that on that measure many of us might not have wanted to listen to apostle Paul on our iPods!

(2) Whatever we make of the best preachers in the world (if we think like that), let us not fail to appreciate the servants of the gospel whom God has used and is using to establish us in the faith, Paul included. Some of them (probably most of them) are unimpressive by some popular measures. But their struggles for our sake, in their prayers for us and their proclamation of Christ, should be very important to us.

(3) In whatever ways we listen to the word of God (and I can't really see anything *wrong* with listening to sermons as you jog!), let us not neglect the deep purpose of God by his word. It is not intended to entertain, or amuse, or even simply excite us, but to encourage our hearts, to knit us together in love, to give us all the riches of the full assurance of understanding and knowing God's secret, to present us before him holy and blameless and above reproach.

Study Questions

1. Now that we have come to the end of the introduction to Paul's letter, try to summarize, in a few sentences, what he has said in Colossians 1:3–2:5, making clear the flow of the argument.

2. Do you agree that the 'great struggle' Paul wants his readers to know must include
   a. his praying for them; and
   b. his proclaiming Christ?

   If so, consider how and why each of these activities would be a 'great struggle'. Can you think of anyone who has struggled like that for you (in addition to Paul!)?

3. Consider the three dimensions to Christian maturity described in Colossians 2:2, and the ways in which you know each of these in your own experience.

4. Reflect on the claim that in Christ 'are hidden all the treasures of wisdom and knowledge'. Explain (perhaps with examples) how knowing Christ gives wisdom and knowledge for life.

5. Can you recognize any instances of 'persuasive speech' (or 'plausible arguments') that have the potential to deceive Christian believers today?

6. Looking at your life, do you think Paul would rejoice to see 'your good order' and 'the firmness of your faith in Christ'? What precisely would he see that display these things?

8

The Christian Life
(Colossians 2:6, 7)

Someone has said that in Christian circles what is taken for granted in one generation is very likely to be ignored in the next and denied in the third. The wisdom of this adage could be illustrated many times over in the history of churches, denominations and other Christian groupings. There are many sad stories to be told. Churches that once stood firm and were faithful under terrible pressure of one kind or another can in time come to take for granted the gospel that their fathers preserved at such a high cost, and eventually reject that gospel altogether. All such stories, no doubt, are more complex than 'taken for granted in one generation, ignored in the next and denied in the third', but there is enough truth there to sensitize us to the importance of reflecting on what is being taken for granted in the Christian circles of which we are part today.

Things that are taken for granted can easily be very important matters that were emphasized by a previous generation. Perhaps taking them for granted is a reaction to that emphasis. It is not easy to identify something that is being taken for granted, and so in danger of soon being ignored and even rejected – precisely because we are taking it for granted! One possible candidate for the 'being taken for granted' category today in some Christian circles is *the Christian life*.

The first piece of evidence I would advance that I just might be right about this is that many reading these words are wondering what precisely I am talking about. The Christian life? How could we be taking the Christian life for granted? We are Christians, aren't we? And we are alive! So what more is there to be said? That sounds like something that is being taken for granted to me!

Consider a typical healthy evangelical church today. There is probably a regular programme for enquirers explaining the gospel message and how to *become* a Christian. We have names for the programmes: Christianity Explained or Explored, Introducing God, and so on. The emphasis on clear and attractive presentations of the gospel of Christ to people with no previous knowledge of these things is marvellous. It has been a right response to the decline in our society of any general knowledge of the Bible's message. Then for those who become Christian believers, or who have been Christians for years, it is very likely that there will be *training* programmes in various kinds of ministry: sharing the gospel, leading Bible Studies, welcoming, and so on. Indeed, in my part of the Christian world we have become very big on 'training' in a myriad of forms. This emphasis has also undoubtedly done a great deal of good, equipping many Christians to serve others in a variety of important ways. This too has been a right response to our times, in which there is so much work to be done if we are going to multiply and grow churches, rather than be content with a static (or declining) institutional Christianity. Yet the point I want to draw to your attention is that I am not sure I very often see these days a training course in *the Christian life,* in what we might call (to take up some New Testament terms) Christian *growth,* or Christian *maturity,* or the Christian's 'walk'. Is it the case that we expect that these things do not need to be specifically addressed, they can be *taken for granted*?

Now *either* I am missing something, *or* this really is a subject that we do not have to talk about, *or* we are taking it for granted. Is it too much of a caricature of today's evangelical Christianity to see the assumption that if you get a person converted, and teach them to share the gospel, the Christian life will look after itself? That is what I mean by 'taken for granted'.

This leads me to think that there may well be a sharp edge to the relevance for us of Paul's letter to the Colossians. For, as we work our way through this amazing letter, we come now to what has often been considered (and I agree) its theme sentence. The powerful introduction (1:3–2:5) is done. The body of the letter now begins. Its first sentence sums up everything that Paul has been preparing to say, and everything that he will unpack in the rest of the letter. And we discover that what Paul was writing about to the Colossian believers was *the Christian life*.

> Therefore, as you received Christ Jesus the Lord, so walk in him, rooted and built up in him and established in the faith, just as you were taught, abounding in thanksgiving (2:6, 7).

In this one sentence Paul manages to give us three perspectives on the Christian life, each linking the ongoing life of the Christian to its beginnings, while distinguishing the ongoing *from* the beginning. So the beginning is described three times: 'you received Christ Jesus the Lord', 'rooted (in him)', and 'you were taught'. The threefold portrayal of the ongoing life is: 'walk in him', 'built up in him', and 'established in the faith'.

Paul's whole letter, summed up in this sentence, is a call to give careful attention to 'walking in him', being 'built up in him', and 'established in the faith'. I will call these three dimensions to the life of a Christian: Christian *living,* Christian *growing* and Christian *understanding*.[1] We must first notice how the long introduction we have been following for some time has been leading to this statement.

'Therefore'

Therefore is a longish word in English. The Greek word has just three letters. It is nonetheless always worth noticing, particularly in Paul's writings. The 'therefore' at the

---

[1] This way of putting it I have adapted from R.C. Lucas, *Fullness and Freedom: The message of Colossians and Philemon* (Leicester: Inter-Varsity Press, 1980), p. 87.

beginning of Colossians 2:6 is very important. In the flow of the letter, it seems to link not just verse 6 to verse 5, but the whole letter from 2:6 on to the whole introduction that concluded at 2:5.

We will only really understand what lies before us in Colossians 2:6, 7 (not to mention the rest of the letter) if we understand that it is based on and flows out of all that we have heard in chapter 1 and verses 1-5 of chapter 2. Put the other way round: we only really understand what we have been hearing from this letter up until now, if we understand that the consequences are what we hear in 2:6, 7.

We should, therefore, briefly review what we have heard in the letter's introduction. There have been three big points.

First, in 1:3-14 we heard that something extraordinary was happening, for which Paul could not stop thanking God (1:3), and could not stop praying that it would continue (1:9). The gospel was bearing fruit there in Colossae and also in the whole world (1:6, 10): the fruit of faith in Christ Jesus, love for all the saints and the hope laid up in heaven (1:4, 5). What had happened there in Colossae, when Epaphras had taught them the gospel message (1:7), was tremendously significant. It was of worldwide importance.

Paul was constantly praying for the believers in Colossae, that they would grasp and be grasped by the huge thing that God was doing, that they would be filled with the knowledge of God's will, and themselves bear fruit in lives fully pleasing to the Lord, joyfully giving thanks to the God who had qualified *them* to share in the inheritance of the saints, which he summed up as *the forgiveness of sins* (1:9-14).

Second, in 1:15-23 we were shown that the astonishing significance of these Colossians coming to faith in Christ Jesus lay in *who he actually is*: the one on whom all things depend for their very existence and coherence (1:15-17). Furthermore, the forgiveness of their sins (1:14) was part and parcel of the reconciliation of all things to Christ through the blood of his cross (1:18-20). This reconciliation looks forward to the day when they will be presented before him holy and blameless and above reproach (1:22). Nothing therefore matters more than their continuing in the faith, stable and steadfast, not shifting from the hope of the gospel (1:23).

Then, thirdly, in 1:24–2:5, Paul elaborated on his own role in all this as a servant of the gospel. Strange as it may seem, God has chosen to accomplish his plan for all creation under heaven by servants, like Paul, who labour strenuously to make Christ known in the nations, to every possible person. In this work these servants suffer (1:24).

The stunning introduction to Paul's letter has shown us what God is doing in the whole world by the gospel message (1:3-14), because of what he has done for all of creation in Christ by his death (1:15-23), and the surprising way in which he is doing it through servants of the gospel like Paul (1:24–2:5). The conclusion he draws ('Therefore,' 2:6) is the call to live the Christian life, to live in the light of these momentous realities. The call in 2:6, 7 will be elaborated through the rest of the letter. Here we will reflect on the three perspectives Paul provides on the Christian life in 2:6, 7.

1. Christian living (2:6)

One of the New Testament's delightful words for living life is 'walking'. How you 'walk' (that is, how you conduct yourself, what you say and do, how you behave) as a believer in Christ Jesus matters enormously. It needs to flow out of what happened when you became a believer: **as you received Christ Jesus the Lord.**

a. The receiving

This is what happened when you became a believer: 'you received Christ Jesus the Lord'. We need to be careful that our contemporary Christian jargon is not read back into the New Testament. Paul is not referring here simply to 'receiving Christ' into your heart or into your life. That is certainly involved. But the word 'received' here is almost a technical term for receiving *teaching* that has been delivered to them. You 'received Christ' when 'you heard [the gospel] and understood the grace of God in truth' (1:6). It was not *simply* a matter of inviting Jesus into your heart. It was receiving the message about him, and believing it. This is important. The New Testament speaks of the 'tradition'.[2] The tradition is that which is *received* from those who went before and *passed down* or *delivered* to others, who in turn *receive* it. The tradition (in this New Testament sense) is what Paul called in 1:5, 'the word of truth, the gospel'.

From the very beginning the Christian faith has not been a matter of self-discovery or simply personal illumination. It is a matter of *receiving* something that is *passed down* or *delivered* to you. For example, Paul says in 1 Corinthians 11:23: 'For I *received* from the Lord what I also *delivered* to you.' What did he deliver?

> For I *delivered* to you as of first importance what I also *received*: that Christ died for our sins in accordance with the Scriptures, that he was buried, that he was raised on the third day in accordance with the Scriptures, and that he appeared to Cephas, then to the twelve (1 Cor. 15:3-5).

The 'tradition' is the gospel itself and the teaching that surrounds the gospel. So Paul wrote in 1 Corinthians 11:2: 'Now I commend you because you remember me in everything and maintain the *traditions* even as I *delivered* them to you.' Unfortunately the term 'tradition' has taken on meaning and significance over the centuries quite different from the idea in the New Testament. 'Traditions', in this sense, are not old customs, ideas or practices that have become institutionalized. The traditions are the *teaching* the apostle had received and passed on. So Paul wrote to the Thessalonians:

> Finally, then, brothers, we ask and urge you in the Lord Jesus, that as you *received* from us how you ought to live and to please God, just as you are doing, that you do so more and more (1 Thess. 4:1).

> Now we command you, brothers, in the name of our Lord Jesus Christ, that you keep away from any brother who is walking in idleness and not in accord with the *tradition* that you *received* from us (2 Thess. 3:6).

---

[2] 'Tradition' translates a Greek word related to the verb 'to hand down', 'to deliver'.

In due course the tradition was passed down in writing, in what we call the New Testament. This is what has been *delivered* to us from the apostles, ultimately from the Lord Jesus Christ. The tradition we have received is the New Testament (more accurately, the whole Bible).

So in 2:6 Paul points his readers back to the experience of 'receiving' the tradition, the teaching of the gospel. You 'received' Christ Jesus the Lord by hearing, understanding and believing what you were taught about him (see 1:6, 7). The idea is echoed at the end of 2:7: 'just as you were *taught*'.

What were they taught? The indications are that they were taught quite a lot! While we cannot know exactly how much Epaphras had taught these Colossians (1:7), it is clear that the content of the gospel as it had been taught to them was very substantial. Unlike much of today's evangelism that seems to work at keeping everything as simple as possible (the *briefest* gospel outline is the *best*!), it seems that Epaphras taught them a great deal.

'Christ Jesus the Lord' in 2:6 is an unusual phrase. Literally it is 'the Christ, Jesus, the Lord'. This is Paul's summation of what you *received* when you learned the gospel: 'Jesus is the Christ; Jesus is the Lord.' This wonderful *summary* of the gospel that the Colossians heard and learned and understood (what they 'received') is full of meaning and significance. To speak of 'Jesus' to these people of Colossae would have involved telling something about who he was, where and when he lived, what he said and did. To tell these Gentiles of Colossae that Jesus was 'the Christ', the Messiah, would involve an extensive explanation of the promises of God in the Old Testament. Then to teach them that Jesus is 'the Lord' would involve the kind of teaching Paul has given in the introduction to this letter, especially 1:15-20. Furthermore, Paul reminded them earlier that they had 'heard and understood *the grace of God in truth*' (1:6). What they were taught about Jesus, who is both the Christ and the Lord, told them of 'the grace of God in truth'. They must have learned, therefore, not just who Jesus is, but something of what he has done, particularly in his death (1:20, 22). Furthermore, Epaphras could not have spoken of Christ Jesus the Lord without speaking of his resurrection and its significance (1:18). We might add that in this word of truth they had heard of the hope laid up for them in heaven (1:5, cf. 22b). What they learned about Jesus from Epaphras did not stop short of hearing about heaven! All this is what the servant of the gospel teaches when he proclaims Christ, 'warning everyone and teaching everyone with all wisdom, that we may present everyone mature in Christ' (1:28).

Therefore, we should recognize that what Paul is about to say about Christian living is based on the believers having received and believed a substantial body of teaching, summed up as receiving the Christ, Jesus, the Lord. Solid teaching is not an alternative to evangelism, it is the proper means of evangelism. Christ is received with *understanding*. We may well find far fewer problems down the track if people were better taught in the beginning, that is, if they really learned that Jesus is the Christ and that Jesus is the Lord and what that means.

b. The walking

Now, says Paul: *As* you received the Christ, Jesus, the Lord, **so walk in him.** The receiving is not the whole, but the beginning of the Christian life. The Christian life is to be lived, however, not on some other basis, nor with some new discovery, nor on some other level from the beginning, but *as* you received the Christ, Jesus, the Lord, *walk in him*.

Paul told us in 1:10 of his praying that they would '*walk* worthily of the Lord … fully pleasing to him'. He is talking about the actual conduct, the behaviour, of the Christian person: what you do, what you say, what you don't do, what you don't say. No longer can I walk for myself, as I please. I have received Jesus, the Lord and the Christ. I must walk 'in *him*'. Wherever I am, whatever I am doing, Jesus is the Christ and the Lord.

What it means to 'walk *in him*' will be explored in detail in chapter 3. It includes such things as getting rid of sexual immorality, evil desires, covetousness, anger, malice, slander, obscene talk (see 3:5-10) and showing kindness, patience, love, forgiveness (3:12-14), husbands loving their wives (3:19), wives appropriately submitting to their husbands (3:18).

This is the Christian life. So simple to state; so good to see and experience; but a very big thing to do. This is what we have received Christ Jesus the Lord *for*. He is the one (and no other) who is to shape all of our character and behaviour. As you received the Christ, Jesus, the Lord, so walk in him. In every situation, behave with Jesus as the Christ and Lord he is. It would be strange, don't you think, to take that for granted!

The second perspective on the Christian life shows us that it is a process.

2. Christian growing (2:7a)

Again we find two expressions ('having taken root' and 'being built'[3]) which point us to the beginning of the Christian life and its ongoing experience. 'Taking root' and 'being built' may be a mixed metaphor. Paul was comfortable with such things. The beginning may be pictured as a planting, the roots being placed in the rich soil of the gospel, ready for healthy growth. The ongoing Christian life is then pictured as a building being constructed on a well-laid foundation, a firmer and more stable structure as each day passes.[4] It is also possible that we have one metaphor, because the language of putting down roots was sometimes used for the process of sinking the foundations of a building. It is also possible that the metaphorical associations of the language should not be pressed. The ambiguity, such as it is, makes little difference to what is being said.[5]

a. The roots

We are reminded that the beginning of the Christian life was a fundamentally new beginning. We have been brought into a new environment. Our lives have been given a new basis and foundation. We have been **rooted** *in him* – in the Christ, Jesus, the Lord.[6]

---

[3] The change in tense of the Greek verbs is missed by the ESV with 'rooted and built up'. 'Having taken root' and 'being built' is an attempt to represent the Greek tenses a little more clearly.

[4] Douglas J. Moo, *The Letters to the Colossians and to Philemon* (Nottingham: Apollos, 2008), pp. 179-181.

[5] See Peter T. O'Brien, *Colossians, Philemon* (Waco, Texas: Word Books, 1982), p. 107.

[6] The phrase 'in him' applies to both 'rooted' and 'built up'.

It would therefore never be adequate to think of Christian faith as *merely* the acceptance of certain teachings. It is not a *philosophy* we have received, but a *person* whose significance is so gigantic that I have come to understand my complete and utter dependence on him for my very existence (1:16), for my reconciliation to him (1:22a), and for my future presentation before him (1:22b). If I am like a plant, then I have taken root 'in him'. If I am like a building, then the foundations have been laid 'in him'.

The idea seems to be our utter dependence on him. How good it is to be dependent on one so good and wise and powerful (note 2:3!). We who have been planted in such rich soil should, of course, be conscious of the fact. The energy for my Christian growth comes from the Lord Jesus Christ, into whom I have been planted, so to speak.

b. The building

and built up in him. The purpose of being planted is to grow or, to change the imagery, to be built. The image of growth was used in Paul's prayer in 1:10: 'bearing fruit in every good work and increasing (better, *growing*) in the knowledge of God'. The point now would appear to be that even as we have been planted 'in him' so we are to grow (or be built) 'in him'. Christian growth will not occur in some richer soil, or on some stronger foundation than the Lord Jesus Christ. All the treasures are to be found in him (2:3)!

To be built[7] 'in him' will certainly mean exploring all that Jesus Christ is, and growing stronger and wiser from our dependence on him. There is no limit to the scope for growth 'in him', but the all-important thing is that he remains the source of our growth, the foundation on which we are built. Do not be deceived into looking elsewhere.

There are two things to avoid. One would be to think that you can be planted 'in Christ' and not grow. You could have the foundation laid, but no building. I wonder if this

---

[7] The Greek compound verb seems to suggest being built *upon*, rather than built *up*. The implication is that Christ is the foundation upon which the building is constructed. This is difficult to express in an English translation. In English 'built up' has an unfortunate psycho-emotional connotation that should not be read into the text here.

sometimes happens when churches strive to be always evangelistic. Everything we do is laying the foundations. Could it be that we are taking Christian growing for granted? Again this subject will be taken up in more detail at the beginning of chapter 3.

The other thing to avoid is pursuing growth that is not 'in him'. Growing intellectually (even in theological or biblical knowledge) may not be being built *in him*. There may certainly be other kinds of personal, even spiritual, growth that should not be confused with being built *in him*. In the rest of chapter 2 we will be warned of some of these possibilities. Here we learn the principle: it is *from* Christ, *with* Christ and *in* Christ that we are to be built, that we are to grow. That is the Christian life. It would be strange, don't you think, to take this for granted!

3. Christian understanding (2:7b)

The third description of the Christian life emphasizes that *understanding* is fundamental. This time the description of the ongoing Christian life is mentioned *before* its beginning.

a. The establishing

and [being[8]] established in the faith. The Christian life is more than being taught the gospel. It is being *established* in the faith, that is, in the faith you were taught. Of course, there is always more to learn. A growing Christian will be keen to go on learning, eager to be taught more. The point here is that it will be more of what you were taught. The Christian life is not *just* learning the faith, but *being established* in the faith. A deeper grasp of the faith must be a firmer stability in the faith: growing confidence in Christ Jesus the Lord. This is precisely what was described in 1:23: 'continue in the faith, stable and steadfast, not shifting from the hope of the gospel that you heard'.

There are too many Christians (and Christian leaders) who grow away from their gospel beginnings. They think that they have outgrown such simplicities, which is precisely the kind of thing Paul will warn against in the

[8] Again two Greek tenses are used, the sense of which is a little clearer by translating the first with a continuous present.

rest of chapter 2. The Christian life is growing strong *in* the gospel beginnings.

b. The teaching

just as you were taught. Paul repeats the emphasis implied in the *receiving* in verse 6. What you were *taught* at the beginning (assuming you had as faithful a servant as Epaphras) continues to be the shaping influence on your life. We have already considered at some length what this teaching was.

Thanksgiving

This wonderful one-sentence call to the Christian life is rounded off with a marvellous flourish: **abounding in thanksgiving.** Overflowing with thanksgiving. This is what Paul had prayed in 1:12, that they would join him (1:3) in giving thanks to the Father of our Lord Jesus Christ. This is the opposite of spiritual pride. The Christian life is the experience of God's grace from beginning to end (see 1:6). Other kinds of human growth, development and achievement easily lead to self-satisfaction, self-importance, or superiority. Walking in Christ Jesus the Lord, being built in him, being established in the faith leads to *thankfulness.* Irrepressible thankfulness. I do not believe we should ever take it for granted.

Study Questions

1. What do you think is in danger of being taken for granted in the Christian circles to which you belong?
2. Look back over the introduction to Paul's letter (Col. 1:3 – 2:5) and consider how understanding and believing what Paul has said there should help us take Christian living more seriously.
3. Why is it important to understand that 'receiving Christ Jesus the Lord' means more than 'receiving Jesus into my heart'?

4. How does Paul's summary of what the Colossians 'received' ('Jesus is the Christ; Jesus is the Lord') compare with what you 'received' when you became a Christian believer?
5. In what ways might Christian believers be tempted to 'walk', 'be built', or 'be established' that are not 'in him'?
6. Think about your life and conduct recently. In what ways has your living been shaped by Jesus who is the Christ and the Lord? In what ways has it failed to be so shaped?
7. How can growing as a Christian involve 'abounding in *thanksgiving*', and avoid spiritual pride?

9

You've Been Warned
(Colossians 2:8)

No one likes being warned. Most warnings feel like a kind of put-down. When I warn my adult children (as I still do, poor things) to 'drive carefully', is it not clear that I think they are likely to drive irresponsibly? When someone tells me I should watch my diet, I am not unusual (am I?) to feel a little annoyed.

We have less of a problem with *general* warnings, because they apply to everyone *else*! In the College where I teach we have been encouraging students and faculty to participate in a programme of accountability for internet use. I have noticed that my emphasis with the students has been that they should join up in order to help others. I have not wanted to get them off-side by suggesting that internet pornography is a threat to *them*. Yet since we all know it is a threat to *everyone else*, I encourage them all to join the programme, because that will help those *other* people, who need the help, to join up. That has all been true. But I can see that I have been doing the easier thing, by not directly *warning* the students themselves. I should say, 'If you think that *you* are in no danger from this menace, then you are very foolish. Do this to protect *yourself*.' General warnings are easier. I can apply them to everyone but myself.

Paul explained to the believers in Colossae in 1:28 of his letter to them, that *proclaiming Christ* involves *warning* everyone. Proclaiming Christ is what Paul did, as a servant of the gospel. This was and is God's way of bringing reconciliation to the whole world, the hope of glory (1:27). Paul wanted them to know that this was very hard work (1:29; 2:1). He toiled and struggled to do it. Warning every person is not easy. No one likes being warned.

The whole letter Paul wrote to the Colossians is a wonderful case study of Paul *proclaiming Christ*. In this very letter he is doing what a servant of the gospel does. We should not be surprised, therefore, that after the letter's marvellous introduction (1:3–2:5), and his brief statement of the letter's theme (2:6, 7), we find Paul, for the rest of chapter 2, *warning everyone*. There are three specific warnings – 2:8: 'See to it that no one takes you captive …'; 2:16: 'Therefore let no one pass judgment on you …'; and 2:18: 'Let no one disqualify you …'

As we come to the first of these warnings my suspicion is that it will be a struggle for all of us to listen properly and to take the warning seriously, because *no one likes being warned*. This makes it all the more important to give the apostle our full attention! Here is the warning: 'See to it that no one takes you captive by philosophy and empty deceit, according to human tradition, according to the elemental spirits of the world, and not according to Christ' (2:8).

In 1:28, Paul said that proclaiming Christ involved not only warning every person but also teaching every person. It is clear that these are not two unrelated things. The warning of 2:8 here will be backed up by the teaching of verses 9-15. The teaching of verses 9-15 has its point in the warning of verse 8. We will see the same pattern when we come to the second (2:16, 17) and third (2:18, 19) warnings in due course.

1. Warning One: The kidnapper (2:8a)

A warning points out a danger. The purpose of a warning is to get us to take the danger seriously and to take whatever steps are necessary to escape the danger.

What is the danger Paul has in mind here? He describes it in rather graphic terms: **See to it that no one takes you captive.** The Greek word translated 'take captive' is a rare one, but vivid. Suggested meanings include kidnapping, carrying off a person bodily as a slave trader does.[1]

One of our problems (if it is right to call it a problem) in reading Paul's letters is that we only have *his* words. Any assumed common understanding between Paul and the Colossian recipients of this letter has to be deduced from what Paul has written.

One popular approach to Paul's warning here is to suppose that he is alluding to someone, or some particular people (the Colossian Christians would know very well who it was) who would lead them seriously astray if they were not very careful. On this approach we can put together an identikit picture of the people Paul had in mind. From 2:4 we could conclude that they were people with plausible arguments (or, persuasive speech), and so on. If this is correct, then the shocking point, I suspect, would have been the word that Paul used to describe these nice people, likening them to kidnappers or slave traders!

It was not uncommon in the early Christian communities for misleading teachers of one kind or another to come along and threaten the faith of the young believers. The letter to the Galatians, and those to the Corinthians, are quite clear that there were people who came into the Christian communities teaching something different from the apostolic gospel (see, for example, Gal. 1:6-9; 2 Cor. 11:3-5).

Yet (as I have previously indicated) I am inclined to think that the evidence for such persons in Colossae is quite thin. It seems to be at least equally likely that Paul, from his imprisonment in Rome, had heard of the Colossians' solid and firm faith in Christ (2:5), their genuine Christian lives (1:8), and so he wrote this encouraging letter, designed to show them the huge significance of their new faith and of the work the gospel was doing in the whole world, and to warn them of the dangers believers face. Of course, he was well aware of the intellectual climate of the time, and therefore the general form such dangers were likely to take. This, rather than the presence of particular false teachers,

[1] C.F.D. Moule, *The Epistles of Paul the Apostle to the Colossians and to Philemon* (Cambridge: Cambridge University Press, 1968), p. 90.

seems to have shaped the terms in which he expressed his warnings.[2]

One approach or the other does not make a huge difference to how *we* should hear Paul's words, except that if he was not speaking about a specific and actual first-century problem, but rather a potential one, then perhaps we will not be surprised to see how directly his words address us.

'Beware that no one takes you captive.' To hear this warning means to wake up to the fact that there is a real danger for Christian believers. The shock will be to realize that there *are* kidnappers around with the means to 'take you captive'.

2. His means (2:8b)

The rest of verse 8 describes the means by which a believer could be 'taken captive'.

If we were trying to put together a portrait of supposed false teachers in Colossae, we might conclude from these words that they were philosophers who emphasized human tradition and something called 'the elemental spirits of the world'. Perhaps these things were being put forward as alternatives or additions to Christ as a means of finding spiritual fulfilment.

Nevertheless, if (as seems probable to me) Paul did not have particular teachers or a particular teaching in mind, then he is giving *his* estimate of *any* teaching or system of thought that does not have Christ in his rightful place. Such ideas he lumps together: **by philosophy.** 'Philosophy' was a term used in Paul's world for a wide range of ideas and teachings, including, interestingly enough, the ideas of various parties in Judaism. 'Philosophy' itself is not a negative term, but philosophy that is 'not according to Christ' (whatever it is) is **empty deceit.** It lacks content of value, is without truth, has no firm basis, and is devoid of

[2] As indicated previously, this approach has been argued (to my mind convincingly) by M.D. Hooker, 'Were there false teachers in Colossae?' *Christ and the Spirit in the New Testament: Studies in Honour of Charles Francis Digby Moule*, eds. B. Lindars and S.S. Smalley (Cambridge: Cambridge University Press, 1973), pp. 315-331. The commentaries have generally taken some kind of 'mirror reading' approach.

power for good. All it can do is lead you astray, take you captive, kidnap you. Such teachings are **according to human tradition.** This, I take it, is another dismissive shrug.[3] How different are such traditions from what *you* 'received', when you 'received Christ Jesus the Lord' (2:6).[4]

The final insult Paul throws (if I am hearing him right) is that such teachings are **according to the elements of the world**.[5] The phrase is difficult to pin down, and has been the subject of much scholarly debate, but it may well simply be a rather derogatory dismissal of such teaching as 'elementary', 'materialistic', bound up with this world alone.[6]

3. The real danger (2:8c)

The crucial thing that Paul says about the teaching that has the potential to take you captive is, simply, but profoundly, that it is **not according to Christ.** It is not the proclamation of Christ, as you have been hearing from Paul in this letter. It is not the gospel that you heard from Epaphras. The Christ in whom are hidden all the treasures of wisdom and knowledge (2:3), on whom the existence and the reconciliation of all things depends (1:15-20), is the measure of every philosophy. By that measure any human ideas about life and the world that fail to grasp the significance of Christ, particularly of his death on the cross, are empty deceits, no matter how venerable their human origins, or persuasive the speech with which they are presented.

It seems to me that we are hearing Paul's put-down of *any* such teaching, rather than an allusion to some particular and specific problem in Colossae. It is a put-down that I believe fits the intellectual fads of any age, as well as the long-established ideas of any culture or institution.

---

[3] James D.G. Dunn, *The Epistles to the Colossians and to Philemon: A Commentary on the Greek Text* (Grand Rapids and Bletchley: Eerdmans and Paternoster, 1996), p. 148.

[4] 'Human tradition', by the way, is precisely the phrase that Jesus used to denounce the teaching of the Pharisees (Mark 7:8).

[5] While the appropriate English phrase is much disputed, the Greek expression does not have a word corresponding to 'spirits'. 'The elements of the world' is a simple (although far from clear!) rendering of the Greek.

[6] C.F.D. Moule, *The Epistles of Paul the Apostle to the Colossians and to Philemon* (Cambridge: Cambridge University Press, 1968), p. 92.

This should give us reason to pause. A real danger for Christian people (can you feel yourself already deflecting the warning to everyone *else*?) is to be *taken captive* by ideas, teachings, philosophies, ideologies, and even theologies, movements, spiritualities that are not in fact *according to Christ*, but (whatever they may claim for themselves) are empty deceits because they have nothing but a human origin and deal with nothing but this world.

I want to draw your attention carefully to what Paul does not say. It is not unusual for Christian people *either* to be afraid of engaging with ideas with which they are not comfortable, *or* to think there is no point in understanding anything beyond what they consider 'sound'. If that is you, don't think you can appeal to Paul's warning here. Paul does not say we should not understand the false philosophies, or not read any books that are not by our favourite authors, or even not to think that we could learn some worthwhile things from the non-Christian or non-evangelical thinkers. He does not say the danger to be avoided is hearing such things, or understanding them, or even taking an interest in them. That really is not the way for Christian people to relate to the world of ideas around them. The Christian community is not to be an intellectual ghetto any more than it is to be isolated from the world around us physically, socially or culturally. What Paul says is, do not be *taken captive*. Do not be *deceived*. *That* is the danger. And it is a real danger.

Study Questions

1. Are you aware of real dangers you face as a Christian? Describe some of them.

2. Consider some of today's 'philosophies' (in the very general sense of 'ways of thinking about life and the world' – such as, capitalism, materialism, democracy, individual freedom, feminism, postmodernism ...). Think about how each of the following phrases might apply to these views:

a. 'empty deceit';
b. 'according to human tradition';
c. 'according to the elements of the world';
d. 'not according to Christ'.

3. What ways of thinking have the potential to 'take you captive'?
4. What should Christian people do to avoid being 'taken captive'?

10

Teaching Everyone ...

(Colossians 2:9-15)

Serious Christians (and by that expression I do not mean *sombre* Christians, but Christians who take their faith and their being Christian seriously) are, in my experience, often anxious about two related things.

On the one hand, there is an anxiety about our *failures*: we do not live up to what we perhaps think that a serious Christian should. We do not *do* all the things we think that a Christian should. And there are things we *do* that we think a Christian should *not* do. Does this reflect that in some ways we are not what a Christian should *be*? And there is an anxiety. There is something very reasonable about this anxiety. There is an honesty about it. Yet it is a deep frustration. Every effort to be more spiritually minded, every attempt to be more prayerful, every resolution to be more holy, every decision to speak, to act, to love, to think, to give, to serve in a less self-centred way, and a more Christ-like way, every effort seems to disappoint.

On the other hand, there is a related anxiety about what we might be *missing*. Is there more to the Christian life than we have discovered? From time to time we meet Christians who seem to have a level of spiritual experience or godly insight or God-centred living (or *something*) that is way beyond our Christian life and experience. The question can come to our minds: Are we *complete* Christians? Am I living fully as a Christian should? Is there a secret that some have discovered, but I have missed?

This anxiety is also very reasonable and honest. Haven't you often found yourself mixing with, meeting or perhaps just hearing about Christian people who seem to be living at a level far above where you are? Perhaps it is their conversation that is more spiritual than yours. Perhaps it is their evangelistic zeal that is more courageous than yours. Perhaps it is their prayers: more faithful than yours.

Responding rightly to these anxieties is not a simple matter. It would be foolish to *dismiss* them or to deal with them by some kind of denial or suppression. To cope by pretending that you are something that you know you are not would be a mistake. To overcome the anxiety with a smug kind of determined, complacent self-satisfaction or even cynicism would be worse still.

While some of us may well need to be warned not to shrug off these real concerns, we also need to understand that another danger is to seek relief, or answers, somewhere other than the gospel we have received: Jesus, the Lord and the Christ. Remember Paul's counsel we heard in 2:6, 7 (the theme sentence of this letter): 'Therefore, as you *received* Christ Jesus the Lord, so *walk* in him, rooted and built up *in him* and established in the faith, *just as you were taught*, abounding in thanksgiving.' Paul spoke similarly in 1:23 of 'not shifting from the hope of *the gospel that you heard*'. Indeed Paul has insisted that his own energies have all been directed to this one task: 'Him we proclaim, warning everyone and teaching everyone with all wisdom.' By this means, and no other, Paul aims to 'present everyone mature in Christ' (1:28). This is because Christ is the one 'in whom are hidden all the treasures of wisdom and knowledge' (2:3).

It calls for careful wisdom to distinguish between *being built up in him* (as Paul put it in 2:7) and being *deluded by persuasive speech* (of which he warned in 2:4). It is not necessarily a simple matter to tell whether you are discovering 'all the riches of the full assurance of understanding and the knowledge of God's mystery, which is Christ' (2:2) or being taken 'captive by philosophy and empty deceit, according to human tradition, according to the elements of the world, and not according to Christ' (2:8). The difficulty lies in the fact that the latter is a deception or delusion. We may presume that whenever Christian believers are deceived in the way Paul envisages in this letter, they think that they are growing in Christ. That, you see, is the delusion!

In our last chapter we reached the point (2:8) where Paul issued the sharp warning about being taken captive by 'philosophy and empty deceit'. The warning is now supported by teaching about Christ in 2:9-15. This 'warning' and 'teaching' is how Paul proclaims Christ with a view to presenting every person perfect in Christ (see 1:28). The key to distinguishing persuasive (but deceitful) ideas, experiences and teachings from actually growing *in Christ* will lie in listening carefully to the apostle's teaching. The key to walking *in Christ*, to being built *in him* and being established *in the faith* also lies in this teaching.

> For in him the whole fullness of deity dwells bodily, and you have been filled in him, who is the head of all rule and authority. In him also you were circumcised with a circumcision made without hands, in the putting off the body of the flesh, in the circumcision of Christ, having been buried with him in the baptism, in whom you were also raised with him through faith in the powerful working of God, who raised him from the dead. And you, who were dead in your trespasses and the uncircumcision of your flesh, God made you alive together with him, having forgiven us all our trespasses, by canceling the record of debt that stood against us with its legal demands. This he set aside, nailing it to the cross. He disarmed the rulers and authorities and put them to open shame, by triumphing over them in him (2:9-15, slightly modified from the ESV).

1. Why is 'human tradition' so dangerous? (2:9, 10)

The opening word of verse 9 (**For**) connects the whole passage (vv. 9-15) to the warning of verse 8. The teaching in 2:9-15 is therefore presented as the answer to the question: Why is there such a danger in 'human tradition' (to use Paul's term in 2:8) that does not have Christ at its centre?

Paul supports the seriousness of his warning in 2:8 by pointing, not at the danger, but to Christ and the truth about him. This is one of the problems for those who suppose that there was a particular 'false teaching' that had arisen in Colossae, and which Paul's letter is designed to counter. If that were the case (and it is, of course, possible), Paul's tactic frustrates attempts to reconstruct the nature of the false teaching simply because he gives no direct attention to it. His focus and emphasis is firmly on the positive teaching that will protect believers from the dangers. This tactic is also consistent with the view that the dangers of which he warns are general, the kind of thing believers should expect to encounter in one form or another, without there in fact being any particular expression of these dangers current in Colossae and known to Paul.

The horror of being deceived (2:4), and being taken captive away from Christ (2:8), which would mean that you are not walking *in him* and being built *in him* and being established in your faith *in him* (2:6, 7) lies in just how wonderful he is, and how important is what God has done in him, and what it means to live *in him*. The best protection against being taken captive is to know Christ deeply.

The teaching in 2:9-15 consists of three truths about Christ which are briefly stated in verses 9 and 10, and then expanded in verses 11 to 15. The three truths we might sum up as:

(1) God in Christ (v. 9, about which we will hear more in verse 14);

(2) You in Christ (v. 10a, about which more is said in verses 11-13); and

(3) Christ over all (v. 10b, elaborated in v. 15).

a. God in Christ

First: **in him the whole fullness of deity dwells bodily.** This picks up what was said in 1:19: (literally) 'in him all the fullness was pleased to dwell.' Paul will unpack this remarkable statement in verse 14 (just as he unpacked 1:19 in 1:20) by showing us what God *did* in Christ. Yet we start with the basic, but infinitely important point that if you move away from Christ, if you are kidnapped by ideas that take you from Christ, you are being taken away from *God*.

Here is the enormous claim of the Christian gospel, simply stated. The God who had once 'dwelt' on Mount Sinai (Exod. 24:16), in the tabernacle (Exod. 25:8; Num. 5:3; 2 Sam. 7:6; 1 Chron. 17:5; Ps. 78:60; Jer. 7:12; Hosea 12:9) and subsequently in the Jerusalem temple (2 Sam. 7:5; 1 Kings 6:13; 8:13; 2 Chron. 36:15; Ezra 6:12; Ps. 26:8; 84:1; 132:5, 7; cf. 1 Kings 8:27, 30, 39, 43, 49; 1 Chron. 17:4; 2 Chron. 6:18, 21, 30, 33), who was pleased to 'dwell' on Mount Zion (1 Chron. 23:25; Ezra 7:15; Neh. 1:9; Ps. 43:3; 68:16, 18; 74:2, 7; 76:2; 132:13, 14; 135:21; Isa. 8:18; Ezek. 43:7; Joel 3:17, 21; Zech. 2:13; 8:3), now dwells *bodily* in Jesus Christ. In other words, the God who had made himself known and was present among his people in the history of Israel (Exod. 29:45, 46; Lev. 26:11; Num. 35:34) and promised to dwell among them again (Isa. 57:15; Ezek. 37:27; 43:9; Zech. 2:10, 11) was now fully present in Christ in bodily form.

The claim is radical. Remember that it was the Jewish Paul who was writing to these gentile Colossians. He did not allow any notion that Jesus was *a* divine figure, or that *something* of divinity was present in him, certainly not that he was one among many religious figures. 'All the fullness of deity' means that there is no *more* of deity to be found elsewhere.

The idea of God 'dwelling' should remind us of the Old Testament language of *God's name* 'dwelling' in the place that the Lord God chose (Deut. 12:11; 14:23; 16:2, 6, 11; 26:2). That reality whereby God was present with his people by his *name* (in the land, or the tabernacle, or the temple, or on Zion) has given way to *this* reality, where the whole fullness of deity dwells bodily in Jesus Christ.

The words 'in *him*' speak of the absolute uniqueness of Christ Jesus. In our time (as in the first century) this claim must be made in the face of numerous rival religious claims. The exclusive nature of the claim must be appreciated. It is not that 'deity' is the kind of thing that one might encounter in various ways, and to varying degrees, in a variety of religions and spiritualities. The gospel claim is that 'the whole fullness of deity' – all there is to deity – is to be found *in Jesus Christ*.

Moreover, the whole fullness of deity 'dwells *bodily*' in him. This speaks of the real, substantial, even tangible and visible presence of God. The whole fullness of deity has chosen to be present in this created world, not just in the general sense of what we sometimes call 'omnipresence', but in *bodily* form, in the historical person Jesus Christ. It is physical! This is what was said earlier in the words, 'He is the image of the invisible God' (1:15).

Some speculate that there may have been a teaching in Colossae that was suggesting that Christ was one among many powers all sharing something of deity. You will only find the fullness of deity by dealing with all the powers (or something like that). Paul responds with an emphatic 'No.' *The whole* fullness of deity dwells *in Christ*. He is speaking of the one who has come among us in *bodily* form, in flesh, and indeed who in his body of flesh has died on a cross (1:22). In *him* all the fullness of deity dwells bodily!

Yet (as I have been suggesting) it is probable that Paul said this, not because there was someone in Colossae explicitly denying it, but because all the fullness of deity *did* dwell bodily in him! In other words, the reality of who Christ is, and what has happened in and through him, really is enough to generate statements like this about him. The truth is the truth before it is ever denied! This truth is important enough to be said without needing to be a reaction to a particular false teaching.

We will have to wait until we get to verse 14 to see the *purpose* of all the fullness of deity dwelling *bodily* in him. But the first basic truth, briefly stated in verse 9, should make us firm and clear that any philosophy or tradition that is not centred on Jesus Christ and fully satisfied with him will be an empty deceit, no matter how plausible it may sound. That is why Paul struggles with all the energy God gives him to *proclaim Christ* (1:28, 29). That is why we must walk *in him* and be built *in him* (2:6, 7).

b. You in Christ

The second point is: **and you have been filled in him.** The TNIV puts it, 'in Christ you *have been brought to fullness*'; the REB, 'in him *you have been brought to fulfilment*.' These are attempts to get across the sense of the Greek tenses here.[1] The point is that Paul is not speaking of a future possibility, or an unrealized ideal. This is a reality: 'in him you have been filled'.

What does Paul mean by this expression? In context he seems to be saying, 'you have been filled with the whole fullness of God' (cf. Eph. 3:19; 1:23). That is what happens if you are *in Christ,* you see, for in him all the fullness of deity dwells bodily and in him *you* are filled! This is not easy to take in and the truth briefly stated here will be unpacked wonderfully for us at some length in verses 11-13. However, the brief statement is enough for us to see why we must take care not to be taken in by any ideas that would move us from Christ, or on from Christ, no matter how persuasive or impressive. If you move away from Christ, no matter what you are promised, be very clear: you lose.

c. Christ over all

The third point, briefly stated, is that Christ is the one **who is the head of all rule and authority.** Again Paul is picking up a major theme from the introduction, especially 1:16 (where he mentions 'rulers' and 'authorities'). There is no power or authority that can rival Christ. More will be said about this in verse 15, but already we must see that there is no power, no authority that is independent of Christ, or that is not under Christ. No human philosophy whatsoever, no human tradition, no human values, or human insight that is not 'according to Christ', can begin to compare to him. They are delusions and empty deceits. That, again, is why you must not be taken captive by any such thing (2:8). What a disaster that would be!

These three briefly stated truths (*God in Christ, You in Christ* and *Christ over all*) are not simply elements of an abstract philosophy or theology. They are the historical realities of the gospel that you have heard. Paul will now unpack the meaning of each of these three truths, taking the second one first, and at greatest length.

---

[1] There is a present tense of the verb 'to be' and a perfect participle of 'to fill'.

2. You in Christ (2:11-12)

Here we find a truly remarkable description of the fullness of our experience in Christ in the form of a stark and vivid extended metaphor. In what follows, the wording of verses 11 and 12 when reproduced in bold type will be slightly modified from the ESV, reflecting points where a more literal rendering will help our understanding of this unusual statement. These changes from the ESV are in italics.

In him (literally here 'in whom') echoes the phrase 'in him' that we have already heard twice in this passage (2:9, 10). 'In him' or 'in Christ' is a favourite expression of Paul in this letter, and runs like a thread through the argument. Paul began the letter by addressing his readers as brothers 'in Christ' (1:2). Their faith is 'in Christ' (1:4; 2:5). 'In him', Paul says, we have redemption, the forgiveness of sins (1:14). Yet these things are only rightly understood when we see that 'in him' all things were created (1:16, literally); 'in him' all things hold together (1:17); 'in him' all the fullness of God was pleased to dwell (1:19; cf. 2:9). Paul's labour as a servant of the gospel had the goal and purpose of presenting everyone perfect (or mature) 'in Christ' (1:28). 'In him' all the treasures of wisdom and knowledge are hidden (2:3). Therefore, we are to walk 'in him' (2:6) and be built 'in him' (2:7). For we have been filled 'in him' (2:10).

Paul's dramatic description of what has happened to those who are 'in Christ' takes us to the heart of what it means to be 'in Christ'. We will consider the three parts of this extraordinary description in turn.

a. Circumcised

It begins with the arresting words: **also** [or perhaps better, even] **you were circumcised.** Addressing readers who were mostly gentile, these words would have sounded very strange (hence, '*even* you!'). The Gentiles were known (at least to Jews) as 'the uncircumcised' (see 3:11; also Rom. 3:30; 4:9; Gal. 2:7; Eph. 2:11). It is obvious that Paul is not suggesting that they have now been literally circumcised, for he adds: **with a circumcision made without hands.** In other words, not with a literal or physical circumcision, not a circumcision accomplished by human action.

In what sense then have those who are 'in Christ' been 'circumcised'? Paul is apparently using circumcision as a metaphor for death. He puts this starkly by saying that the circumcision of which he is speaking was not performed in the foreskin, but ***in the*** **putting off the body of the flesh.** 'Here is a circumcision which entailed not the stripping off of a small portion of flesh but the violent removal of the whole body in death.'[2]

This hardly makes matters clear! If by saying 'you have been circumcised' Paul means 'you have died a violent death', our question becomes, In what sense have those who are 'in Christ' *died*? The answer is that they have died ***in*** **the circumcision of Christ**, that is (since 'circumcision' is being used as a metaphor for death), in the death of Christ. We have heard earlier that we have been reconciled 'in [Christ's] body of flesh by his death' (1:22). Now, using similar language, Paul says that in Christ's death (his 'circumcision', his putting off the body of the flesh) believers also died (were 'circumcised').

In other words, Paul is teaching the same truth as we hear from him elsewhere. When Jesus died on the cross 'our old self was crucified with him' (Rom. 6:6). While Paul does not explicitly use the language of substitution ('for us', 'in our place') in Colossians 2, it appears to be the idea just beneath the surface. Christ's death was so effectively *for us* that it was *our death*. He died *in our place* so truly that when *he* died, *we* died. 'One died for all, therefore all have died' (2 Cor. 5:14). This truth (often referred to in theological discussions as the doctrine of penal substitutionary atonement[3]) is as profound as any the Bible teaches.

The question raised by Paul's presentation of the profound significance of Christ's death in 2:11 is, Why use such a strange (to us, at least) metaphor? Why did he say, 'you were circumcised … in the circumcision of Christ' instead of 'you died in Christ's death'? One possibility is

[2] Peter T. O'Brien, *Colossians, Philemon* (Waco, Texas: Word Books, 1982), p. 117.

[3] For an important and wide-ranging examination of this doctrine, see Steve Jeffery, Mike Ovey and Andrew Sach, *Pierced for our Transgressions: Rediscovering the glory of penal substitution* (Nottingham: Inter-Varsity Press, 2007).

that in Colossae there were people who were urging that the Gentiles who had come to believe in the Messiah (the Jewish Messiah!) should be circumcised, accepting the God-given sign of his covenant with Abraham (Gen. 17:1-14). Something like that happened in Galatia (see Gal. 6:12 and *passim*). Perhaps, then, Paul is insisting that by their union with Jesus Christ by faith in him, these Colossian Gentiles *have* been circumcised, and indeed their circumcision is superior to the merely physical. 'Made without hands' suggests that this circumcision is not a human act, but a work of God (cf. Eph. 2:11). 'A circumcision made without hands' may remind us of Jesus' contrast between the temple 'made with hands' and the one 'not made with hands' (Mark 14:58),[4] or the description of idols as 'gods made with hands' (Acts 19:26).[5]

While this thesis is possible, we still lack concrete evidence that such teaching was in fact present and a problem in Colossae. It seems at least as likely that Paul chose the language of 'circumcision' because of the fact that wherever the gospel of Christ Jesus was proclaimed among the nations, it was important to understand the relationship between the physical descendants of Abraham ('the [literally] circumcised') and those whom God had now 'qualified to share in the inheritance of the saints in light' (1:12) 'in [Christ's] body of flesh by his death' (1:22). As far as Israel was concerned the human race had two parts: the *circumcised* and the *uncircumcised*: *Israel* and the *nations*. The wonder is that there in Colossae, and indeed wherever the word of the truth of the gospel was being proclaimed in the whole world, people from the *nations* were now being *circumcised* with this remarkable new kind of circumcision.[6] The issue did not need to be raised by false

---

[4] Cf. Acts 7:48; 2 Cor. 5:1; Heb. 9:11, 24.

[5] Cf. Deut. 4:28; 27:15; 2 Kings 19:18; 22:17; 2 Chron. 32:19; Ps. 115:4; 135:15; Isa. 2:8; 17:8; 31:7; 37:19; Jer. 1:16; 10:3, 9; 25:6; Micah 5:13; Acts 7:41.

[6] We should also remember that Moses spoke of a circumcision more profound than the physical mark Israelites bore. He said to them: 'And the LORD your God will circumcise your heart and the heart of your offspring, so that you will love the LORD your God with all your heart and with all your soul, that you may live' (Deut. 30:6).

teachers advocating the physical circumcision of Gentiles. One of the questions inevitably provoked wherever the gospel was preached among the Gentiles was, Is a gentile believer in Jesus fully qualified to belong to God's people, the descendants of Abraham to whom circumcision had been given as a sign of the covenant between God and his people (Gen. 17)? Paul answers this question, not (in my opinion) because he has heard someone was giving a wrong answer, but simply because the answer is important. 'In Christ *even you* have been circumcised.' The death of Jesus Christ on the cross is your circumcision! You died with him.

Here is the powerful significance of Jesus' death, even for Gentiles like most Christians today. Christ's death was so fully and effectively *for us* that each of us have to say that what happened to Christ, in awful, physical, bloody reality (his terrible 'circumcision') has happened to me, in reality too, though not physical and bloody.

This is something that I fear has become a cliché in many Christian circles. One benefit of Paul's stark and graphic language may be to break through the clichés. We are to *consider* the death of Christ, that astonishing 'baptism', with which he was 'baptized', his 'circumcision'. We are to understand that there an extraordinary thing happened *to us*. Our old life came to an end. The necessary consequences of this will come later in Paul's letter (see 3:5-9).

This dramatic description of the believer's death in Christ's death closes with the words, **having been buried with him in *the* baptism.** The majority of commentators see here a reference to the Christian rite of baptism.[7] This is not certain.

In the first place, we should note that the Greek word does not necessarily refer to what we now call 'baptism'. Indeed, it is important to realize that 'baptism' is not

[7] So, for example, C.F.D. Moule, *The Epistles of Paul the Apostle to the Colossians and to Philemon* (Cambridge: Cambridge University Press, 1968), pp. 96, 97; Peter T. O'Brien, *Colossians, Philemon* (Waco, Texas: Word Books, 1982), p. 118; N.T. Wright, *The Epistles of Paul to the Colossians and to Philemon* (Leicester: Inter-Varsity Press, 1986), pp. 106-108; Douglas J. Moo, *The Letters to the Colossians and to Philemon* (Nottingham: Apollos, 2008), pp. 200-203; 158-160.

a *translation* of the Greek word, but a *transliteration*.[8] Meanings that have subsequently been associated with the word 'baptism' in English are no sure guide to the meaning of the Greek words used in the New Testament. Greek had a number of cognate words based on the root *bapt-*. These words had meanings in Greek independent of any rites or ceremonies. The word translated 'baptism' in 2:12,[9] depending on the context, could mean 'engulf', 'overwhelm', 'dip', or 'wash'. Note, for example, that the Septuagint translates a Hebrew phrase in Isaiah 21:4 meaning 'wickedness *overwhelms* me' with the verb *baptizo,* while what Naaman did in the Jordan River according to 2 Kings 5:14 is represented with the same verb. It is possible that the sense of the phrase in 2:12a could be conveyed in English as 'having been buried with him in *the overwhelming experience* (that is, in the experience referred to in the previous phrase, namely, Christ's death itself).'

Secondly, there is an important precedent for the *bapt-* vocabulary being used to refer to Christ's death. Jesus referred to his death as 'the baptism with which I am baptized,' better: 'the overwhelming experience with which I am overwhelmed' (Mark 10:38). He said that his disciples, James and John, would be 'baptized' with this 'baptism' of his (Mark 10:39). By this he was not referring to what we call Christian baptism, but in some sense to their sharing in his suffering and/or death.

In the context of 2:12, therefore, where the death of Jesus is clearly in mind but there is no other allusion at all to 'baptism' as Christians usually understand that term today, it seems probable that 'the baptism'[10] to which Paul refers is, again, Jesus' death, or possibly the believers' participation in that death ('overwhelmed with the overwhelming

---

[8] I am grateful to my friend Dr Barry Newman for this important observation.

[9] There is a textual uncertainty whether the word is *baptismos* or *baptisma*. There are good arguments for the former. Peter T. O'Brien, *Colossians, Philemon* (Waco, Texas: Word Books, 1982), p. 118.

[10] The definite article in the Greek text (not represented in most English translations) is consistent with the understanding presented here, but not decisive.

experience with which [he was] overwhelmed'). In neither case would the reference have anything to do with a literal washing or immersion in water. 'In Christ' believers have shared in his death, fully and completely: they have been 'buried with him'.[11]

b. Made alive

More than that: **in *whom*[12] you were also raised with him.** To be joined with Christ in his death cannot stop with the burial. He was raised from the tomb! The one who raised him from the dead is the one who has also raised you to new life. You have this new life in your union with him whom God has raised. The union is accomplished by faith: **through faith in the powerful working of God, who raised him from the dead.** Faith in Christ is at the same time faith in God, the Father of our Lord Jesus Christ (cf. 1:3, 4). United to him by faith we share in his resurrection life. This faith is the sure sign of new life, just as it is the means of taking hold of that new life. It is the *breath* of this new life. Your faith in the working of God who raised Jesus from the dead will animate a whole new life, as new and as substantial as the resurrection life of Jesus. At the beginning of this letter we learned that news of these Colossians' 'faith in Christ Jesus' had stirred Paul to constant thankfulness (1:3). Continuing in this faith, stable and steadfast, was more important than anything else (1:23). The firmness of their faith in Christ gave Paul joy (2:5). In this faith he called on them to be established (2:7).

---

[11] On the interpretation of Colossians 2:12a see the important argument of D.W.B. Robinson, 'Towards a Definition of Baptism,' Chapter 23 in Peter G. Bolt and Mark D. Thompson, eds, *Donald Robinson: Selected Works, Volume 2: Preaching God's Word* (Camperdown, N.S.W.: Australian Church Record, 2008), pp. 252-270, especially 261, 262; originally published in *Reformed Theological Review* 34/1(1975): 1-15.

[12] The Greek (which is exactly the same as the phrase translated 'in him' at the beginning of verse 11) could be translated 'in which' (so ESV), referring to 'the baptism'. However, I agree with Peter T. O'Brien, *Colossians, Philemon* (Waco, Texas: Word Books, 1982), p. 119, and others in seeing the phrase as a further instance of the 'in Christ', 'in him', 'in whom' theme that runs through this passage.

The very same power (God's own powerful working!) that raised Jesus from the dead has brought us to life in Christ. This striking assertion is elaborated in verse 13.

The wonder of what has happened to these gentile believers who are now 'in Christ' is only fully appreciated when we remember their former condition. **And you, who were dead.** He is not now speaking of their having 'died' with Christ as in 2:11, 12a, but of their condition before coming to faith in Christ. The language is being stretched beyond its normal capacity in order to describe something beyond our full comprehension. Those who have died with Christ were already dead people!

The sense in which they were dead is defined with two expressions. First: **in your trespasses.** Earlier, Paul had described their former life as 'alienated and hostile in mind, doing evil deeds' (1:21). This is what Paul now calls 'dead'. As guilty sinners they were without life, being alienated from the source of life.

To this Paul adds, **and the uncircumcision of your flesh.** They were, of course, literally 'uncircumcised', being Gentiles. This signified that they were, as Paul puts it elsewhere, 'at that time separated from Christ, alienated from the commonwealth of Israel and strangers to the covenants of promise, having no hope and without God in the world' (Eph. 2:12). This is what Paul means by 'dead': alienated from God.

But now the death of Christ has been the circumcision ('a circumcision made without hands') of these uncircumcised people (2:11). The outcome? **God made *you* alive together with him.** The dead ('uncircumcised') people died (were 'circumcised') with Christ in order that they might be made alive with him.

c. Forgiven

The heart of all this is: **having forgiven us all our trespasses.** The forgiveness of sins is the powerful reality that makes possible deliverance from the domain of darkness and transference to the kingdom of Christ (see 1:13, 14). It is the reality that makes people who were dead in trespasses alive. It is what turns alienation into reconciliation (1:21, 22).

Do not overlook the word 'all'. The heart of the new life we have been given is the forgiveness of *all* the trespasses. The essence of our old dead existence being discarded is the forgiveness of all our trespasses. Some of us are more aware of our trespasses than others. Some of us have more sensitive consciences. But in Christ the truth is: ALL FORGIVEN.

A small but significant point: at the end of 2:13 Paul shifts from speaking of 'you' (Gentiles) to 'us'. While the language 'uncircumcision' and 'a circumcision made without hands' of verses 11-13a was particularly fitting for his gentile readers ('you'), the forgiveness of all 'our' trespasses is something Paul and other Jewish believers in Jesus share with the faithful brothers in Christ at Colossae (1:2).

All of this (2:11-13) is what Paul meant when he said 'you have been filled in him' (2:10). He does not for a moment mean to encourage spiritual complacency by this. You are to *walk* in him, to be *built* in him, to be *established* in your faith in him (2:6, 7). You are to continue in this faith, stable and steadfast, not shifting from the hope of the gospel that you heard (1:23). The point now is the completeness of what has been given to us *in Christ*. The fullness of life (as all the treasures of wisdom and knowledge, 2:3) is *in him*. I am not sure what you are looking for in life, but what you *should* be looking for is what has been given to you in Christ, in the death of Christ and his resurrection. That is why you must see to it that no one takes you captive away from Christ (2:8).

Verses 14 and 15 now, elaborate the other two truths about Christ that were briefly stated in verses 9 and 10, and show us why *in him* we are filled. Verse 14 spells out the point of the whole fullness of deity dwelling bodily in Christ (2:9). Verse 15 then spells out how it is that he is the head of all rule and authority (2:10).

3. God in Christ (2:14)

Verse 14 shows that the point of the whole fullness of deity dwelling bodily in Christ lies in what was accomplished in his death. In 1:19, 20 it was made clear that 'all the fullness (of God)' dwelt in Christ with the purpose of reconciling all things to him by the blood of his cross. In 2:14 we are given a further description of what God did in Christ's death on the cross that resulted in the forgiveness of all our trespasses.

a. Wiping clean

Verse 14 is one of the most vivid descriptions in the New Testament of what happened when Jesus died. Consider a document that records all of our indebtedness to God (the indebtedness of those who were dead in trespasses, alienated, hostile in mind and doing evil deeds). What a disturbing document that would be! It would not be the kind of a certificate that you would want to frame and put on your wall for all to see! This is a document you would want hidden in a secret place, where no one would find it. The trouble is that hiding it would not change the facts that were recorded on it.

The forgiveness of all our trespasses was accomplished **by cancelling the record of debt.** It is reasonable to see Paul's thought being expressed here in terms that apply particularly to himself and his fellow Jews (note the 'us' in the next phrase). They had entered into covenant with God to obey his law. They had failed to do so. The Law of Moses was therefore a 'record of debt' **that stood against us.** This makes good sense of the phrase **with its legal demands.** Yet it is unlikely that Paul was thinking only of Jewish people as being indebted to God. In some less clearly defined way, we are right to understand that there is a record of the debt all people owe to God (see Rom. 3:23 in context).

This debt was 'cancelled'. The word is strong; it means 'obliterated'. The record of the debt no longer exists. The slate has been wiped clean. The record has been completely expunged.

b. Nailed to the cross

How could that happen? **This he set aside, nailing it to the cross**. 'The cross' has already been mentioned in 1:20. God who was pleased to dwell in Christ reconciled all things to him, 'making peace by the blood of his cross'. Now Paul says, all our trespasses were forgiven (2:13) when the record of our debt was obliterated by Jesus being nailed to the cross (2:14).

As we considered 1:20 we reflected on the fact that the claims of the Christian faith are nowhere more remarkable than in what is claimed to have happened when Jesus died on the cross. In 1:20 Paul presented Christ's death as a sacrifice which effected the reconciliation to him of 'all things, whether on earth or in heaven'. In 1:22 we heard that Paul's Colossian readers are part of this, having themselves been 'reconciled ... by his death'. In 2:11-14 this truth has been elaborated: you died in his death (v. 11-12a); you were also raised with him (v. 12b); made alive, all your sins having been forgiven (v. 13); your debt to God has been obliterated by Jesus' death on the cross (v. 14). Once again (as we noted in 2:11) the idea that is just beneath the surface here seems to be that of substitution. The debt was cancelled when Jesus died precisely because he paid the debt *for us* by dying *in our place*. It is sometimes objected that the death of one man cannot possibly pay the debt that others owe. How could that be just? The answer involves understanding that this was not simply one man taking the punishment deserved by others. In him all the fullness of deity dwells bodily (2:9). The one to whom the debt was owed was fully involved in the payment of the debt. As Paul puts it elsewhere, 'in Christ God was reconciling the world to himself' (2 Cor. 5:19).

4. Christ over all (2:15)

In 2:15 Paul concludes his explanation of why his readers must see to it that no one takes them captive (2:8) by filling out the statement that Christ is 'the head of all rule and authority' (2:10b). He points to the cosmic scope of what God has done in the death of Christ. He says a little more than in 1:20, where we heard that the peace accomplished by the blood of Christ's cross embraces 'all things ... in heaven and on earth, visible and invisible, whether thrones or dominions or rulers or authorities' (1:16, cf. 20). It is now made clear that the peace made with the 'rulers and authorities' involved what we might call 'pacification'. Not all of creation has submitted gladly to this peace.

a. Disarmed

He disarmed the rulers and authorities. It is most natural grammatically to understand 'He' as a reference to God (see verse 13b), rather than Christ, although it is inappropriate to make too strong a distinction (see, again, 2:9). While the precise identity of 'the rulers and authorities' has been the subject of much scholarly discussion, the context suggests that Paul is referring to spiritual powers that were opposed to God. More precise definition is unnecessary except to observe that these 'rulers and authorities' were, it seems, 'disarmed' by the cancellation of the record of debt that stood against us. Satan (who we must assume is the power behind the rulers and authorities) is 'the accuser ... who accuses ... day and night before God' (Rev. 12:10). With no accusation that can legitimately be made (the record of debt has been cancelled!), Satan and his minions have been stripped of their power against us.

b. Shamed

More than that: **and put them to open shame.** By being stripped of their power to accuse, the 'rulers and authorities' were 'exposed to the universe in their utter helplessness'.[13] They now have no power or authority. As rulers and authorities, they are a joke!

c. Triumphed

All this was accomplished **by triumphing over them in him.**[14] Through his death on the cross all things have been put back in their place. Insofar as they have usurped God's place, they have been stripped and put to shame. A mighty victory has been won over them.

This is deeply ironic, of course. The 'rulers and authorities' most obvious in the first-century Mediterranean world, namely the Romans, had put Jesus to death. They had no trouble doing it. They met no resistance. They suffered no

---

[13] Peter T. O'Brien, *Colossians, Philemon* (Waco, Texas: Word Books, 1982), p. 128.

[14] Note that 'in him' could be 'in it', that is, 'in the cross' (So AV, NIV, TNIV). The ambiguity of the Greek is attractive, for of course both meanings are true and important.

injury. He was the one who was stripped naked. He was the one shamefully hung on the public gallows. The triumph, if you judge by appearances, was all theirs.

But it wasn't. The truth is that the triumphant one was the one who died. If you still cannot see that, perhaps you had better go back and read this passage carefully again.

The whole of creation has been pacified by God in the death of Christ. In particular there is no power (if I may put the same point in different words of Paul) in all creation that will be able to separate us from the love of God in Christ Jesus our Lord (Rom. 8:39). In the cross they were stripped of all power to do harm in a mighty triumph.

Anxious Christian: I do not ask you to ignore your concerns about the inadequacies of your Christian life. But look to Christ. Consider again who he is. Consider again what he has done. And understand how in him you are filled. That is why you must see to it that no one takes you captive with anything that takes you away from this Christ.

Study Questions

1. How can each of the three truths about Jesus Christ taught in Colossians 2:9-15 protect Christian believers from the danger of which Paul warned in 2:8?
2. What is the value for gentile Christians today of the unusual language Paul uses to describe the significance of Jesus' death for us in Colossians 2:11, 12?
3. Explain to a new Christian the sense in which he or she has 'died' and been 'raised'.
4. Explain to a non-Christian enquirer the sense in which he or she is 'dead', and the sense in which God makes such dead people 'alive'.
5. Consider how the phrase 'having forgiven us all our trespasses' sums up all that Paul teaches in Colossians 2:9-15.

6. List (in your own words) everything Paul says about Jesus' death in Colossians 2:9-15, and give thanks to God!

11

Shadows and Substance
(Colossians 2:16, 17)

As the assembly of relatively new believers in Christ Jesus gathered in Philemon's house in Colossae listening to Tychicus reading the letter that he had brought from Paul in Rome, it is reasonable to suppose that by this stage they would all have picked up the tone of the letter: joyful, confident *thankfulness*, combined with a note of serious *warning*. That combination is striking and important.

For example, they had heard Paul's words: 'And you … he has now reconciled in his body of flesh by his death, in order to present you holy and blameless and above reproach before him' (1:21, 22). What a reason for thankfulness! However, this was immediately followed by these words of serious warning: '… if indeed you continue in the faith, stable and steadfast, not shifting from the hope of the gospel …' (1:23)

Again they had heard Paul's joy expressed: 'For though I am absent in body, yet I am with you in spirit, rejoicing to see your good order and the firmness of your faith in Christ' (2:5). No wonder he was constantly thanking God! However, immediately before these words they had heard the note of warning: 'I say this in order that no one may delude you with plausible arguments' (2:4).

In our last chapter we were listening to 2:9-15 which presents, in some detail, the wonder that *in Christ the whole fullness of deity dwells bodily* (and what was therefore accomplished by his death, 2:9, 14), and that *in him you have been filled* (because in his death your old life died, and you have been made alive with him, fully forgiven, 2:10a, 11-13), and that *he is the head of all rule and authority* (because the death of Jesus was a mighty victory over every power in all of creation, 2:10b, 15). The tone of 2:9-15 is clearly joyful, confident thankfulness!

It is important to notice that this joyful passage begins with the word 'For' (meaning 'because') and is presented as the reason for the warning that immediately precedes it: 'See to it that no one takes you captive by philosophy and empty deceit, according to human tradition, according to the elements of the world, and not according to Christ' (2:8).

The brilliant news of 2:9-15 is then followed by the second warning in the main body of the letter (the first was 2:8), presented as the conclusion to be drawn from the preceding words:

> Therefore let no one pass judgment on you in questions of food and drink, or with regard to a festival or a new moon or a Sabbath. These are a shadow of the things to come, but the substance belongs to Christ (2:16, 17).

This linking of joyful, confident *thankfulness* with *warnings* that are to be taken seriously continues as the texture of the letter. The seriousness of the warnings is the complement of the joyful thankfulness. It is precisely because what God has done in Christ Jesus is so good, important and brilliant that it would be a monumental disaster not to continue in this faith, or to be deceived by plausible arguments, or to be taken away from Christ in any way.

It is a mistake to set these things over against one another. We may imagine that the joyful confidence believers have in Christ somehow cancels out any serious warning. Perhaps we think that to take too seriously the danger of shifting from the hope of the gospel, or the threat of being deceived would undermine our joyful confidence. On the other hand, when confronted with the stark and real possibilities of our faith being weakened or shaken, perhaps we think that joyful, confident thankfulness is unrealistic.

There is an intellectual challenge here. In terms of categories sometimes employed by theologians, we are talking about the relationship between the *preservation* of the saints and the *perseverance* of the saints. The issue could be expressed in terms of the supposed tension between divine sovereignty and human responsibility in salvation. The connection between grace and works would be another way of looking at it.

This intellectual struggle (important as it is to consider) is an expression of the existential tension we easily feel: between (a) joyful confidence in God's sovereign and free grace towards us for our full and complete salvation in Jesus Christ and (b) our efforts at godliness. Frankly, when we focus on the latter, what confidence can we have? When we concentrate on the former, what real dangers could there possibly be?

Many Christians could be categorized along these lines. There are those of us who are not yet shaped as persons by the overwhelming goodness of God towards us in Jesus Christ. For all our genuine Christian profession, there is an underlying lack of confidence, an absence of joy, a nervous need to prove ourselves (to ourselves, if not to everyone else). The warnings of the gospel are very real to those like this. Will we continue in the faith? Will we ever be established and firm?

On the other hand, there are some of us who are so confident, so assured, so bold that the warnings have no more than a theoretical impact on us. They are the things we gladly apply to others, but can hardly imagine that we need to hear. There is no realistic prospect of my being deceived and taken away from Christ, I might think.

I am describing this situation because in a commentary like this we find ourselves listening to Paul's letter to the Colossians rather slowly (you may have noticed!). No apology is needed for this, in my opinion. It is important to give our attention to the details of the Bible text. Nevertheless, the problem that can arise is that we miss the way in which the *joy* and the *warnings* belong *together*. As we look at one small section of the letter we may have an exposition for the nervous Christians (aiming to bring them to more joy and thankfulness). The next section may seem to be more for the smug Christians (warning them of their spiritual peril).

We need to appreciate that this is not how Paul's letter works. He was not addressing two groups of believers. The joyful thankfulness and the warnings are consequential. The one entails the other. The warnings are the warnings *of the gospel,* the very gospel in which we hear and understand *the grace of God in truth.* In this letter Paul is doing precisely what he said he does in 1:28: he is proclaiming Christ which means '*warning* everyone AND *teaching* everyone ... that we may present everyone perfect in Christ'.

These considerations should help us feel the weight of the first word of 2:16: **Therefore.** Strange as the warning that follows may sound to our ears, it is the conclusion drawn by Paul from the wonder of what God has done in Christ, of our death in his death, our new life in his resurrection, our full forgiveness in his triumph over every power that might conceivably threaten us (2:9-15).

1. Warning Two: The judge (2:16a)

In 2:16 the Colossian believers are warned of a possibility that I suspect seems about as remote from most of today's readers as anything we have ever heard. Yet, as we will see, it is worth thinking more carefully and giving our attention to this warning: **let no one pass judgment on you.** The possibility of which Paul now warns his readers is that of being judged by other people in certain matters. We will come to those matters shortly, but first we need to grasp the sense of the imperative.

Paul does not mean, 'Do not *allow* anyone to judge you,' in the sense '*Take some action to prevent* anyone who might judge you from in fact doing so'. Put technically, this is not a second-person imperative telling his readers to do something, or not to do something. It is a third-person imperative, indicating something that a third party (here *anyone*) ought not to do. The sense, I take it, is that you, the hearer of these words, are not to give any legitimacy or credence to anyone who passes this kind of judgment on you. You are not to be disturbed by such a thing in any way. Any who pass such judgments ought not to do so. They are the ones in the wrong.

Put to one side for a moment the particular things Paul will mention over which judgments may be made, and consider the experience of being judged by others. This is a rather sensitive area for many for whom what others think of them matters a great deal. This is often a problem for the Christian life, and indeed for Christian ministry. In another context Paul insisted that in his preaching of Christ he repudiated seeking the approval of man. The approval of God was what mattered to him. Seeking God's approval and seeking man's approval were mutually exclusive as far as he was concerned. 'Am I trying to please man? If I were still trying to please man, I would not be a servant of Christ' (Gal. 1:10; cf. Rom. 2:29; Eph. 6:6; 1 Thess. 2:4).

There is a general danger in allowing the judgments of other people to push you around or unsettle you, to be the shaping force on your life, the motivation behind your decisions and behaviour, how hard you work, what you choose to work hard at.

2. The kind of judgment on view (2:16b)

The warning in 2:16, however, is more specific. The kind of judgment on view is specified. This is what makes the warning sound remote and irrelevant today. The kind of judgments Paul has in mind are **in questions of food and drink, or with regard to a festival or a new moon or a Sabbath.**

Almost certainly these words refer or allude to a range of requirements of the Old Testament law. There were the various food laws of the book of Leviticus (see Lev. 11), specifying kinds of food that may be eaten, and other kinds of food that may not be eaten by the people of Israel. There were the annual festivals, the monthly days and, of course, the weekly Sabbaths that were to be observed by them. Indeed 'festival, new moon and Sabbath' is a direct echo of a number of Old Testament texts that refer to these three elements of Israel's calendar (see 1 Chron. 23:31; 2 Chron. 2:4; 8:13; 31:3; Neh. 10:33; Isa. 1:13, 14; Ezek. 45:17; Hosea 2:11). It is true that the Old Testament law does not have any general prohibition of any particular drink, but we do have the example of Daniel resolving not to defile himself with the wine that the king drank (Dan. 1:8), and a few other particular examples of people who were not permitted some forms of drink (see Lev. 10:9; 11:34-36; Num. 6:1-3; Jer. 35:1-19).[1] Therefore, we might paraphrase Paul's warning as: Don't let anyone pass judgment on you for not keeping the Old Testament dietary laws, or for not observing the Old Testament calendar.

The problem for today's reader of these words is obvious. The warning hardly seems to have any relevance. I do not know anyone who is ever likely to criticize me for failing to maintain the ritual requirements of the Old Testament! If I ever worry about what others might think of me, the truth is that I have never been greatly troubled that someone might think less of me because of what I had for lunch, or because last month I overlooked the new moon.

Whenever we encounter this problem as we read the Bible it is important to be patient. In order to grasp today's relevance of God's Word at this point we must go back to Colossae, and try to appreciate why Paul would follow up his earlier warning in 2:8 ('See to it that no one takes you captive by philosophy and empty deceit') with *this* warning to let no one pass judgment on you over the kind of matters mentioned.

Commentators often deal with this question in the manner we have now noted several times. The suggestion is that there may have been a particular problem in Colossae. Was there someone, or some group of people, presumably Jewish Christians, who were zealous to force the gentile believers to keep the law of Moses? We do know that this kind of thing happened in various places where the gospel was bearing fruit among the Gentiles, notably in the churches of Galatia (see Gal. 2:4; 6:12; cf. Acts 15:1, 5; also Phil. 3:2). That is worth keeping in mind (and I am sure Paul had not forgotten the problem in the Galatian churches[2]). However, we should observe again that the very generality of Paul's warning in 2:16 (no particular requirement of the

---

[1] Douglas J. Moo, *The Letters to the Colossians and to Philemon* (Nottingham: Apollos, 2008), p. 219.

[2] The letter to the Galatians was probably written a decade or so earlier than this letter.

Law is focused on) and the very different tone of this letter from that found in the letter Paul wrote to Galatia (no one is actually criticized here) cast some doubt on the theory that the warning is a response to an actual problem that had arisen in Colossae (as distinct from a potential problem that could arise there or anywhere else).

It is far preferable to suppose that Paul wrote the warning of 2:16 simply because what he points to here is the kind of criticism to which believers in Christ Jesus were susceptible. Paul knew this well. He had learnt it from bitter experience in Galatia and elsewhere. What gave rise to Paul's warning here (on the evidence we have) is the character of the Christian faith, and the kind of thing that can threaten the Christian faith, and could shift believers from the hope of the gospel that they had heard (1:23), that could delude them (2:4), and take them captive (2:8).

If this is correct we do not need to reconstruct a supposed false teaching, which Paul was combating, in order to understand him. We need to ask what it is about faith in Christ Jesus that made *this* a danger.

I am suggesting therefore that, even today, believers should pay attention when they hear the apostle say, in effect, 'Do beware of any suggestion that your faith in Christ must be expressed in things like abstaining from certain foods and observing certain days. Beware of any criticism that supposes that believers in Christ Jesus really should adopt practices of the kind required of Old Testament Israel.'

We understand, of course, that the way Paul expresses his warning in 2:16 would have had a force back there in Colossae that we may not immediately feel in the twenty-first century. Today's Christians have largely forgotten that the Christ in whom we have found so much is *Israel's* Messiah. We are hardly aware of the ethnic origin of the gospel we have heard. This was not so in A.D. 60 in Colossae, or in many other places where this gospel began to bear its fruit (see 1:6). To believe the gospel was to acknowledge Israel's Messiah. How could that be done without honouring Israel's religion? How could you have one (the Messiah/ Christ) without the other (the religion with its practices)?

If today we do not feel the appeal of such reasoning, it is because we have forgotten (if I can put it like this) the Jewishness of the gospel. That does not mean that we are immune from the danger behind Paul's warning. We need to see what it was (and what it *is*) about the Christian faith and life that made Paul see this warning as necessary. What was at stake here?

3. Why this warning matters (2:17)

Verse 17 confirms that verse 16 *does* point to the practices of Old Testament religion. What is at stake is *the shadow* (**These are a shadow of the things to come**) versus *the substance* (**but the substance belongs to Christ**).

If you have died with Christ (circumcised in the circumcision of Christ, as we heard in 2:11), and been made alive with Christ (through faith in the powerful working of God who raised him from the dead, 2:12), and have been forgiven all your trespasses (the record having been cancelled by Christ's death, 2:13, 14), and have been delivered from every power that could threaten you (because they were defeated in Christ when he died, 2:15), then do not be intimidated by anyone who wants you to go back to shadows.

This is not a denigration of the religion of Israel, or the Old Testament scriptures. Paul values them for what they are: the shadow of things to come. Yet the gospel announces that the substance of which they are the shadow has *come*. It is no longer the time to live in shadow land.

There is a remarkable translation challenge at the end of verse 17. The words translated in the ESV as 'the substance belongs to Christ' are, more literally rendered, 'the body of Christ'. There is no doubt that the context requires us to see the shadow/substance contrast here (and so the translation is appropriate). Nonetheless the original hearers would not miss the echo of the references already made by Paul to 'the body of Christ'. He has spoken of this 'body' in two senses. One is 'his body of flesh' which died on the cross to reconcile all things (1:22; 2:11); the other is the 'body' of which he is now the head, namely, the assembly of believers (1:18, 24). The body of Christ (in both of these senses) is the substantial reality of which the religion of Israel was the shadow.

It matters very much that we live in the substantial reality and do not exchange it for shadows. What is stated so briefly in 2:17 is developed into a major theme in the letter to the Hebrews: 'For since the law has but a shadow of the good things to come instead of the true form of these realities, it can never, by the same sacrifices that are continually offered every year, make perfect those who draw near' (Heb. 10:1). The concern of the writer of those words (like the concern of Paul writing to the Colossians) was to persuade his readers to recognize the substantial and solid realities they now possess in Christ.[3] The important question is not, Do you abstain from certain food or drink?, but, Are you in Christ? It matters nothing whether or not you observe certain days. Are you in Christ?

We need only a little awareness of church history to understand that the tendency to move back to some form of shadow land (and therefore at least implicitly to pass judgment on those who abandon the shadows) has been constantly present. Most obviously, I suppose, it has been in the historical reintroduction of a human 'priesthood' in church practices. A human priesthood has only ever been a shadow of the priesthood of Christ. To suggest that we need any priest other than Christ is (at best) to give up the substance for a shadow. The letter to the Hebrews, of course, addresses that issue rather directly.

We could reflect on the wide range of ways in which Christian people so easily shift into patterns of religious behaviour that reflect the religion of Israel in one way or another. Church life can be full of such things as holy places, holy times, holy rites. Even if they are not exactly the places, times and rites of the Old Testament, they have the same character as Old Testament Israel's religion: shadows. Paul says, let no one pass judgment on you concerning such things. Are you *in Christ*? That is what matters.

Of course, having the substance is not simply a matter of repudiating the shadows. I cannot help wondering whether

---

[3] R.C. Lucas, *Fullness and Freedom: The message of Colossians and Philemon* (Leicester: Inter-Varsity Press, 1980), p. 114.

some of our church life these days imagines otherwise. Do we sometimes simply assume that we will have the substance by *getting rid* of priests, religious dress, rituals, religious symbols, and so on? That is absurd.

The reality of a joyful, confident, thankful faith in Christ, and love for the brothers and sisters, and the hope of heaven, will drive out the shadows. But you don't make the reality merely by doing away with the shadows. That is why the warning of 2:16, 17 has force for us regardless of the particular 'shadows' that are mentioned. The point is to know and live in the substantial reality that Christ is for us. The day of shadows is past.

There is much we could explore positively about what we do as Christians and as churches to express the solid reality of our life in Christ. We will hear more on that subject later in Paul's letter, especially in chapter 3. At this point Paul's warning should direct us to rejoice in and love the reality that is ours in Christ, not the shadows, whatever form they may take.

Study Questions

1. Are you a Christian who focuses more on God's grace or on your responsibilities? How should Paul's letter to the Colossians change this?

2. Can you think of particular experiences where the judgements of others have mattered to you more than they should? Are there other circumstances in which the judgments of others should be taken seriously? What's the difference?

3. Does it matter that many Christians today have lost any awareness that the gospel they believe is about the Messiah of *Israel*?

4. In your experience what are some of the ways in which Christians or Christian churches have introduced 'shadows' which (at least sometimes) can *overshadow* the 'substance' of Christ?

5. What steps might Christians take to ensure that they do not allow anyone to move them back into 'shadows'?

12

Disqualified by Spirituality
(Colossians 2:18, 19)

Despite the edgy interest in our society in things paranormal, and in many forms of spirituality and the like, we remain a deeply secularized society. I am writing as an Australian living in the prosperous and pleasure-seeking city of Sydney. It is not possible for anyone to live in this society, I believe, and be unaffected by secularism. We who have come to faith in Jesus Christ know that the secularist creed is false. Not only is it false, it is feeble. We have noted this obvious fact earlier in our study of Paul's letter to the Colossians. Nothing exposes the error of secularism more than knowledge of the person and work of Christ. When you come to know Christ, you see *all things* differently, as we learnt in 1:15-20. The *beginning* of all things (1:16) and the *end* of all things (1:18) are dependent on Jesus Christ. We look forward to the day when *all things* will be brought finally under him as head. That day will certainly come, because by his death on the cross the rebellion in creation has been put down. Peace has been won, God has reconciled all things to Christ (1:20; 2:15).

As we come to the third warning in the body of Paul's letter to the Colossians (the first was in 2:8; the second in 2:16; and the third is in 2:18), it may be helpful to reflect on a profound tension in *our* experience between our secularized outlook on life, ingrained into us through education and many other influences of our culture, and our faith in Christ.

If you are a Christian believer, you can see the dark ignorance that secularism is. Claiming to be enlightened, the God-denying philosophy can offer no hope, no purpose and meaning, no basis for right and wrong, no judgment and no forgiveness, no truth and no grace. Therefore, we rightly want to escape from secularism. We do not want to see the world and our lives through the dark deceptive glasses of secularism. We do not want to see our circumstances, our sorrows and joys, our fears and hopes, distorted by secularism. We want to be filled with the knowledge of *God's* will in all *spiritual* wisdom and understanding, to walk in a manner worthy of *the Lord*, fully pleasing to *him*, bearing fruit in every good work, and growing in the knowledge of *God* (Col. 1:9, 10).

One problem is that *secularism* and *the knowledge of God* are not the only two options available. The poverty and inadequacy of secularism has led to a resurgence in our society of an interest in almost any and every *alternative* to secularism. We even have a general word for any and every alternative. We call them all 'spirituality'.

For someone keen to escape from secularism and find something better, various kinds of 'spirituality' can have a powerful appeal. Indeed they can seem and feel more appealing and more powerful than faith in Jesus Christ.

That, it seems to me, is a fair description of today's expression of the general area of concern addressed in 2:18, 19. These verses are difficult in a number of respects, as we will see, but they belong to the series of warnings that we have been hearing Paul issue to the Christian believers in Colossae.

These warnings were anticipated and their purpose made clear in 1:23. It was that the Colossian believers would continue in their faith in Christ Jesus, established and firm, not shifting from the hope of the gospel they had heard. Nothing in all of life mattered more than that. That is why Paul sounds these warnings against the kind of thing that *could* rob you of your faith in Christ, *destabilize* you, or *shift* you from the hope of the gospel you have heard. He warned them in general terms in 2:4 against being deceived by persuasive speech. They had come to trust in Christ by believing the word of the truth of the gospel (1:5). The basic danger was the possibility of being deceived to believe something else. The kind of persuasive speech that could do that was then characterized in 2:8 as 'philosophy and empty deceit, according to human tradition, according to the elements of the world, and not according to Christ'. Recognize the messages that you may hear for what they are, he said. Anything that is not according to Christ, that does not have Christ in his rightful place, no matter how impressive or persuasive, is a deceit, derived from human thought, and therefore dealing only with this world. A more specific example was identified in the warning of 2:16, 17. This was the possibility of shadows instead of substance; religious forms in place of the solid reality of Christ.

The third warning is expressed in these words:

> Let no one disqualify you, insisting on asceticism and worship of angels, going on in detail about visions, puffed up without reason by his sensuous mind, and not holding fast to the Head, from whom the whole body, nourished and knit together through its joints and ligaments, grows with a growth that is from God (2:18, 19).

1. Warning three: 'disqualification' (2:18a)

In the first place, the danger of which Paul's readers are being warned here sounds a bit like the warning we heard in verse 16, 'Let no one pass judgment on you.' Now, in verse 18, Paul says, **Let no one disqualify you.**

Both warnings touch the common human problem of being subject to the opinions of others, unduly enslaved to being well thought of by others, or unsettled by being thought ill of by others. The reiteration of the theme suggests that this is a matter of some seriousness.

The verb has changed ('pass judgement', 'disqualify'), but the idea seems to be very similar. The Greek verb represented by 'disqualify' is rare and the precise meaning is not certain. The nuance of the word in the context seems to be well expressed by the English versions with: 'Let no one *disqualify* you.'

There is a difference between verse 18 and what was said in verse 16. What Paul seems to have in mind now is not so much someone *passing judgment* because you don't do this, or because you do that (particularly in religious kinds of practices, that are at best *shadows* of the substance). This time it is the suggestion that you do not *measure up to the mark*. You are *inadequate*. You are a *failure*, really. At best you are second rate.

Before we get into the real difficulties of understanding the rest of this warning, we should try to feel the force of the first words of verse 18. This will set us on the right path for hearing the rest.

A summary of Paul's message that sets the warning of 2:18 in context might go like this: 'I have heard about the firmness of your faith in Christ. I have heard about how you are living in that faith, loving one another, with your hope set on heaven. Don't let anyone make you feel a failure. Don't let anyone suggest that you are inadequate. Let no one disqualify you.'

'Do not misunderstand,' Paul might continue. 'The reason you are not to allow yourself to be disqualified in this way is not because you are such a wonderful success at living the Christian life, but because you are *in Christ*.' The important teaching of 2:9-15 lies behind the warnings of 2:16 and 2:18. The purpose of the warnings is that Paul's readers will appreciate and not forget the truth of what it means to be in Christ. In him the whole fullness of deity dwells bodily, and in him you are filled (2:9, 10). So do not let anyone suggest that you are, or make you feel, inferior. You are not. You are in Christ.

Such 'disqualification' is the kind of thing that can happen in many different ways. When I am confronted with one of those success stories of a huge spectacular church, do I feel that I belong to a hopeless, little, weak and pathetic church? When I see one of those success stories, do I sense that I have had a feeble and dismal ministry? Paul sounds a warning. Do not respond like that. Is that (possibly small and unimpressive) church you belong to the body of Christ, or is it not? Don't dare let anyone malign it! Has your ministry presented Christ, or has it not? Don't let anyone denigrate it. That is the sense of the words at the beginning of 2:18: 'Let no one disqualify you'.

2. 'Spirituality' (2:18b)

Yet the kind of 'disqualification' experience Paul had in mind was a little more specific. It seems to be what we might call the 'spirituality disqualification'.

In general terms, I suspect that we are familiar with this. When I hear of the experiences of some Christians, I can find myself thinking what a poor and weak Christian I am, what an unspiritual believer! I try to trust in Christ, to love his people and hope for heaven. But I have had no visions. I have experienced no miracles. I have nothing really to boast about – unlike so-and-so. Have you heard about his prayer life? Have you heard about her remarkable dreams? Have you seen their worship? I'm a spiritual pygmy. Paul sounds a warning. Do not respond like that. Are you or are you not *in Christ*? Then: 'Let no one disqualify you'.

While that seems to be the general gist of verse 18, we have some trouble understanding it more precisely. It is nonetheless worth the effort.

Paul seems to have his tongue firmly in his cheek (so to speak) in what follows. This is *his* description of the kind of person he has in mind by whom you might be tempted to allow yourself to be 'disqualified'. It is a description designed to help us to see the absurdity of being intimidated by such 'spirituality'.

a. The humility

First, Paul describes them as **insisting on asceticism.** The phrase could be translated 'delighting in humility'. Various translations try to interpret the word 'humility' here. The ESV's 'asceticism' is one such attempt. The NIV/TNIV has 'false humility', and this probably captures something of Paul's intention, even if at the expense of destroying his subtlety. The word is exactly the same as he uses in 3:12 for something that should characterize all Christians. The ESV probably presses the meaning too far with 'asceticism', and in fact takes the whole phrase in a particular direction ('*insisting* on asceticism').

Taking a minimalist approach, which I think takes us to the basic thing Paul is pointing to here, I prefer the quite literal translation, 'delighting in humility'. This is a superior kind of humility! I wonder whether you have encountered something like this. It is a kind of self-denial in the face of which you feel hopelessly inferior. Perhaps it is expressed in some form of asceticism (as the ESV has it), never indulging in such unspiritual things as enjoying yourself, or enjoying things, or any luxury – or perhaps even any rest. What a second-rate Christian I seem when I see such people!

'Wrong!' says Paul. Do not let anyone disqualify you, delighting in humility, insisting on asceticism.

b. The worship

Paul's adds to his picture of the disqualifier: **and** [insisting on/delighting in] **worship of angels.** This phrase is rather more difficult. Does Paul have in mind people who delight in directing their worshipping to angels? The fact that I have never met such a person does not, of course, mean that there were no such people in the first-century Mediterranean world, but there is not much evidence that there were. Perhaps we should remember that the Greek word for 'angel' can also mean, simply, 'messenger'. If we allow that Paul is giving *his* view of things in this portrayal, then he could be characterizing the would-be disqualifier as one who in reality worships no more than 'messengers'.

Yet Paul could be saying something a little different that would be easier for us to recognize. That, of course, is not a good criterion for assessing an understanding of anything in the New Testament, but neither is it a good reason for dismissing an interpretation. It is possible that by 'worship of angels' Paul does not mean making angels the *object* of worship, but rather the worship which angels *do*. 'Do not let anyone disqualify you … delighting in/insisting on *angelic worship*.' He would be speaking of persons whose worship (the word refers to ritual or religious acts) is so spiritual, so uplifting, so heavenly, that they think they are joining in with the angels.

We should not press the point with a phrase that is rather obscure (at least to us), but the context suggests that

Paul is speaking of a kind of 'worship' that in some way is intimidating, just as he was picturing an expression of 'humility' that can be intimidating.

How dismal is our worship of Christ, we may think. We merely try to trust in him more, to love his people and to look forward to heaven. Pitiable really, when you see the *worship* of some. O how *they* worship! These thoughts are at least in the same general field as the picture Paul is painting. 'Let no one disqualify you … insisting on/delighting in angelic worship.'

c. The experience

Paul's description of the menacing behaviour which must not be allowed to disqualify those who are in Christ continues to be a little perplexing. The third element in his picture is difficult to translate. The difficulty is illustrated by the range of translations. The ESV has **going on in detail about visions**. Other English versions include: 'Such people also go into great detail about what they have seen' (TNIV); 'access to some visionary world' (REB); 'claiming access to a visionary world' (HCSB). A quite literal translation would be: 'going into things he has seen'.

Paul seems to be referring to some kind of visionary experiences playing a role in what makes the pictured person intimidating. Again, I suspect that many of today's readers have experienced something in the same general field of experience. Many of us have met Christian people who have had (or at least claim to have had) extraordinary experiences of such things as dreams, visions, voices, inner convictions telling them something important that they could not otherwise have known. On the one hand, there is nothing in a biblical understanding of life and the world that suggests that such things cannot happen. There is nothing in the Christian understanding of God that rules out such experiences. On the other hand, it is a simple matter of fact that many Christian believers have never had such experiences. How should a believer who has no personal knowledge of such things respond to a brother or sister who speaks freely of these experiences? Do they sense their own unspirituality and Christian inferiority?

I am not trying to reconstruct the first-century experience Paul had in mind, but suspect that what I have described may well be closely related to his thoughts here. He says, 'Let no one disqualify you … going on in detail about visions.'

d. The superiority

At this point Paul intensifies his attack on the would-be disqualifier. The fourth and last element in the picture he is presenting is not calculated to avoid offence: **puffed up without reason by his sensuous mind.**

For all the delighting in humility, elevated worship and claimed visionary experience, if that is what you encounter in this imagined person, Paul describes him as 'puffed up'. This is a word (also translated 'arrogant') Paul used a number of times when writing to the Corinthians (see 1 Cor. 4:6, 18, 19; 5:2; 8:1; 13:4). This dangerous sense of superiority was rather too much in evidence in the Corinthian believers. This is what makes such people intimidating. It is what makes you feel inferior. They are superior, in their own eyes at least, for the kind of reasons that Paul has been describing. I am sure they never *say* they are superior. After all, they delight in humility! But superior is how we encounter them.

Paul now says two shattering things about their superiority. First, it is 'without reason'. Excessive display of humility is not something to be proud of! Angelic worship does not elevate a person above others. Visionary experiences, if they are granted to someone, does not make that person in any way superior to someone to whom such experiences have not been given. The 'puffed up' is 'without reason'.

Second, what then is the cause of their superiority? What is it that puffs them up? 'His sensuous mind', literally: 'the mind of his flesh'. There could not be a more devastating put-down than that, to the one who overawes you with his spirituality. His sense of superiority comes entirely from his fleshly mind. It is not 'spiritual' at all!

Verse 18 has been difficult in its details, but the general picture painted by Paul is clear enough, and (in my opinion) familiar enough to be taken seriously by today's Christian readers. Those who are in Christ (who have died with him and been made alive with him, whose trespasses have all been forgiven – do not forget all we learned in verses 9-15), take care not to be threatened by what might look like superior spirituality, however it might be expressed.

Before we come to verse 19 and see why such spirituality can be such a serious problem, two comments about what we have seen in verse 18 are important.

First, this is a critical verse for the common approach to this letter (we have noted already several times) that supposes that there was actually a group of false teachers in Colossae, or perhaps a particular false teacher. The theory is that Paul's rather unusual vocabulary in verse 18 derives from the fact that he is describing that person (or persons) specifically, possibly using some of their own words. While that remains possible, it seems to this reader more likely that Paul is drawing on his years of experience, perhaps recalling many times when this kind of thing had happened to believers, and describing, not an actual person there in Colossae, but the *kind* of person, the kind of presence, the kind of claims that he wants to alert them to. Do not let *any* such person disqualify you.

The second comment is that while Paul is here strengthening his hearers to have confidence in all that has been given to them (given to us!) in Christ, it would be a mistake to think that being in Christ is a claim we can make lightly, or casually, or in any way that treats this as a small thing. The consequences of our being in Christ will be explored in detail in chapter 3, therefore it will be very important for us to read on. Of course, being in Christ has consequences for our lives and our experience. But before we get to them Paul is warning of various kinds of persuasive speech (2:4) that could deceive you. Those in Christ must not be threatened by apparently superior spirituality.

3. The problem with such spirituality (2:19)

The pattern of 'warning' and 'teaching' (see 1:28) we have observed since 2:8 is followed again in 2:18, 19. The warning of verse 18 is supported by the teaching of verse 19. The teaching is necessary if the seriousness of the warning is to be appreciated. Verse 19 answers the reasonable question: What precisely is wrong with the kind of spirituality that has been pictured for us? Why should such a super-spiritual person not show me up as a second-rate (or third-rate!) Christian? If my spiritual experience, worship and life are in fact inferior to that of other believers, what is wrong with being disturbed by the superior example of others?

a. Christ is the head

The problem is simple, but devastating. The issue with the kind of spiritual intimidation Paul had in mind is that the person concerned is **not holding fast to the Head.**

Christ is the 'head' of all rule and authority (2:10), but the body of which he is the 'head' is the assembly (ESV 'church', 1:18, 24). Here is the horror. The super-spiritual person has attracted your attention to him/herself. You are threatened because you are comparing yourself to him/her. But *Christ* is the head! Let go of him and you have lost everything, no matter how humble or spiritual you are. Hold fast to him and you are not under threat. Displays of humility or asceticism, elevated worship practices or remarkable spiritual experiences are of no value without Christ. With Christ as your head, they are unimportant.

b. Christ is the source of life, unity and growth

Misunderstanding here is all too easy. Of course, Christian people should be concerned about their Christian lives and the assembly (church) should care about its unity. The warnings that we have heard ('see to it that no one takes you captive', 2:8; 'let no one pass judgment on you', 2:16; and 'let no one disqualify you', 2:18) must not be taken as excuses for spiritual complacency. We are not to respond to the intimidation of the super-spiritual with our own kind of self-satisfaction ('I'm OK – I'm an evangelical' – or whatever my self-description might be). As we considered 2:16, 17 we saw that while we must not allow anyone to push us back into a shadow-land religion of forms and ritual, the substance of really living in Christ is not secured simply by abolishing such forms. Likewise, while we must not allow anyone to draw us from Christ into some superior spirituality that does not have him as head, we must not imagine that a general antagonism to spiritual experiences is itself the mark of maturity in Christ. The reality of Christian living, growth and stability matters for each of us and for us all. Paul prays constantly for this (1:9-14). He is writing this letter as a means for this to happen (2:6, 7). He will say much more on this matter directly in chapter 3. The vital point that Paul brings us to now is the solid truth that Christ is the one **from whom** our life, unity and growth come.

The whole body is the whole assembly of believers (as we have imagined them gathered there in Philemon's house listening to this letter being read to them). Christ is the source of this body's sustenance (**nourished**) and the source of this body's unity (**and knit together through its joints and ligaments**), as well as its growth (it **grows with a growth that is from God**).

Each part of the body (each Christian believer) lives and functions properly from his/her connection to the head. Believers are to be knit together by their shared dependence on Christ. Together they are to be nourished by their faith in Christ. That is how the growth that comes from God happens.

It is all too common for a form of superior spirituality, when it takes hold in the Christian fellowship, to shatter the unity, weaken the life and stunt the growth. Your faith in Christ is the source, power and life force of everything that matters. Faith in Christ will certainly transform you and continue to do so, but if you are trusting in Christ, do not let anyone 'disqualify' you.

Study Questions

1. What are the main alternatives to secularism that seem to have some appeal in the society in which you live?

2. Can you think of particular experiences where others have considered your Christian life or ministry to be, in some way, inadequate? How did you respond? What have you learnt from Paul's letter to the Colossians about such experiences?

3. Are there areas in which you feel spiritually weak, or incompetent? How does Paul's teaching in this letter help you to respond to this?
4. What do you think is the difference between the 'humility' that Christians should display (Col. 3:12) and the intimidating 'humility' he refers to (using the same word) in Colossians 2:18 (ESV 'asceticism')?
5. What would your advice be to a church member who complains that the 'worship' at his or her church is inferior to another church nearby?
6. If you are a Christian who has never experienced visions or other such things, how do you react to those who claim they have? If you are a Christian who has experienced visions or other such things, how do you react to those who have not?
7. From Colossians 2:18, 19, how is the Christian assembly united and what might threaten that unity?

13

Dictated to by Rules
(Colossians 2:20-23)

There are many ways in which a Christian life can be destabilized. In chapter 2 of Paul's letter to the young believers in Colossae, he has been addressing this subject. His concern has not been with the direct and obvious pressures of moral temptation. Those forces ought not to be underestimated: the pressure to simply abandon, in some area of behaviour, any semblance of the Christian manner of life for a life of flagrant disregard for God and Christ. That pressure is real enough and is felt at various times and ways in every Christian's life. Nevertheless, there is something more fundamental than blatant moral failure, and usually more subtle. It can undermine a Christian life, and more often than not precedes any more obvious change in external behaviour. It can sneak up on you and unsettle your faith in the Lord Jesus Christ well before that instability comes to be expressed in palpable moral stumbling.

We have been listening to the series of warnings that have run through Colossians 2 about things that could undermine the firmness of your faith in Christ, and therefore the good order of your life (2:5). These warnings started in 2:4 with the very general description of the danger in terms of being deceived: 'I say this in order that no one may delude you with plausible arguments.' If today's Christian readers of Paul's letter are to benefit as we ought from this part of Scripture, then, like those Colossian believers, we must give careful attention to the apostle's teaching, study his divinely inspired instruction and learn from him so that we will not be deceived. That is the purpose of our study of his writings. Sometimes we may have to struggle to understand what he was saying. Yet the purpose of our efforts is far more important than we may realize – it is that we will not be deluded.

In case his readers were slow to see the importance of this, the possibility of being so deceived was vividly presented as a kind of kidnapping: 'See to it that no one takes you captive' (2:8). This was Paul's characterization of the kind of 'persuasive speech' or 'plausible arguments' (2:4) that have the power to deceive. Learn to recognize it for what it is, and do not be taken in by it.

Then, after a very important teaching about the work of Christ in 2:9-15 (we will have reason to look back at that shortly), Paul presented a second warning: 'Therefore let no one judge you' over matters that are a shadow of the reality that has come in Christ (2:16, 17). He was speaking about the persuasive speech of those who gave much importance to external religious practices.

A third warning was advanced in 2:18, 19 about the arrogance of superior spirituality: 'Let no one disqualify you'. He had in mind the persuasive speech from those who think they have found something superior to Christ and his death and resurrection.

While the language used in these warnings is no doubt strange to us, reflecting as it does ideas, beliefs and practices in the first-century Mediterranean world, we have been finding that the apostle's words nonetheless sound a contemporary warning that we need to hear. Learn to recognize the voices of false spirituality, no matter how impressive, and hold fast to Christ.

We come now to the warning that concludes Colossians 2. This time some of the language is *very* difficult, some almost impossible to translate. Yet, as we will see, it is nonetheless a word again with the power to stabilize Christian faith against destabilizing influences.

Here is the ESV set alongside a quite literal translation of 2:20-23.

> If with Christ you died to the elemental spirits of the world, why, as if you were still alive in the world, do you submit to regulations – 'Do not handle, Do not taste, Do not touch' (referring to things that all perish as they are used)— according to human precepts and teachings? These have indeed an appearance of wisdom in promoting self-made religion and asceticism and severity to the body, but they are of no value in stopping the indulgence of the flesh. (2:20-23, ESV)

> If you died with Christ out from under the elements of the world why, as if living in the world, be dictated to – 'Do not handle, Do not taste, Do not touch' – which things are for decay as they are used – according to the commandments and teachings of men which have indeed a reputation of wisdom in self-made religion and humility and severity to the body but they are of no value against the indulgence of the flesh. (2:20-23, my translation)

1. The basic reality of the Christian life (2:20a)

a. you died with Christ

We begin by being reminded again in verse 20 of the basic reality of the Christian life: the believer's profound involvement in the death of Christ (see 2:11-15). The ESV **If with Christ you died** should not be understood as indicating uncertainty about the fact. Although this reality does require persistence in the faith (see the 'if' in 1:23), Paul does not doubt that his readers really have 'died with Christ' (see 1:21, 22; 2:11, 12). 'If' here almost means 'since' (so TNIV).

The brief phrase 'you died with Christ' points to the heart of the Christian life. Paul has expounded this central truth of Christian existence in 2:9-15, providing the teaching that supports the series of warnings running through this chapter. In that 'circumcision of Christ' (his death), you were 'circumcised' (2:11). In that 'baptism' of Christ (his death), you were 'buried with him' (2:12). His death was so truly *for me* that the reality is I died *with him*. My life is so dependently united to him that I *died* with him.

The context of 2:9-15 links each of the warnings Paul issues in this chapter to this reality. Precisely because *you died with Christ*, do not let anyone take you captive by any human philosophy (2:8). For the same reason, do not let anyone pass judgment on you because of scruples about such things as food and drink, festivals or Sabbaths (2:16). Likewise, do not let anyone 'disqualify' you with their superior spirituality – *you died with Christ* (2:18). In 2:20 Paul is about to spell out another consequence of dying with Christ.

b. to the elements of the world

He draws attention to this aspect of our death in Christ's death: you died **to** [literally 'from'] **the elemental spirits of the world.** Paul has used this phrase earlier (2:8), where we noted that it is perhaps better translated, simply, 'the elements of the world'. In 2:8 the expression seemed to be Paul's rather derogatory dismissal of merely human philosophy as 'elementary', at best, dealing only with this world. Now he uses the same phrase to underline that, in dying with Christ, believers have been liberated from bondage to this world, from the basic forces, powers, structures and inevitabilities of this world. This world, and the fundamental 'elements' of which it is constituted, no longer hold us, own us, or control us. 'You died with Christ out from under the elements of the world.'

Strange as Paul's way of putting this may be to our ears, the reality of which he is speaking is important. Earlier in the letter he spoke of how we have been *reconciled to Christ* (and thus to God) in his death (1:22). The blood of his cross that has made peace between God and us has also made peace with all powers in the whole of creation by triumphing over them (1:20; 2:15). Therefore your dying with Christ has released you from bondage to this world and its forces – whatever those forces might be.

2. The denial of the basic reality (2:20b)

This is huge. Since we died with Christ, our life is now to be lived in an entirely new context, about which we will hear much more in chapter 3. Here Paul wants us to see the foolish nonsense of *denying* this basic reality. **Why**, he asks, would you go on living **as if you were still alive in the world** – as if you were still living *in the world*?

We know very well from all that Paul will say in the rest of this letter (let alone his teaching in every other place) that he does not for a moment mean that Christian people should not live 'in the world' in any sense. But when you have died with Christ, why would you live with the world as the shaping influence on you? Why would you live, in other words, as though your life is still held by the world, controlled by the forces of the world, subject to the elements of which the world is constituted?

Did you die with Christ, or didn't you? Your answer to that question has massive consequences for how your life is related now to 'the world'.

3. Living out the denial (2:21)

This vital truth could be taken in several different directions. The denial of the basic reality of the Christian life can be lived out in many ways. 'Since you died with Christ out from under the elements of the world', why would you be anxious about your life in this world, about such things as your possessions and your prosperity? 'Since you died with Christ out from under the elements of the world', why would you fear the powers of this world – the power of status or lack of it, of reputation or lack of it, of admiration or scorn? 'Since you died with Christ out from under the elements of the world', why is it that this world can still terrify you?

We could profitably pursue many such important consequences of having died with Christ. I hope that you might do so in your own serious response to God's Word in 2:20. Nevertheless, Paul pushes us in an unexpected direction, a direction we would not, I think, have taken without his instruction. 'Since you died with Christ out from under the elements of the world, why, as if living in the world, **submit to regulations**?'

One reputable understanding of all of the warnings in Colossians 2 (as we have noted a number of times) is that Paul has in mind a particular teaching that someone was presenting to the Colossian believers. This suggestion is attractive, because any difficult language of Paul can be explained as his specific response to that teaching, perhaps even using its own terms. On this view, someone in Colossae was advocating a life of self-denying rules for believers in Christ. The existence of that teaching would explain what Paul says here. He is mocking the prohibitions advocated by the false teaching.

Several English translations (ESV is an example) support this view by rendering 2:20 as 'why … *do you* submit to regulations …?' Yet (as I have said a number of times now) I doubt that this letter is a response to a particular teaching in Colossae, or that Paul is suggesting that the Colossian believers have actually fallen into some error. If Paul is speaking (as I strongly suspect) in general terms about the kinds of pressure that believers can experience, his words are perhaps better translated, 'why … submit to regulations …?' – without suggesting that they necessarily were doing so. If I may interpret him quite simply, he is asking, 'Since you died with Christ out from under the elements of the world, why would you allow your life to be controlled by rules about stuff in the world?'

Paul's parody of such rules, **'Do not handle, Do not taste, Do not touch,'** suggests that *the kind of thing* he had in mind would include Jewish food laws (as in verse 16: 'let no one pass judgment on you in questions of food and drink'). Such rules are *not* the kind of thing that shapes your life in Christ. You died with Christ, remember, out from under the elements of the world.

If it is right that Paul is speaking about *the kind of thing* he has seen again and again, rather than a particular problem known to be present in Colossae, we (today's readers of Paul's letter) should reflect on *the kind of things* in our experience that would in principle be the same.

This may not be easy in the Christian circles of many readers of this commentary because many of us think that we have learnt rather well from the apostle. By and large we are people who have little patience for anything we regard as arbitrary rules – and Paul does seem to be implying a certain arbitrariness about the kind of rules he is talking about: 'Do not handle, Do not taste, Do not touch.' Indeed, perhaps partly under the influence of Paul's teaching here, it reasonably may be suggested that many of us today have little patience with rules of any kind. Who among us wants to be dictated to by rules?

This is where we should pause and reflect. Is it clear that the aversion to rules felt by many of today's Christian believers is really a consequence of our having died with Christ? I am far from persuaded that rejecting any role for any kind of rules in the Christian life or the Christian fellowship is itself a sign that we have learnt the lesson of this passage of Scripture.

Let me illustrate. Suppose we distance ourselves from the Christian who has observed the damage caused by alcohol in our society, and the number of Christians (including Christian ministers) who have alcohol problems and addictions, and who decides not to handle, not to taste, not to touch alcohol, perhaps encouraging others to do the same. Do you think our liberty is necessarily a consequence of the apostle's injunction here?

There are many similar instances of rules playing various roles in our lives. Consider how part of a response to the horrendous cases of sexual misconduct and abuse in some churches has been the drawing up of a formal set of rules about what is and is not acceptable behaviour by people in public ministry. Such codes of conduct have been made public and Christian ministers in many churches have been required to abide by them. Do you think that a person who refuses to be bound by such rules is necessarily showing that he or she has died with Christ? What would you want to say to a minister today who responded to such a code of practice by saying, 'Since I died with Christ out from under the elements of the world, I will *not* be dictated to'?

Perhaps such a person should be reminded that it was the same apostle Paul who could say elsewhere, in another context, 'This is my *rule* in all the churches' (1 Cor. 7:17). Paul clearly did not reject any kind of rules or commands in the Christian life. *Obedience* is a feature of Christian living! (See Col. 3:20, 22; Rom. 6:16; 13:9.)

Then what did Paul mean by his sharp critique of the life dictated by rules in 2:20, 21? There is something important to be learnt here even about sensible, wise and responsible rules.

4. The problem of such living (2:22, 23)

Verses 22 and 23 spell out the problem of a life regulated by rules. Unfortunately these verses become progressively more difficult to translate and understand in detail. Yet, as is often the case in such biblical texts, there is gold here for those who will take the trouble to dig! Paul makes four points that we will try to see without getting lost in the difficulties.

a. The rules are all about stuff that decays!

First, the kind of rules people put themselves under deal with things that all decay with use. They are **referring to things that all perish as they are used.** This is obvious if Paul has in mind rules like Jewish food laws. He is speaking very much as Jesus did (see Mark 7:18, 19). If he has in mind a wider range of rules that can regulate life, then he is highlighting a general problem with such rules. By their nature they can only deal with this decaying world. If you have died with Christ out from under the elements of the world, rules must be seen in perspective. They are extremely limited in what they can encompass. They cannot even begin to do for you what Christ's death has done for you!

b. The rules are only human!

The second problem with rule-dictated living is that such rules are only human. They are **according to human precepts and teachings.** Again Paul sounds like Jesus when he quoted Isaiah 29:13: 'in vain do they worship me, teaching as doctrines the commandments of men' (Mark 7:7). You died with Christ out from under the elements of the world! Why would you allow your life now to be shaped by human rules?

c. The rules may appear impressive …

The third problem with rule-dictated living is that the reputation does not match the reality. The Greek of verse 23 is very difficult. No doubt this is compounded by the fact that Paul had in mind first-century expressions that are unfamiliar to us.

The point, however, appears to be that rules and regulations can appear impressive. **These have indeed an appearance of wisdom in promoting self-made religion and asceticism and severity to the body.** Even today rules can impress. You can see them. You can see their effects. A code of conduct can produce a pattern of life. Regulations can shape a religion. Rules can shape a piety. Rules can be hard on the body. If your life is regulated by rules, they will have an effect, and it may even be impressive.

That is their attraction, of course. Paul, however, is reminding his readers: you died with Christ. What do you really think rules can do for you?

d. ... but are of no value in what matters

The fourth thing Paul says about rule-dictated living (v. 23b) is really very difficult in Greek, but most would agree that it is a comment on the worthlessness of rules for what really matters: **but they are of no value in stopping the indulgence of the flesh.** Rules simply do not solve the problem of human living. The problem is so much deeper than we like to acknowledge. It is our fallen, self-indulgent, God-ignoring, pleasure-craving, self-absorbed nature we all know so well, that Paul often calls simply 'the flesh'. We might hope to control it with a set of rules, a code, some regulations, strict discipline. It will not work. And you, of all people, should know that, says Paul. You died with Christ out from under the elements of the world!

The consequences of what we have heard here from the apostle are considerable. I do not think for one moment that the conclusion to be drawn is that there is no place at all for rules of any kind or that there is no benefit at all that rules can ever bring to the Christian life or the Christian fellowship.

On the one hand, Paul seems to be saying very strongly that there *are* rules that are useless. There are rules that can deceive you into thinking that you are pious and godly. Or, indeed, rules that can intimidate you into thinking that you are not pious and godly! That is not what Christ died to accomplish.

On the other hand, even when rules are wise and sensible, do not be deceived into thinking they can achieve much. Rules don't change people. Rules don't change hearts. Rules can't curb the flesh. That is what Christ's death was about.

Did you, or did you not, die with Christ? If the answer is Yes, then the power that is to shape your life is not rules. The true power of the Christian life is the subject Paul takes up in chapter 3 of his letter.

Study Questions

1. Look back over the first two chapters of Colossians and note each way in which Paul has explained the significance of the death of Jesus Christ for believers in him. How has Paul's letter deepened your appreciation of this?
2. In what ways has the death of Jesus Christ freed you from 'the world'? In what ways do you find it easy to forget this freedom?
3. Think of some of the rules that play a role in your life. Do they have any or all of the problems Paul speaks of in Colossians 2:22, 23? In what ways, then, are they helpful? In what ways could they be unhelpful?
4. What is the difference, do you think, between the kind of rules Paul seems to be criticising in Colossians 2:20-23 and the kind of thing that Paul says later in this very letter, like 'Children, obey your parents' (3:20), 'Masters, treat your slaves justly and fairly' (4:1)?
5. How ought Christians ensure that rules do not have an inappropriate role in our lives?

14

The Power of the Christian Life
(Colossians 3:1-4)

> If then you have been raised with Christ, seek the things that are above, where Christ is, seated at the right hand of God. Set your minds on things that are above, not on things that are on earth. For you have died, and your life is hidden with Christ in God. When Christ who is your life appears, then you also will appear with him in glory (3:1-4).

I wonder whether you think of the Christian life in terms of *power*. In some circles that would be almost a ridiculous question. *Of course* the Christian life is about power, it might be said. The Christian life is about God, isn't it? Whatever else God is, he is powerful. Therefore, to deal with God is to deal with power. Remember Paul's prayer for the Colossian believers in 1:11 that they would be *strengthened* with *all power* according to *God's glorious might*! The only kind of Christian life that is not about *power* is a Christian life that is not about God! Is that not what Paul meant on another occasion when he spoke of 'having the appearance of godliness, but *denying* its power' (2 Tim. 3:5)?

I am not sure we would find *that* response in other circles, where we would be more likely to hear that the Christian life is about contentment and patience, about love and goodness. It involves suffering and serving. Paul's prayer in 1:11 was that they might be empowered with all power according to God's glorious might *for all endurance and patience*! It is misleading to think of the Christian life in terms of unqualified *power*.

Put like that, it is difficult to dismiss either of these basic attitudes to the Christian life. We might well hope that the person who begins with firmly believing in the power of God will come to understand that the Bible shows us the power of God in the most unexpected ways: power that confounds all of our concepts of power. The power of God we encounter in Jesus Christ is the power of the cross, the power of his death, the power of the unimpressive word of the cross, 'power ... made perfect in *weakness*' (cf. 2 Cor. 12:9). *Power* Christianity (or Power Religion, as it has sometimes been called), where power is *just power*, is not the Christianity of the New Testament. For the second attitude is *right*. The Christian life *is* about contentment, patience, love, goodness, suffering and serving.

Yet we might also hope that the person who begins with *that* understanding will not make the mistake of denying God's power. It is not as though God's power *disappears* in weakness. It is not that God's power is *displaced* by weakness. The centrality of the cross does not marginalize the resurrection! Could we be so committed to the way of contentment that we do not seriously pray for the miraculous? Do we pray for patience, but *not* for healing? Do we pray for faithfulness, but not for anything astonishing? Or if we do, do we really think that God would (or perhaps even could) grant our request?

The reaction to *power Christianity* (whether in the form of prosperity teaching, or other distortions of the gospel that promise that God's power *will* do or *must* do things that the Bible does not promise God will do) can very easily become a practical denial of the power of God. Those who glory in the cross of Christ long to know the power of his resurrection (Phil. 3:10).

The subject we come to as we begin the third chapter of Paul's letter to the Colossians is the power of the Christian life. I want to introduce our consideration of this part of the letter by pressing the question about power in the Christian life a little further. It is not a merely academic question. I am not just asking about your theology of the Christian life, important though that question is. I am asking about *your Christian life*. Where is the power? What is the power? What do you know of power?

I want to press these questions, because power plays such an important role in human life. There are many forms of power that shape our lives, just as there are many forms of power that our lives exhibit. There is the power of a personality. It might be yours, or it might be a powerful personality that has its impact on you. There is the power of human energy and drive and vision, the ability to get things done and powerfully inspire others. There is the power of human confidence. There is the power of oratory. Many powerful forces shape human lives. My little list is just a beginning. These are forces, by and large, that can be good or bad in their influence. The powerful personality, the person with energy and vision and drive, may be a person sanctified by God's Spirit. Then we can be thankful for these God-given powers and the good they do. Almost certainly you will be able to see such powerful influences that have played a role in your life for good. Your own life may in fact be powerful in some of these ways.

We have an interest these days in other kinds of power. Assessment of Christian ministry these days is not dominated by the old qualities of faithfulness, humility, service, courage and hard work. These things are not so much being denied, as being taken for granted. More attention is given to the power of good strategies, the power of technology, cultural relevance, innovation and flexibility. Again, it is clear that these things can be good and worthwhile, and can serve the cause of Christ. Not necessarily so. But they can be.

Any and all of these powerful things can also be substitutes for the power that matters more than all of them put together. When Paul prayed that the Colossian believers would be empowered with all power according to the might of God's glory, he was not talking about the power of personality or the power of innovative strategies. Quite the contrary. There is a power that all Christians are to know in their experience that puts all of our experiences of human and worldly power in their place. If *this* power has been, or is in danger of being, *overshadowed* in our thinking, concerns, hopes and experience, then Chapter 3 of Colossians is a word we need to hear, and hear well.

1. The power of the Christian life (3:1a)

The chapter begins with a brief reference to the indispensable power of the Christian life. **If** does not suggest uncertainty about the fact about to be stated (see 2:13). As in 2:20, 'if' in this context almost means 'since'.

What is about to be said is the positive side of all that has been said since 2:8 in the form of warnings. The logical connection is indicated by **then** (or 'therefore'[1]). The essence of the positive teaching of chapter 2 is summed up in the words **you have been raised with Christ**. All that will follow in this chapter flows from this remarkable statement.

It is difficult to imagine a more dramatic thing that could be said about a human life. The chapter division between Chapter 2 and Chapter 3 must not obscure the fact that 3:1 is closely tied to the statement a few lines earlier in 2:20: 'If with Christ you *died* ...' The two statements belong together: With Christ you died, *and* you have been raised with Christ.

It is not easy for us to grasp the enormity of this. The death and resurrection of Jesus Christ are events of massive importance in the history of the world. Paul has already spoken in this letter of the entire creation being put back together again, reconciled to Christ – the one in whom all things were created, and for whom all things exist (1:15-20). In the death and resurrection of Jesus, God has pacified a deep alienation that has disrupted the order of all things (1:20). The new age of God's kingdom has begun, in the death and resurrection of Jesus. And you, who have come to trust him, have been so united to him that you *died with him* and you were *raised with him* (see 1:21, 22).

What does that mean? In 2:12 Paul said, 'you were ... raised with him through faith in the powerful working of God, who raised him from the dead.' As you trusted in the one who raised Jesus from the dead, you were brought into a new life along with him. In 2:13 this was elaborated: 'And you,

---

[1] The Greek word translated 'then' is the same as that translated 'therefore' in 2:6 and 16.

who were dead in your trespasses and the uncircumcision of your flesh, God made alive together with him, *having forgiven us all our trespasses.*' This new life has at its heart *the forgiveness of all our trespasses*. What a massive thing the forgiveness of all our trespasses is! It is the beginning of the restoration of all things. It is being raised with Christ. It has eternal consequences. It is, without question, the most powerful thing that has ever happened to you.

Consider the resurrection of Jesus. What an amazing event! How astonished those witnesses were who saw the risen Jesus! Imagine if you had been there, on the road to Emmaus (Luke 24:13-35), or in the locked room with Thomas (John 20:24-29), or with Peter by the lake (John 21:1-14). You may not have grasped the full significance of what had happened, but you would not have thought it a small thing. Then understand: the forgiveness of your sins is of that order. You have been raised with Christ. Take time to reflect on this extraordinary and powerful reality.

2. Living the Christian life (3:1b, 2)

a. Seek

What has happened to you has huge consequences for your life. And it begins with what you now **seek**.

Jesus said that the life of the Gentiles (by which he meant the pagan nations who do not know God) is characterized by what they 'seek'. 'The Gentiles *seek* after all these things', he said. 'What shall we eat?' 'What shall we drink?' 'What shall we wear?' (Matt. 6:31, 32). A person *seeks* what they are anxious about (see Matt. 6:25-34), what matters to them, what they know they need, or perhaps just what they very much want.

If we had adequate self-understanding and could see our own hearts clearly, we would see how *what we seek* is what dominates and shapes our lives. *What we seek* determines what we think about, how we spend time, the decisions and choices we make.

Here, then, is the power of the Christian life: having been raised with Christ, our 'seeking' is given a whole new direction. Seek **the things that are above**. Look upward. Paul spoke earlier of 'the hope laid up for you in heaven'

(1:5). Your new life has a direction and a goal, a purpose and an end that is magnificent. Lift your eyes. Lift your heart. Look where you are headed. Seek the things above.

The reason we who are united to Christ can and must do so is that 'above' **is where Christ is**. To seek the things above is to seek Christ, to seek all that Christ is. Since we have been raised with him, the whole of our lives must be reordered to 'seek' him.

Christ is **seated at the right hand of God**. The allusion is to the messianic Psalm 110: 'The LORD says to my Lord: "Sit at my right hand, until I make your enemies your footstool"' (Ps. 110:1). The Old Testament promise that God would give his Messiah the place of honour and power at his right hand has been fulfilled in the resurrection and exaltation of Jesus. He has begun his reign. To seek the things above is to seek Jesus' reign. It is to long for and set your heart on Jesus' reign. It is to cling to him. It is to find in him the centre and source of all our joys.[2] It is what you do if you have been raised with Christ.

b. Set your minds

To help us to grasp this, Paul says it again, in slightly different words. It matters a great deal that we understand, and understand truly, the heavenly Christ. **Set your minds on** means consider, think, put your mind to.

It would be a misunderstanding (and one that will be quickly dispelled as we move through this chapter) to think that the words **things that are above, not on things that are on earth** encourage a detachment from the realities of life in this world, as though Paul were advising that the Christian believer may not give serious attention to the things of this world. Could he be suggesting that if you are going to take your Christian life seriously you cannot possibly be a tradesman, or a lawyer, or a businessman or, for that matter, a mother, a father, a husband, a wife? All of these require serious attention to things in this world. The unfolding of the Christian life that we are going to see in due course in the rest of this chapter will make quite clear that to set your minds on the things above and not on the

[2] R.C. Lucas, *Fullness and Freedom: The message of Colossians and Philemon* (Leicester: Inter-Varsity Press, 1980), p. 135.

things on the earth does not in fact mean lack of interest in life in this world. What he means by 'the things that are on earth' becomes clear when he uses that exact phrase again in verse 5 (ESV 'what is earthly'). There is earthly stuff that we are not to fill our minds with. Our minds, our thinking, our understanding is to be focused and informed by the things above, by Christ, the reigning Messiah. Understanding the things above will transform and empower our lives in this world.

How are we going to do that? It will involve the *deliberate* turning of our minds and our affections to Christ, in such a way that he becomes the shaping power of our lives. The words before us are a call to do so.

This, I am sure, is where the Christian practice of regular, daily Bible reading and prayer comes from. It is a practice that has proven, for generations of believers, to be an effective way of seeking the things that are above, where Christ is, seated at the right hand of God, and setting your minds on the things that are above, not on the things that are on the earth. A daily 'Quiet Time' is not prescribed anywhere in the Bible, and it is certainly possible to have such a discipline *without* doing what is spoken of in 3:1, 2. Furthermore, seeking the things that are above could not possibly be limited to a few moments each morning. There are many other ways in which we respond to the call here, including times of meeting together in the fellowship of believers in ways that will be described later in this chapter (see 3:12-17). The conversations of believers with one another ought to stimulate us to seek the things that are above. At the same time, the value of daily reading of God's Word and thoughtful prayer should not be underestimated. Setting your mind on the things that are above is not something that just happens. It is something to which we are called, because we have been raised with Christ.

There has been, in some Christian circles, an abandoning of such disciplines. It has been, in part, a reaction to perceived legalism. That has been the excuse, but it is a poor one. Certainly having a regular 'Quiet Time' (as many Christians have come to call it), or not managing to do so, should not be motivated by or a cause for guilt and shame. It is also true that an empty ritual of reading a Bible passage and saying a prayer may be of limited value. Even so, the apostle encourages us to see the inestimable value of seeking the things that are above, where Christ is, seated at the right hand of God. The importance of giving deliberate and concentrated thought to 'the things that are above' is his concern here. Taking time, daily, with the Scriptures, and in prayer is a well-proven way of doing this.

How will such upward directing of our thoughts and desires affect our lives here and now? We will be hearing more about that in very concrete terms as chapter 3 of the letter unfolds. Yet the imperatives of verses 5 and following will be misunderstood if we do not come to them through the imperatives of verses 1 and 2.

3. The power of the Christian life (again) (3:3, 4)

How is this redirection of our thinking and our affections possible, and why is it so important? In verses 3 and 4 Paul supports his exhortation in verses 1 and 2 with a fuller statement of the powerful reality of the Christian life. He unpacks the brief reference at the beginning of verse 1, this time in terms of your past and your present and your future (cf. 1:21, 22).

a. Your past

As for the past, Paul tells us again, **For you have died**. He means, of course, that you have died *with Christ*. There has been a decisive end to your old life. This is what we heard in 2:20, and it was the subject of 2:9-15. The new life we have in Christ cannot be thought of as an add-on to the old life. The new life only comes on the other side of a death. As we trust in Christ, his death is our death. The old life is over.

We do need to be reminded of this. The important gospel truth that Christ died *for* us does not mean (as it could logically be understood to mean) that we are therefore spared from death. As Paul puts it elsewhere, 'one died for all, therefore [not all are *spared from* death, but] *all died*' (2 Cor. 5:14). The power of his death *for us* means that in his death *we died*.

b. Your present

Paul's concern at this point in his letter is not with our past death with Christ as such, but with the consequence of this death, namely, our new life with him in the present. We who have died with Christ have been raised with Christ (see 2:13). That is how the paragraph began (3:1a). The difficulty for believers in the present is that it is not obvious for all to see that we have 'died' and 'been raised'. That is not how it now appears, nor is it how it feels (at least much of the time). That is because **your life is hidden.** Your new life in God is, for the time being, hidden, just as Christ is hidden (for now) from our eyes.

Make no mistake, however. Your new life is real. It is as real as the forgiveness of all our trespasses (2:13). And it is known. It is known by God and by the believer: your new life is **with Christ in God**. It is just that it is not now seen for all that it is. That is why we need to look up to 'where Christ is' (v. 1), to seek and consider the things that are above. We cannot and must not live simply by present appearances.

c. Your future

The day is coming when the reality will be revealed. **When Christ who is your life appears**, when he is revealed, because you have died with him and been raised with him, **then you also will appear**, you will be revealed, **with him in glory**. What is now hidden will no longer be so. Paul is speaking of that day when Jesus Christ will come in glory. On that day he will be seen as he really is, and your now-hidden life in him will also be seen for what it really is: glorious!

The point is that what will be revealed on that day is already real. We have died *with Christ*. We have been raised *with him*. We live *with him*. We will appear *with him*. The power of the Christian life that puts all other powers in their place is the death and the resurrection of Jesus Christ, who now reigns at God's right hand, and will one day appear in glory.

What do you know of that power?

Study Questions

1. Reflect on some of the powerful influences that have made you the person you are. Which, do you think, have been the most significant, and what have been their effects?
2. Consider how the death and resurrection of Jesus Christ have affected you. In what ways have these events been a powerful influence on your life?
3. In the context in which you live what do people 'seek'? Can you see substantial differences in the lives of Christian believers? Think back over the last few years of your life: What have you been 'seeking'?
4. In your experience what have been some of the ways in which you have been helped to 'set your mind on things that are above' and 'seek the things that are above'? What might you do to increase this influence on your life?
5. Why is it important to understand that 'your life is (now) *hidden*'?
6. How will 'seeking the things that are above' also mean looking forward to the future?

15

The Victory of the Christian Life
(Colossians 3:5-11)

The opening lines of Colossians 3 have spoken of the power of the Christian life, which is the power of the death and resurrection of Jesus. The Christian life participates in the power of the death and resurrection of Jesus Christ. 'You have died [with Christ]' and 'you have been raised with Christ' (3:3, 1). Just as by the blood of his cross God has acted to reconcile all things to Christ, making peace in the whole creation (1:20), so we, who were once alienated and hostile in mind, God has reconciled by Jesus' death (1:21). The one who raised Jesus from the dead, has raised us with him, has made us alive with him, forgiving us all our trespasses (2:12, 13). Our union with Christ is a union with him in his death and in his resurrection.

Therefore, in the opening lines of Colossians 3 we hear the call to *look up*! Set your heart and mind on *Christ*, who is seated at the right hand of God, reigning until all his enemies are made a footstool for his feet (3:1, 2; cf. Ps. 110:1). Your life is *with him* (3:3). When he comes again he will be seen in all his glory, and your new life with him, which is now hidden, will also be gloriously seen (3:4).

The call to *look up* in 3:1-4 is a call to know the *reality* of which the apostle speaks here: the *present hidden* reality of your life with Christ in God, and the *future manifested* reality of your life with Christ. It is reasonable to ask what the consequences are *now* (until Christ appears) and *here* ('below', on the earth) as we still live our 'ordinary' lives that are not hidden. It is not at all unusual for Christian believers to misunderstand the real power of the Christian life in ways that mean that its connection with the here and now is distorted or misconstrued.

The questions we were asking in the last chapter should now be pursued a little further. How do you experience the power of the resurrection of Jesus Christ now? In what ways do you know, here and now, the death of Jesus, and your death with him, and the rising of Jesus, and your new life with him? How does the *hidden* reality (if it is more than mere words, which of course it is) affect the *visible* reality of our here-and-now lives?

The answer is that here and now, in this present and visible existence, we who have died and been raised with Christ are to experience a remarkable victory.

> Put to death therefore what is earthly in you: sexual immorality, impurity, passion, evil desire, and covetousness, which is idolatry. On account of these the wrath of God is coming. In these you too once walked, when you were living in them. But now you must put them all away: anger, wrath, malice, slander, and obscene talk from your mouth. Do not lie to one another, seeing that you have put off the old self with its practices and have put on the new self, which is being renewed in knowledge after the image of its creator. Here there is not Greek and Jew, circumcised and uncircumcised, barbarian, Scythian, slave, free; but Christ is all, and in all (3:5-11).

1. The victory - I (3:5-7)

Therefore, at the beginning of verse 5, ties what is now said as closely as can be to the powerful reality of which Paul has been speaking in verses 1-4. *Because of that reality*, you are to **put to death what is earthly in you**. The implication of 'therefore' is that there is no way that you could do this apart from the power of having died with Christ. 'You have died' (v. 3), *therefore* (v. 5) 'put to death what is earthly in you.' This is going to be very different from a call to mere moral effort. There is certainly an imperative here, and it is a summons to effort. Yet it is set in the context of a power that is not from us: the power of what Christ has done for us in his death (and therefore our having died with him) and of our new life in him (we have been raised with him).

a. Victory over …

The call is to defeat ('put to death') 'what is earthly in you'. This phrase is a little difficult to translate, but in Greek it clearly echoes the words in verse 2, 'the things that are on the earth'. What Paul means by the phrase here is in no doubt, because he elaborates with five nouns.

The first is **sexual immorality**. Here is an astonishing surprise. The power of Christ's death and resurrection changes your sex life! That may be a rather direct way to put it, but no more direct than the words of Paul. The five nouns in verse 5 are all, I think, coloured in their meaning by the first. The Greek word *porneia* refers to any and all kinds of improper sexual relations. *Porneia* is, to be perfectly clear, any sexual intercourse outside of the marriage relationship.

Only a short time ago (a few decades at most) Christians were not regarded as weird for thinking that sex belonged exclusively to marriage. That was because of centuries of influence of Christian teaching. This has now all but been forgotten, and Christians are today regarded as strange as they must have seemed in the first-century gentile world. How bizarre! No sex until marriage. No sex outside of marriage. Without marriage, no sex.

Worse than bizarre. Some accuse Christian teaching of being infinitely cruel, and uninterested in human happiness, for advocating this: sex for marriage and only for marriage.

To see this as other than bizarre, you have to believe God's Word. But once you have believed him, he is not hard to believe. The teaching of the Bible about sex is confirmed in experience. It is not a negative view of sex. Far from it. Instead it is the highest view of sex. Sex is a purposeful gift of God, so good for its purpose that it is to be guarded and used for that purpose. So powerful is sex for its purpose of binding a man and a woman together in lifelong marriage (and because it has that remarkable purpose it has to be very powerful), its misuse can do incalculable damage. You do not need to know much of life to know something of the powerful goodness of sex in its intended context, and something of the damage done by sex misused.

The astonishing surprise is that if you have died with Christ, the first thing mentioned in Colossians 3 is that you are to destroy any and every spoiling of sex.

With *porneia* as the lead word, the other nouns in verse 5 belong to the same context of ideas. **Impurity** is a general word, wider than *porneia*, perhaps picking up sexual misbehaviour which is not quite *porneia*. **Passion** perhaps in this context should be translated 'lust'. **Evil desire** here probably means wrong sexual desire. **Covetousness** can certainly be wider than sex, but I think it likely that here Paul is tracing wrong sexual behaviour back to an uncontrolled desire for more and more pleasures that are not yours to take. That is covetousness. It is not necessary to tease out distinct meanings for Paul's fivefold list here, but to take in its scope. It is all of the perversions of our sexuality, where something pure is made impure, where powerfully good desires are made into lust and evil desires, no better than greed or covetousness.

Which is, Paul says, **idolatry**. Living for self-indulgent pleasure is the basic human alternative to loving God.

As I hear these words, I must confess that my first thought is of the tragedy, harm and truly devastating consequences that flow from those occasions when Christian people (and even more so when Christian leaders) do *not* in fact put to death what is earthly in them. When Christians (and even more when Christian leaders) fall into sexual immorality, nothing but harm is done – to individuals, families, marriages (including future marriages), ministries, churches and the reputation of the gospel. My first thought is, how important this word is for us all, because I am thinking of those I know who have not heeded it.

People sometimes ask why it is that the Bible so often puts sexual behaviour high on the list of things that matter in human conduct. Isn't that a rather stupid question? We are sexual beings. God has made us male and female. As we go around messing up life because of our alienation from God, pretty high on the list of things we mess up is sex. It is a big thing to mess up.

I cannot help noticing the wisdom of these words. If I don't deal with my covetousness, I am likely to be in trouble with my desires. If I don't deal with my desires, I will be in trouble with my thoughts. If I don't deal with my thoughts, then I am asking for trouble in my actions. 'Put to death what is earthly in you.' Decisive, firm, radical action is called for.

Nevertheless, that first thought must not be my last thought. For while I find it devastating every time I hear of a brother or sister who has failed in the area of sexual morality, I too easily take for granted the astounding phenomenon of believers who do not. If you doubt the power of the death and resurrection of Jesus Christ, take careful account of the Christian people who *do* do away with sexual immorality, who *are* pure in their sexual lives, who repudiate lust, who put down evil desire, who love God rather than self-centred pleasure. I do not want to pretend that we Christians are better than we are in all of this. I do not want to suggest that any of us experiences complete victory over 'what is earthly in us' here and now. But neither do I want to overlook the powerful work of Christ among us. When you see a believer put to death sexual immorality, impurity, lust, evil desire and greed, you are seeing the power of the death and resurrection of Jesus Christ. It is no small thing! It is the very power that is putting the creation back together at work in a human life!

b. Victory because ...

Just in case we need to be convinced that these things are to be put to death, Paul adds in verse 6: **On account of these things the wrath of God is coming**. The heart of the believer's new life in Christ is the forgiveness of all our trespasses (2:13; 1:14). You have been delivered from the dominion of darkness (1:13). The wrath of God is indeed coming, but not on you. In Christ you have left the way of life that is bringing God's wrath to the world. So, of course, you must be done with that way of life.

In other words, **in these things you yourselves walked once, when you were living in these things**. But (by implication) that was a thing of the past. These things characterize the life of those who have not died with Christ or been raised with him. I sometimes wonder whether we are a little unrealistic when we Christians agitate for Christian morality in our pagan society. I don't mean we should not do so, but our expectations should not be high. It is natural for the unredeemed to live immoral lives. What else can they do? That is what you and I would do apart from Christ.

2. The victory - II (3:8)

Verse 8 begins with those wonderful gospel words of comfort and encouragement: **But now**. What was 'once' the case (v. 7) is 'now' (v. 8) no longer so. How could we deny what has happened to us in Jesus Christ? How could we live *now* as we *once* lived?

Therefore in verse 8 Paul returns to his theme, with a shift. Slightly less graphically, but no less definitely, instead of 'put to death' (as he said in verse 5), he now says, **you must put them all away**.

If he stopped there you would think he meant the things in verse 5. I think he still has the idea of 'what is earthly in you' in mind, but this time he elaborates with five different nouns. Just as the first of the five nouns in verse 5 coloured the whole list, so the little phrase he adds at the end of the list in verse 8 may apply to all of the preceding five terms: **from your mouth**.

In other words, we are thinking now not of sexual behaviour as in verse 5, but of *speaking*. (I am all too aware that readers will find it difficult to retain the same level of attention with this change of subject. Paul may well have known what he was doing in mentioning sex first!)

The significance of the matters addressed in verse 8 may be illuminated by two observations.

First, we should now understand that what believers have left behind in joining Christ is a whole pattern of life. If Paul can view this pattern of life from the perspective of sexual behaviour (v. 5), and then from the perspective of speaking behaviour (v. 8), we are to understand that it is the whole way of life that is to be put to death, not just one or two areas of moral struggle.

Second, just as sex was an entirely appropriate subject to raise when the subject is redeemed human life, because God has made us sexual beings, so God has also made us speaking beings. Furthermore, just as the Christian life is far from having a negative view of sex, so it is not negative about speech. Yet as alienated and hostile people (1:21), we have perverted our speaking just as we misused our sexual behaviour.

The surprise (again) of the Christian life is this: the death and resurrection of Jesus has power to change what comes out of our mouths.

Just as Paul's direct words about sexual behaviour and thoughts strike a chord with today's readers, so must the words in verse 8.

The first is powerful: **anger**. In the original this is the same word as is translated 'wrath' in verse 6: 'the *wrath* of God is coming'. How peculiar it is that the very people who have brought the wrath of God to the world think that they have the right to be the angry ones at any wrong, or perceived wrong, they might suffer. In the original the second word is perhaps a slightly gentler version of the same: **wrath**.[1] The third word is hard to precisely define, but **malice** is a good rendering: speech that expresses ill will to others, hastily spoken words, nasty and hurtful. The fourth word, **slander**, in another context, would be translated 'blasphemy'. It is the opposite of praise: defaming and damaging the reputation of another person. The fifth word is a compound word in the original which means disgraceful speech, or **obscene language**. Such is often employed, of course, in anger and malice and slander.

The Christian view of how we are to speak is no less bizarre in a pagan world than our view of sex. It is only that the pagan world is more obsessed with sex, and so it notices our weirdness more there. Yet the very idea that

---

[1] It would be preferable for the English translation to pick up the echo of verse 6 by putting 'wrath, anger' in verse 8 instead of 'anger, wrath'.

speech is not for putting others down, nor for expressing your frustrations and annoyances, nor for lashing out, but for building *others* up, for expressing kindness, for turning attention away from yourself, is as strange to an unbelieving world as anything that Christians believe about sex!

If you died with Christ, you are to put away all such damaging speech.

Once again, I confess that my first thoughts as I hear these words are of the damage that I see done (and indeed that I have done) when this call goes unheeded. Even in Christian churches there are times when people are spoken to, or spoken about, in anger, even malice, sometimes slander, and perhaps occasionally (when you are quite sure certain people cannot hear) obscenities. Are you aware of the harm that is done when and if you speak to others like that? My first thought is that this word from God is needed by us, perhaps particularly by some of us. Put away these things.

Nevertheless, as before, that first thought cannot be my last thought. To focus on the failures (distressing as they may be) is to miss the powerful wonder. If you doubt the power of the death and resurrection of Jesus Christ, take careful notice of the quality of the speech you do hear from the mouths of Christian people. I do not want to ignore the failures, but neither do I want to take for granted the powerful work of Christ among us. When you see believers put away anger, wrath, malice, slander and obscene talk from their mouth, you are seeing the power of the death and resurrection of Jesus Christ. It is no small thing! It is the very power that is putting the creation back together at work in a human life!

3. A strategy (3:9-11)

To this point it would be reasonable to hear what Paul has been saying simply as individuals. If we are realistic we may have come to see that the claim being made here is extraordinary. There is power to put our individual lives back in good order (see 2:5), even in such persistently troublesome matters as sex and speech.

In verse 9, however, there is a sharp change. The apostle addresses the assembled believers as a body, and says, **Do**

not lie to one another. With these words Paul could be simply extending the list of speech behaviour that must be changed if we have died with Christ. While that is possible, the words that follow suggest that he is doing more. 'Do not lie to one another' seems to be Paul's indication of the strategy by which the victory he has called us to is to be won. If this is so, it is very important.

Having died and having been raised with Christ and received new life in him is not merely an individual experience that happens in isolation from others. There has been a radical change in the identity of a believer. As Paul puts it, **seeing that you have put off the old self with its practices**. It is like discarding an old shabby, dilapidated, worn-out, embarrassing set of clothes. You put off Adam (literally 'the old man'). You discarded your identity in Adam's lost race. **And** [you] **have put on the new self**, like a brand spanking new, smart, classy set of clothes. You put on Christ, (literally 'the new man'). You joined the new human race in him, **which is being renewed**. It is being made what humanity was meant to be **in knowledge** (that is, in knowing God, see 1:10). The renewal of humanity is **after** [or according to] **the image of its creator**. Christ himself is the image of the invisible God (1:15). As we are joined to Christ, as we have died with him, as we have been raised with him, we are being restored, just as the whole creation is being restored. This is not just happening to each of us individually, but to all of us who are in Christ. This is Christ's 'body' Paul spoke of back in 1:18, of which Christ is already the head, pre-eminent there as he will one day be pre-eminent over all things. This 'body' is the assembly (ESV 'church') that Paul serves (1:24) by his suffering proclamation of Christ, warning every person and teaching every person in order to present every person perfect in Christ (1:28).

This new humanity is defined by one thing. **Here there is not Greek and Jew**. It makes no difference if you are a sophisticated Greek or a pious Jew. Indeed it is not a matter of **circumcised and uncircumcised** at all, that is, it does not matter whether you are a Jew or a Gentile. Here it makes no difference if you are even a despised **barbarian** (a term used generally by Greeks for those of non-Greek culture and language), or an even more despised **Scythian** (a term that referred to the lowest classes of barbarians, usually slaves), nor whether you are a **slave** or **free**. No. Christ is *all* that matters here. **Christ is all, and in all.** We may guess that all of the categories of people in verse 11 were present among the gathering of believers in Philemon's house in Colossae on the day that this letter was first read out. Those differences between people are utterly irrelevant. You have received Christ Jesus the Lord (2:6). That is what matters. You have been filled in him (2:10). You have died and been buried with him (2:11, 12, 20; 3:3). You have been raised with him (2:12; 3:1). All your sins have been forgiven (2:13). These are the things that mark you out as God's people, and these things you share with all of God's people.

This presentation of the new humanity, the assembly of believers (elsewhere called the 'body' of Christ, 1:18, 24), provides the context for the victories of the Christian life described in verses 5-8. It is in this context that Paul says in verse 9, 'Do not lie to one another'. Here is the way in which the victory is to be won. The body of believers is the place for speaking the truth to one another. Don't let anyone in this assembly say that evil desires or malicious speech, sexual immorality or foul talk do not matter. That's a lie. Don't let anyone here deny the coming wrath of God. That's a lie. Don't let anyone here undermine your love for Christ, your faith in Christ, your hope in Christ. That would be a lie. 'Do not lie to one another.' The warnings of the previous chapter were all of lies that could be spoken among believers (see 2:8, 16, 18, 20). Let us speak to one another about the Christian life *truthfully*. Let us remind one another of Christ *truthfully*. That is how the new humanity in Christ is being renewed in knowledge after the image of its creator.

Study Questions

1. Explain how Paul's teaching in Colossians 3:5-11 differs from mere moralism (that is, just urging people to stop doing bad things).

2. How is it that there is a connection between the death of Jesus Christ and a Christian believer's sexual (and, for that matter, speaking) behaviour?
3. How would you help a young Christian to understand the importance of sexual purity?
4. What is the point of Christians agitating for Christian moral standards in a generally non-Christian society?
5. In your experience what is the role of the fellowship of Christian people in helping you to live as Paul encourages believers to live in Colossians 3:5-11?

16

The Quality of the Christian Life
(Colossians 3:12-17)

It is difficult for us to imagine how our society could function if *achievement* were not important to at least most people. Much as we might criticize the ambitious, where would we be without those who have the drive to achieve? Those who achieve great things usually bring benefits for many others as well. What a waste of a life if there is no achievement! What a worry it is to the parents whose son or daughter seems to have no desire, will or discipline to achieve.

There are a number of social commentators these days who draw attention to the *downside* of achievement. It has got out of proportion, they say. In our society it matters too much. While old people might criticize some young people for lack of focus, it is generally the parents who have put far too much pressure and expectation on the school examination results – to take one striking example. There is extraordinary anxiety where I live in Sydney, Australia, surrounding the HSC (Higher School Certificate) examinations each year. Most of the apprehension seems to be felt by the parents! It is an expression of how we derive our sense of importance and security from our achievements and, sadly, from the achievements of our children.

That may seem all very well when I am achieving and when I have children who achieve. But what about when, through no fault of my own, my achievements collapse? Or even if it is my fault? What about when my child does not perform up near the top of the class?

What happens to my dependence on achieving when life places before me responsibilities that provide no measurable or obvious achievement criteria? To raise and care for children? To care for a home? To look after ageing parents? Our achievement obsession produces almost unbearable frustration for many who have to leave their achievement path to do other good things, if those good things do not produce measurable, tangible *achievements*.

The Christian life and achievement

There is little doubt that we who are Christians have been infected by the achievement disease. Just as our society thinks of life so much in terms of achievement, so we Christians find ourselves looking at our Christian lives in *achievement* terms.

Consider how this happens. How do you think about your Christian life? How would you *rate* your Christian life? The vast majority of us who are Christians find this a very difficult subject. Why? Because, frankly, we think we are pretty poor Christians. Most Christians have a deep sense of disappointment with themselves. Is that not true? (Or is it only me?) Some Christians, it is true, seem pretty pleased with themselves. I don't meet very many of those (I'm glad to say!).

My question is: *Why* do you think that you are a 'not very good Christian'? For that matter, if you are in the other category, *why* are you so pleased with yourself as a Christian? I make the confident prediction that, in most cases, how you think about your Christian life (how you *really* think I mean) is infected by the achievement mentality. How we think about our Christian lives is dominated by what we *do* or what we do *not* do. The self-satisfied Christian thinks that he or she is 'doing well'. The downcast Christian thinks that he or she is *not* 'doing well'. I am not really a person who prays as seriously as I think I should. I do not read the Bible as consistently as I should. I do not behave in my family as unselfishly as I should. In my work I am not a strong witness to Christ. There is that bad habit I just don't seem to be able to overcome. I'm a very poor Christian. Does this sound familiar?

It is very difficult for us to see how we could think otherwise. After all, what we do *does* matter. What we are like *is* relevant. While it is true that some people may call themselves Christians and yet seem not to care about what they do or say, or how they treat people – it is not a pretty sight! The word 'hypocrite' springs to mind!

So is achievement thinking appropriate for Christians, or not? What alternative is there?

With these questions in mind we return to the third chapter of the letter to the Colossians, where I believe a powerful and important answer to these questions is taught to us.

As we have been seeing, Colossians 3 is a wonderful exploration of the Christian life. The heart, centre and power of the Christian life is Christ and our identification or union with him. We have been raised with Christ (3:1). We died with Christ (3:3). We will appear with Christ in glory (3:4). The Christian life is therefore a life of victory over the things that are bringing down God's wrath on this world (3:3, 6). Our belonging to Christ means that we have taken off the old humanity (3:9 literally; ESV 'the old self'), and have put on the new humanity (3:10), which is being renewed in knowledge according to the image of its creator.

This means, negatively, that there are behaviours to be done away with. This was sketched in 3:5-11. There are also, positively, things to take on. This is the subject of 3:12-17. There are two parts to the passage. The first (vv. 12-14) addresses *each* one of us. The second (vv. 15-17) addresses *all* of us. It is worth noticing the difference.

1. The new 'man' (3:12-14)

> Put on then, as God's chosen ones, holy and beloved, compassionate hearts, kindness, humility, meekness, and patience, bearing with one another and, if one has

> a complaint against another, forgiving each other; as the Lord has forgiven you, so you also must forgive. And above all these put on love, which binds everything together in perfect harmony (3:12-14).

As always, when reading Paul's writings, it is worth taking the trouble to follow his logic carefully. **Then** (or 'therefore', at the beginning of verse 12) is almost always an important word! Here it indicates that this paragraph follows logically from what precedes, in particular from verses 9-10 and verses 1-4 of this chapter. We must learn what has happened to us and what will happen to us because of Jesus Christ. The 'you' who died with Christ (3:3) was your 'old self' (literally 'old man') which has thus been 'put off' (3:9). This old human nature was 'alienated and hostile in mind, doing evil deeds' (1:21). It was at enmity with God, eager to live without God, ungrateful to him. That 'you' has been put to death, judged as you deserved to be judged. But the judgment took place, not by me dying for myself, but by Jesus Christ dying for me. My sins have now been *forgiven* (1:14; 2:13).

Therefore the *new* 'man' (literally, 3:10) is the forgiven one, who wants to live with God, and is thankful to God. This one has been 'made alive' (2:13). That has not been my doing. I have been made alive because Christ has been raised. I have been raised with him (2:12; 3:1).

a. The new identity: given

Therefore I have a new identity. Before we can respond to the imperatives in verses 12-17 we must understand that this new identity has been given to us, not achieved by us. In Christ, it is who we are. This identity is utterly extraordinary. The words used to describe it in verse 12 are heavy with connotations. They describe the most privileged status conceivable.

God's chosen ones. God is the owner of the whole world. He is the maker of all people. And yet among all people, we who are joined to Jesus Christ are his chosen ones, his special possession.

Holy. *God* is holy. Only what is holy can be accepted, welcomed and embraced by God. We, who are joined to Jesus Christ, are holy!

Beloved. Literally, the word is 'having been loved'. We have had love, God's love, lavished on us. We are people privileged beyond all imagination!

Add to these astonishing words the kind of thing that Paul, the Jew, would know well. He would remember the words spoken by Moses to the Old Testament people of Israel:

> And because [God] *loved* your fathers and *chose* their offspring after them and brought you out of Egypt with his own presence, by his great power … (Deut. 4:37)

> It was not because you were more in number than any other people that the LORD set his love on you and chose you, for you were the fewest of all peoples, but it is because *the LORD loves* you and is keeping the oath that he swore to your fathers … (Deut. 7:7-8)

> Blessed is the nation whose God is the LORD, the people whom *he has chosen* as his heritage! (Ps. 33:12)

We could find many, many more such statements through the Old Testament Scriptures. Any Jewish person could tell you that the nation of *Israel* was God's chosen people, God's holy nation, God's loved children. The whole Old Testament testifies to this fact.

Here is the glorious mystery. The secret that is out, *Christ* among the *nations,* as he is proclaimed to all people, is the hope of glory (1:27, 28). Now *you,* says the apostle to those in Colossae who have been united to Christ by faith (Jews, Greeks, barbarians, Scythians, 3:11), are *God's chosen ones, holy* and you have been *loved*.

b. The new character: **put it on**

As such they are to dress as befits their impressive new identity. **Put on** your new clothes. This is an image for the new character those who are in Christ are to have.

Imagine for a moment the most elite, select, exclusive, privileged group of people in the world. What do you expect them to be like? Paul's description of the character of God's chosen ones is surprising, and not what we are used to seeing in 'important' people. The reason for this surprising description of attire to be put on by the most privileged people in the world is that each of the following words is a term that typically describes God or Christ.

Compassion. As God's chosen, holy, loved people, take on a heart like God's: 'The LORD is gracious and compassionate, slow to anger and rich in love. The LORD is good to all; he has compassion on all he has made' (Ps. 145:8-9 NIV).

Kindness (or 'goodness'). As *God's* people, put on goodness, kindness like God's: 'Oh how abundant is your goodness, which you have stored up for those who fear you and worked for those who take refuge in you ...'(Ps. 31:19)

As God's loved people, put on **humility**, like that of Christ Jesus: 'He humbled himself by becoming obedient to the point of death, even death on a cross' (Phil. 2:8).

Meekness (or 'gentleness'). Elsewhere Paul refers to the 'meekness and gentleness of Christ' (2 Cor. 10:1). This is the consideration of others before one's self. Put on gentleness like that of Jesus.

Patience (or the older translation, 'long suffering') is the putting up with wrong rather than flying into a rage or seeking revenge. Again, like God, like Christ.

This is a sketch of the new character that God's chosen, holy, loved people are to don. It is as unlike what we would expect as the character of Jesus is unlike what we would expect for the one for whom all things were created, the King of kings and Lord of lords!

c. The new conduct: **a consequence**

Not only is there an unexpected *character* to be taken, there is the most unlikely *conduct* that will flow from that character, as a consequence. Just as character ought to be appropriate to identity, so there is conduct that ought to express character.

What kind of conduct can we expect from the most privileged class of people in the world? How do you expect the elite of the whole world to behave? Paul's description is again a surprise: **bearing with one another and, if one has a complaint against another, forgiving each other.**

It is an astounding proposition, that the characteristic behaviour of the most privileged people in the world, the chosen people of God, no less, should be no more impressive than putting up with each other and forgiving each other – not giving up on one another, and not holding grievances against one another.

Why should God's chosen people behave like *that*? How *can* we behave like that? Simply, that is how the Lord has behaved towards us – and that is precisely what has made us the most privileged people in the world: **as the Lord has forgiven you, so you also must forgive.**

d. Summing up: love over all

This section of Paul's argument is summed up like this: **And above all these put on love, which binds everything together in perfect harmony.** The image here may be of an overcoat which is to be put on over all the other garments already mentioned. It holds them all perfectly together. Again our expectations are shattered. What would you expect to see in a *perfect* human being? A magnificent physique? A brilliant personality? Extraordinary ability? No. *Love* binds together all that a human is intended to be.

2. The new society (3:15-17)

> And let the peace of Christ rule in your hearts, to which indeed you were called in one body. And be thankful. Let the word of Christ dwell in you richly, teaching and admonishing one another in all wisdom, singing psalms and hymns and spiritual songs, with thankfulness in your hearts to God. And whatever you do, in word or deed, do everything in the name of the Lord Jesus, giving thanks to God the Father through him (3:15-17).

And suggests that the following paragraph continues the subject that has been under discussion, namely, the new life to be enjoyed by believers. Now, however, the focus shifts slightly to the believers corporately, as a congregation or body of God's people. If the character and the conduct described in verses 12-14 are to be displayed in *each* of us, then our life *together* must support this radical new way of being and living.

a. The peace of Christ

Let the peace of Christ. The 'peace of Christ' is not to be reduced to merely a subjective emotional state, 'peace of mind'. It is the peace which Christ has won for us 'by the blood of his cross' (see 1:20). It is cosmic in scope, embracing 'all things' (1:20), and yet is a gift from God our Father particularly to believers in Christ Jesus (1:2). This peace accounts for the fact we are no longer God's enemies (1:21, 22), but God's chosen ones who have been loved by him (3:12). It is the peace that can be described like this: He forgave us all our sins (1:14; 2:13). This peace is now the reality between us and God because of Jesus Christ.

This peace is now to **rule** in the company of believers. It is to hold sway, call the tune, among us. This peace is to determine our relationships with one another. Together believers are to have a deep awareness of the peace with God that each has been given, and therefore the profound peace that is established between those who believe in Christ. We are to see each other, think of each other, speak and treat each other, conscious of this extraordinary peace. This peace from Christ is to be the decisive factor in our relationships with one another.

To be sure, this is to be a deep reality within each person. Christ's peace is to be the controlling reality **in your hearts** where, as we will hear in verse 16, thankfulness to God is to be the dominant disposition. This peace is to make such a difference to the inner being of each believer that the relationships between believers are controlled by it (in the way that has been described in verses 12-14).

This peace, which was established by Christ's death (1:20; 2:15), is a reality **to** [or, into] **which indeed you were called** by God through the gospel. This is the experience described in different words earlier in the letter: 'He has delivered us from the domain of darkness and transferred us to the kingdom of his beloved Son, in whom we have redemption, the forgiveness of sins' (1:13, 14). The kingdom of Christ is the realm where sins are forgiven. This is the 'peace of Christ'.

Although this call has come to each individual believer, the same gospel call has drawn believers to one another, **in one body**. The assembly (or 'church') of believers there in Philemon's home in Colossae (see Philem. 2) is the primary idea here. This assembly was called 'the body' in 1:18, 'his body' in 1:24, and 'the whole body' in 2:19. This 'body' is an actual assembly, where compassion, kindness, humility, meekness, patience, forgiveness and love can be expressed in real and practical ways (3:12-14). It is true that all believers, wherever they may be, who have been united to Christ, are a 'body' of which he is the head. Nevertheless, this is expressed and experienced when believers meet together in a particular place. This is where the peace of Christ must rule.

The words at the end of verse 15 are crucial. **And be thankful.** How could we be otherwise? This is a note that will be repeated in the following lines, and has been prominent in the teaching of the letter earlier. Paul expressed his own thanks to God the Father in 1:3. He prayed the Colossians would share in this thankfulness in 1:12. In an important summary of the purpose of his letter Paul exhorted them to abound in thanksgiving (2:7). Now it is clear that this thankfulness is to characterize their life *together*.

b. The word of Christ

Verse 16 echoes, in different words, the call of verse 15. In this way it provides a further explanation of the exhortation. How are believers to 'let the peace of Christ rule in [their] hearts' so that the body of God's chosen people enjoys peace and thankfulness? Verse 16 elaborates: **Let the word of Christ ...** 'The word of Christ' is the gospel message that the believers in Colossae had heard from Epaphras (1:7). In this message they had heard and understood God's grace (1:6), and the hope laid up for them in heaven (1:5). By this message God had worked among them, evidenced by their faith in Christ Jesus and their love for all the saints (1:4). 'The word of Christ' therefore probably means 'the word about Christ', rather than 'the word from Christ', although the distinction is hardly important. This word of Christ (v. 16) is the means by which the peace of Christ (v. 15) will rule in the hearts of the believers.

This word is to **dwell in you** (that is, among you) **richly**. The image is unusual, but vivid. The word is to live among them lavishly. This word is to be at home in the body of believers. It is to be dominant in their life together, shaping and directing their minds and hearts. The word of Christ is to be extravagantly spoken and heard among them. Churches today that take this call seriously ensure that time and effort is given to taking in and learning the message about Jesus Christ from the Bible. This is not just teaching for teaching's sake, or learning for learning's sake. Its purpose is that the peace of Christ will rule among us.

Yet it would be a mistake to think that the word of Christ is to be spoken and heard only in the form of formal teaching or sermons. Indeed here Paul gives no particular emphasis to such activities (although he does elsewhere). The word of Christ is to dwell richly among the believers by their **teaching and admonishing one another**. This is a clear echo of 1:28 where Paul described the work of a servant of the gospel as '*admonishing* [ESV, warning] everyone and *teaching* everyone'. Therefore just as Christ is to be proclaimed among the nations (1:27) with effort and energy (1:29), so the word about him is to be spoken extravagantly among believers. This will sometimes be a matter of the truth being shared ('teaching'). Often it will involve addressing those who are failing to 'put to death what is earthly' (3:5) or to 'put on' the Christ-like behaviours of 3:12-14 ('admonishing'). Such conversations are to be a big part of the life of those who have been called into the fellowship of Christian believers.

The strong echo of 1:28 in the wording of 3:16 is extended in the words **in all wisdom** (exactly the same phrase in Greek as translated 'with all wisdom' in 1:28). It seems clear that the word dwelling richly among the believers is closely related to the proclamation of Christ in which Paul was so earnestly engaged. The proclamation that aimed at 'presenting everyone mature (or perfect) in Christ' (1:28) is the word that is to be generously spoken to 'one another', with a view to the qualities described in 3:12-14 being perfected. In other words the goal of the preaching in 1:28 is not attained instantly, but over time as the proclaimed word works among those who have received Christ Jesus the Lord (2:6).

It is perhaps a little surprising to find that one means by which this teaching and admonishing is to take place is with **psalms and hymns and spiritual songs**. The word order and syntax of the Greek suggests this. A more literal translation of verse 16b is: 'teaching and admonishing one another with psalms, with hymns, with spiritual songs, with thankfulness singing in your hearts to God'.

Psalms is probably a reference to the Psalms of the Old Testament. Jesus himself (see, for example, Matt. 21:16; 27:46; Luke 24:44; John 19:24) and the New Testament writers (see, for example, Acts 4:25, 26; 13:33; Heb. 1:5; 5:5) understood the Psalms to be spoken by and about God's king (the Christ, see Ps. 2:2, 6), and to have been fulfilled in Jesus. The Psalms were a rich source for teaching about the Christ. We may be sure, for example, that Paul turned to the Psalms when he 'reasoned ... from the Scriptures, explaining and proving that it was necessary for the Christ to suffer and to rise from the dead' (Acts 17:2, 3). The believers in Colossae were to likewise teach and admonish one another with the word about Christ from the Psalms (see 1 Cor. 14:26, where 'hymn' in the ESV should be 'psalm').

Hymns is not as specific, but probably refers especially to songs of praise to God. This would probably include such songs from the Old Testament (the word is used, for example, in the Septuagint of 2 Chron. 7:6; Neh. 12:46; Ps. 6 title; 40:3), but may extend to songs of praise that were being composed among the Christians (see Matt. 26:30; Acts 16:25).

Songs is a less sharply defined category again, and perhaps therefore needs the qualifying word 'spiritual'. This may refer to the subject matter of the songs ('about spiritual things') or the source ('from the Spirit'). In either case they would be songs about Christ, for they are a means by which the word about Christ dwells richly among the believers.

In the first place, these psalms, hymns and songs are a means of the believers 'teaching and admonishing one another'. We should probably not think too quickly of our contemporary church gatherings, with musicians and song leaders. Today's relatively structured and formal church meetings should no doubt take the teaching of this passage to heart. As we conduct such assemblies the word about Christ must be extravagantly spoken to and heard by 'one another', and this is the purpose our songs and hymns should serve. It is likely that the believers who met in Philemon's house in Colossae shared the gospel with one another in a less structured way. Singing was probably more spontaneous than among many Western Christians today (see two striking examples of spontaneous singing in Matthew 26:30 and Acts 16:25).

In the second place, however, our words *to one another* must come from and build up our thankfulness and joy *towards God*. The word order in the Greek ('with thankfulness singing in your hearts to God') suggests that there should be **singing** directed **to God**. This takes place **in your hearts**. Strictly speaking this 'singing' is not identical to the psalms, hymns and songs which are directed to one another, and therefore must be audibly spoken. The distinction should not be pressed, of course, but it is worth noticing that the outward audible speaking and singing is directed to one another, while it is the inward joyfulness of the heart that is directed to God.

This singing of the heart is **with thankfulness**. We have found thankfulness to be a strong theme through the letter (see 1:3, 12; 2:7; 4:2). In these few lines (3:15-17) thankfulness is mentioned no fewer than three times. The Greek word here is not quite the same as the other occurrences of this idea in the letter. This is the word usually translated 'grace'. It often refers to the grace of God, which the believers have learned in the gospel (see 1:2, 6; 4:18; cf. 4:6). It is possible, therefore, that 'with [or, in] thankfulness' should be rendered 'in [God's] grace'. The point will not be materially different, however. The thankfulness of which Paul speaks throughout this letter is thankfulness for God's grace (see 1:3, 12).

The whole experience of which Paul has been speaking is of God's grace. To know that you are chosen, holy, loved (3:12) is to know God's grace. To experience compassion, kindness, humility, meekness, patience, forgiveness and love in the fellowship of Christian believers is a gift of God's grace. Believers who know these things will be characterized by their thankfulness.

c. Summing up

Verse 17 sums up the quality of the Christian life that has been described in this paragraph.

The scope of the Christian life is indicated: **And whatever you do, in word or deed**. There is no part of life that is not changed by your having died with Christ and been raised with him. In particular, the new life which 'is hidden with Christ in God' (3:3) is also lived in the actions and speech of the believer. The Christian life cannot be merely inward and private.

The Lord of the Christian life is emphasized: **do everything in the name of the Lord Jesus**. This is a remarkable expression. The Old Testament often used the phrase 'in the name of the LORD [Yahweh]' (see for example, Deut. 18:5; 1 Sam. 17:45; Ps. 20:7; Isa. 50:10; Micah 4:5). It is astonishing that Paul could extend that phrase to 'in the name of the Lord *Jesus*'. This was an expression of his conviction that 'in [Jesus] the whole fullness of deity dwells' (2:9). To speak and act 'in the name of' Jesus as Lord perhaps deliberately points us back to the theme sentence of the whole letter, with which the body of the letter began: 'Therefore, as you received Christ Jesus the Lord, so walk in him' (2:6). This is precisely what doing everything in the name of the Lord Jesus means.

The manner of the Christian life is underlined again: **giving thanks to God the Father through him**. Again there is a clear echo of that theme sentence which concluded with the words 'abounding in thanksgiving' (2:7). This is the third time in as many verses that this note has been struck ('be thankful', 3:15; 'with thankfulness', 3:16; now 'giving thanks,' 3:17), and the sixth time in the whole letter (see 1:3, 12; 2:7). To give thanks to God the Father 'through the Lord Jesus' means that he is the one who has made it possible for us to give thanks to God as Father (cf. 1:3).

We conclude this study of 3:12-17 by returning to the importance of 'achievement' in human life. The repeated refrain of thankfulness gives us the key for the alternative to the 'achievement' mindset. The Christian life may be compared to marriage. The wisdom of our society tends to think of marriage in 'achievement' terms. You must work at it – and you will succeed or you will fail. The weakness of such marriages is the weakness of the persons involved. The Bible teaches us that *God* joins a man and a woman in marriage. Their unity is *given*. It is a gift. The call is to make the most of it. Live it out. Live up to what God has given. The strength of such marriages is in what God has given. Just so, the Christian life is to find its strength in *thankfulness* to God for what *he* has done and given. In everything the believer is to give thanks to God the Father through the Lord Jesus.

Study Questions

1. In your life (so far), what has given you a sense of achievement? How has the teaching of Paul's letter to the Colossians affected your sense of achievement?
2. If you are one of 'God's chosen ones', is it true that you belong to 'the most elite, select, exclusive, privileged group of people in the world'? How is it possible to really believe that without a sense of arrogant superiority towards others?
3. Compare the description of the character and behaviour of 'God's chosen ones' in Colossians 3:12, 13 with your experience in the Christian fellowship to which you belong. Give thanks to God for the privilege of belonging to this group of people.
4. Consider some examples of how your experience in the Christian fellowship to which you belong sometimes falls short of the description of the character and behaviour of 'God's chosen ones' in Colossians 3:12, 13. How might the peace that Jesus Christ has won (Col. 1:20) change such

things – if it had a greater influence in your life and the life of your fellow believers?

5. In what practical ways does the word of Christ play a role in the Christian fellowship to which you belong? What is the purpose of hearing this word together? How effective is it?

6. Why is music so often a matter of controversy in churches? When this happens how might the teaching of Colossians 3:12-17 help?

7. Why is thankfulness so important? How might the thankfulness of a fellowship of Christian people be a good indication of its spiritual health?

17

Family Life in Christ
(Colossians 3:18-21)

Wives, submit to your husbands, as is fitting in the Lord. Husbands, love your wives, and do not be harsh with them. Children, obey your parents in everything, for this pleases the Lord. Fathers, do not provoke your children, lest they become discouraged (3:18-21).

If you had been among the small gathering of believers in the home of Philemon in Colossae on the day that this letter arrived (all the way from Rome, where Paul was imprisoned) by the hand of Tychicus and Onesimus, I wonder whether you would have felt a jarring change of tone at this point of the letter, as you listened to Tychicus read.

Perhaps unlike the readers of this commentary, those listening to Tychicus would be able to remember the words read only minutes earlier, at the beginning of the letter, which lifted their eyes to the utterly remarkable significance of their faith in Christ Jesus the Lord, their love for all the saints, and their hope laid up in heaven (1:3-8). The letter had spoken in the most dramatic terms of what had happened, and was happening, to these previously pagan people (1:9-14). From utter darkness into the brilliant light. Redeemed. Forgiven. Reconciled. That is what your faith in Christ Jesus means!

This understanding was then supported by the most astonishing assertions about the Christ in whom they had come to believe (1:15-20): 'the image of the invisible God', 'the firstborn of all creation', 'all things were created through him and for him', 'in him all the fullness of God was pleased to dwell'. As you Colossians have come to faith in *him*, the hope of glory has come to the nations (1:27), for this Christ Jesus has acted to reconcile all things to himself. He has made peace and is putting this broken and divided world back together again. He has done this by the blood of his cross (1:21–2:5).

The purpose of this letter was then made clear. It is a call to these believers to stay in this faith, to stand firm in Christ Jesus, not to move from him, to live *in him*, to grow *in him*, to be built up *in him*, and so to abound in thanksgiving (2:6, 7). There was, after that, a warning that, in the world of the Colossians (as in our own world), there are plenty of challenges to this faith. There are forces – people, ideas and teachings – which threaten this faith (2:8-23). That is why this letter was so important.

Then, through the first half of chapter 3, they heard a magnificent description of the life of the one who believes in Christ Jesus: the *wonder* of our union with Christ – past, present, and future (3:1-4); the *transformation* of the life that is united to Christ (3:5-11); the *quality* of that life (3:12-17).

As Tychicus continued reading, they then heard: 'Wives, submit to your husbands ... Husbands, love your wives ... Children obey your parents ... Fathers do not provoke them' (3:18-21). I like to imagine those listening looking up, with a questioning look on their faces. I am not (for the moment) alluding to the awkwardness that we in our society and culture have with the words of 3:18 (a word about that shortly). The more important thing is to sense the apparently astonishing shift of subject from the cosmic work of Christ, reconciling all things to himself, whether things on earth or things in heaven – to the tiny domestic scene: wife, husband and children.

We need to appreciate that when Paul turns to say something about family life for those united to Christ, he is still talking about the consequences of the death and resurrection of Jesus. If that event of immense effect is intended to bring order and peace back to the chaos of *all things* (1:15-20), then we must understand that this same Christ and this same work of Christ brings order and peace to the family: your family and mine.

Before we concentrate on the specific details of these four verses, notice their general shape. The brevity is immediately striking. I do not know that I would like to be asked to say something significant about the Christian family in less than 50 words. In another place (the fifth chapter of Ephesians) Paul does elaborate somewhat on these brief lines. Nonetheless, the very brevity of what Paul says here encourages me to think that he may well be telling us something essential. This is what he chooses to say when he only has 50 words!

The second thing to notice is that these words are about an *ordered* household. The way the wife is to relate to the husband, the husband to the wife, the children to the parents, the fathers to the children. Earlier Paul told his readers that he was 'rejoicing to see your *good order* and the firmness of your faith in Christ' (2:5). Faith in Christ brings order to life, just as he brings order to the totality of all things. One place where this good order is to be seen is the marriages and families of believers.

What is meant by 'order' we will come to when we look at the details of these verses but, even before we get there, notice that the general shape of what Paul says, and the context in his letter, clearly implies that marriages and families *need to be redeemed*. Marriage and the family are not institutions that have escaped the ravages of the Fall. They can be places of terrible chaos, darkness, hurt and even wickedness. We sometimes have a sentimental view of marriage and the family. Those of us who are unmarried need to realize this as well as those of us who are married. Marriage and family is not itself a haven from the chaos, where your sinfulness will do no harm, and you will be unharmed by the sinfulness of others. The married and the unmarried among us sometimes think like that. Either in longing or in pretence we think of a marriage or a family where we could just 'be ourselves', let our hair down and have no need for restraints – a place of safety. Yet everything human needs redemption. We are dangerously deceived if we hope that a life situation (even marriage and family life) will by itself bring us peace, security and happiness.

Sometimes Christians can have the same unrealistic expectations of their church. Come into a Christian community, committed and focused on the things of God, and surely I will grow in sanctification. Surely *here* I can escape from the darkness. What a devastating discovery it can be to find that even the Christian community is in need of redemption, just like each of its members.

Perhaps it is less common to be unrealistic about church. I do suspect, however, that many of us are unrealistic about our marriages and families, or the marriages and families of others.

These days we have our own particular, culturally conditioned kind of sentimentality about family life. This is the view that *freedom from restraint* is the path to fulfilment and happiness. If we cannot be free from restraint in our home, if we cannot be relaxed and unguarded and undisciplined in our own family, then where can we be? The answer that the Bible gives is terribly unsettling to our culture. It is that *nowhere,* this side of heaven, is it safe for us to simply 'be ourselves' – not until 'ourselves' have become the fully redeemed children of God.[1]

This does not mean that there is no difference between life in my home and life outside it. It simply means that it is no safer in my family than anywhere else to pursue happiness simply through personal and unrestrained freedom. The order of life in my family will be different from the order of life outside it. In some ways it will be more difficult, because it is more intimate.[2] The call of the words of Scripture that come to us in 3:18-21 is to know the redeeming power of Christ and his work in our marriages and in our family life.

---

[1] For an insightful reflection on this subject, see C.S. Lewis, 'The Sermon and the Lunch', in *Undeceptions: Essays on Theology and Ethics* (London: Geoffrey Bles, 1971), pp. 236-237.

[2] *ibid*, p. 237.

The question is, What shape does the redemption of Christ bring to marriage and family? Paul provides this brief but profound outline: a word to wives, to husbands, to children and to fathers.

1. To wives (3:18)

It is important for us to appreciate the reason that the words addressed to wives ('Wives, submit to your husbands') sound so appalling to our ears today. It is that two related ideas have become embedded in the consciousness of our culture. The first I have referred to already, namely, that human happiness is found in independent freedom. These words seem to deny that freedom, and therefore the possibility of happiness, to wives. No wonder it sounds offensive! The second idea is that a person who *subordinates* himself or herself to another is thereby diminished as a person. These words seem therefore to make wives *inferior* to husbands. Again, no wonder Paul's words give offence.

The offence of 3:18 (and many similar statements in the New Testament) is *unavoidable* if you accept these two ideas. At least it *should* be unavoidable. Furthermore, the offence should be taken seriously. Sometimes I fear Christian people retain those two ideas and then, insisting that 3:18 (or similar biblical teaching) is the Word of God, accept the offensive conclusions: that husbands have a freedom to pursue their own happiness which wives do not, and that husbands are somehow superior to their wives. The problem is not being offended by such conclusions. We *ought* to be offended by them. The problem is the utterly unchristian thinking that draws these conclusions from the Word of God.

Our new life in Christ is very different from our culture's notions of liberation and happiness. Those who have died with Christ and been raised with Christ and will appear with him in glory are to live lives of *compassion* (not freedom from the demands of others), *kindness* (not self-centred independence), *humility* (not superiority), *meekness* (not assertiveness), *patience* (not impatience) – *bearing with one another* and, if one has a complaint against another, *forgiving* each other, as the Lord has forgiven you. Above all, the new life in Christ puts on *love* (3:12-14). Only with this radical understanding of life as Christ shapes it can we sensibly approach the particulars of family life in Christ.

What, then, does Paul mean by his exhortation to **wives**?

Submit translates a Greek word that could be literally represented as 'order under' (hence 'subordinate'). The word is related to the term translated 'good order' in 2:5. 'Order your lives under' is the general idea here.

It is striking how often this word appears in the New Testament to describe how Christians are to live. 'Ordering our lives under' another is a characteristic, it would seem, of the Christian life. We are to order our lives under God (Heb. 12:9; James. 4:7); under his law (it would seem from Rom. 8:7); under Christ (Eph. 5:24); under the governing authorities (Rom. 13:1, 5; Titus 3:1; 1 Pet. 2:13); under ministers of the gospel (1 Cor. 16:16); slaves are to put themselves under their masters (Titus 2:9; 1 Pet. 2:18); young men under older men (1 Pet. 5:5); children under parents (Luke 2:51); and wives **to your husbands** (Eph. 5:22; Titus 2:5; 1 Pet. 3:1, 5 and of course Col. 3:18).[3] Indeed there is the exhortation to believers in Ephesians 5:21 to 'order yourselves under *one another* out of reverence for Christ'.

On this basis, someone has reasonably argued that the New Testament teaches a 'subordinationist ethic'.[4] This is the way in which the new humanity is constituted. It is the way in which the disintegration of human society is to be redeemed: not by individual liberation from restraints and obligations to others, but by each one gladly placing himself or herself *under* the ones God has placed 'over' us.

In the case of wives, we must notice, Paul affirms that to place themselves under their husbands is **fitting in the Lord**. This is explicitly not presented as an accommodation to the patriarchal society of the day (as some allege), but 'fitting' (that is, in harmony, proper, appropriate) 'in the

[3] Douglas J. Moo, *The Letters to the Colossians and to Philemon* (Nottingham: Apollos, 2008), pp. 299-300.

[4] R.C. Lucas, *Fullness and Freedom: The message of Colossians and Philemon* (Leicester: Inter-Varsity Press, 1980), p. 158. This chapter is indebted to Dick Lucas's masterful exposition.

Lord'. In Christ (cf. 3:17), there is a proper order, and the husband (as Paul puts it elsewhere) is the 'head' of the wife (Eph. 5:23; cf. 1 Cor. 11:3).

There is probably a further nuance to the phrase '**as** is fitting in the Lord'. The subordination Paul calls wives to has a particular character. Subordination, like every human relationship, can be perverted. The standard of what Paul means by subordination is that which is 'fitting in the Lord'.

This requires care. Just as we must not capitulate to secular liberationist philosophies here, we must also be very careful that we are not captive to our own human traditions. In some measure the liberationist philosophies have been in reaction to inexcusable conduct by men (and at times, it must be said, by Christian men). The teaching of which 3:18 is an example has sometimes been taken by men and used to provide a framework for the most appalling chauvinism and self-centred, greedy, assertiveness: a husband requiring his wife to meet *his* needs, to serve *his* interests, to fulfil *his* desires, to bow to *his* selfish will. It can be very ugly indeed. It is no wonder that with such horrors in the background many of us feel a certain attraction to the liberationist philosophies.

But they are a *false* answer. The Bible's answer is to understand the character of the husband's headship, under which the Christian wife is called to order her life.

2. To husbands (3:19)

The word to wives in verse 18 must therefore be understood in the light of the word to **husbands** in verse 19. The husband's responsibility is to **love your wives**. His solemn, God-given duty is the well-being of his wife. It has always been too easy for a man to *say* 'I love you' to a woman. The word to husbands here is not a call to utter the words, but to live the reality. Husbands, love your wives.

Again, in a full recognition of our need for redemption (and that our *marriages* need redemption), the very real tendency from which husbands need to be delivered is identified: **and do not be harsh with them**. We could translate, 'do not become bitter towards them.' How tragically ever-present is the possibility of bitterness in marriage, perhaps particularly for a husband. When a wife disappoints a husband's (possibly self-centred) hopes and ambitions, when she does not live up to his unrealistic ideals for her, bitterness and then harshness are close at hand. Husbands, love your wives, and do not be harsh with them – do not become bitter.

There is no more place for selfishness, self-centred 'liberty', and self-seeking assertiveness in a Christian husband than there is in a Christian wife.

It is important to see that wives are called to put themselves under husbands who are called to love them. The idea, in its context, is not first and foremost for wives to place themselves under the *authority* of their husbands, but to place themselves under their *love*.

I want to explore this distinctively Christian way of understanding life just a little further. We noted earlier that the New Testament is sometimes said to present a 'subordinationist ethic'. We saw the range of situations in which believers are called to place themselves *under* others. In each case the one to whom we are called to submit is one who has a responsibility for our welfare. It goes against the grain of the liberationist philosophies, but the reordering of life that comes with Christ Jesus as Lord involves, not the assertion of *independence*, but the embracing of *dependence*.

This is how it is with Christ himself. He is our saviour. But we receive his salvation by submitting to him as Lord. Of course, this involves accepting his authority, but his authority is *for our good*. It is simply impossible to say, 'I want Christ's salvation, but I want to be independent, I do not want to submit to him as Lord.' He is our saviour *by* being our Lord. *As* our Lord, he is our saviour.

It is the same in all the other areas of Christian submission. Submission is never permission for authoritarian tyranny, or bullying. We are called to submit to those whose responsibility it is to care for us in some way. But care can only be given to the one who submits to the care.

Christian ministry is like this. Christian ministry is service, or care. It is a terrible thing when the authority of Christian ministry is used to bully and boss. Yet there are times when Christians complain that they are not being cared for as they would like to be, even though they are the very people who refuse to submit to the ministry that they insist should be caring for them.

In any Christian fellowship it is appropriate to call on believers to *put themselves under* those who are 'over you in the Lord' (1 Thess. 5:12). This does not give leaders the right to be authoritarian bullies, but at the same time they cannot care for me if I will not trust them. If I pursue a path of independent freedom, just doing my own thing, I cannot complain that I do not receive the care and love I expect.

The problem often emerges in churches. The people with limited commitment to the fellowship, who come when they feel like it, who accept no measure of authority from the pastor over their lives – these will so often be the ones who complain that they are not being cared for.

This is not a one-sided matter. Indeed that is the very point we should see by reading 3:18 and 19 *together*. 'Wives submit to your husbands' makes full sense only *alongside* 'Husbands love your wives'. The fulfilment of each side of this relationship is dependent on the other. A husband must take some responsibility for making his wife's submission to him a good and joyful thing. A wife must take some responsibility for making her husband's loving her a good and joyful thing.

It will be for each husband and wife hearing these words to work out the details in their situation of what it means for Christ to be the Lord of their marriage. The basic shape of the relationship is: 'Wives, submit to your husbands, as is fitting in the Lord. Husbands, love your wives, and do not be harsh with them.'

3. To children (3:20)

The next word is to children. **Children, obey your parents**. I have always liked the T-shirt that has the words in large letters across the front: 'Because I'm the mother. That's why!' It expresses the understandable, normal and very common frustration at the child who (from about the age of three) questions why he or she needs to do as they are told. While I enjoy the T-shirt, I would not like it to be a true statement of my relationships as a parent. The obedience of children is not for the sake of the parents. The obedience of the children is to those who are responsible to care for them. The authority of the parent is to be exercised for the care of the child. That is the context of the obedience required of the child. Disobedient children contribute to a dysfunctional family, chiefly because their disobedience hinders their parents' love and care.

This should help us to see the force of **in everything**, and to understand that this obedience changes as a child grows up. The obedience required corresponds to the parents' responsibility. As the scope of the parents' responsibility changes over time, so does the scope of obedience required. I take it that 'in everything' points to the comprehensive nature of parents' responsibility for children in their dependent years.

The phrase, **for this pleases the Lord** might be better translated 'for this is pleasing in the Lord'. It corresponds and is very close in meaning to 'as is fitting in the Lord' at the end of verse 18.

4. To fathers (3:21)

Finally, Paul turns to fathers. Although this exhortation, no doubt, applies to mothers too, perhaps fathers are more typically in need of this word.[5] **Fathers, do not provoke your children, lest they become discouraged.**

What behaviour on the part of fathers does Paul have in mind here? Most of us (especially fathers) who have any experience of family life probably recognize it: those words and actions (or sometimes absence of words and absence of actions) that make our children fearful and timid, lacking in normal self-confidence. Strong fathers sometimes bemoan the fact that their children are so lacking in confidence, when they have used their strength to crush and undermine them.[6] Fathers especially have a responsibility to support and encourage their children.

In just four sentences, Paul has brilliantly sketched the essential shape of marriage and family under the reconciling Lordship of Jesus Christ. It is only a sketch in bare outline.

---

[5] Lucas p. 163.

[6] *ibid.* pp. 163-64.

It leaves us to work out the concrete expression of these relationships in our own marriages and families. The essential and basic framework of family relationships is, however, vitally important. We need these words because our families and our marriages are as marred and distorted as we are as individuals. These are healing, redeeming and constructive words for wives, husbands, children, parents and all of us who care about Christian marriages and families.

Study Questions

1. Consider some of the ways in which people have unrealistic expectations for marriage and family life? What problems can this cause?
2. Are you offended by Colossians 3:18? Why, or why not?
3. How does the teaching about the Lord Jesus Christ that we have heard in this letter show the error of the ideas that:
   a. human happiness is to be found in independent freedom; and
   b. a person who *subordinates* him or herself to another is thereby diminished as a person?
4. In what particular ways does your life involve 'subordination' to others? Who are they? What is good and what is problematic about these relationships of 'subordination'?
5. In what ways are 'ordered' relationships (of the kind we have seen in Col. 3:18-21) better than the pursuit of individual freedom?
6. If you are a husband, what can you do to make your wife's submission a good and joyful thing? If you are a wife, what can you do to make your husband's love a good and joyful thing?
7. Does Paul's teaching about children and fathers in Colossians 3:20, 21 (though very briefly stated) raise questions about any approaches to parenting with which you are familiar?

18

Slaves of Christ
(Colossians 3:22–4:1)

One of the two men who brought this letter from Paul in Rome to the gathering of believers in Colossae was Onesimus (4:9). Onesimus was a slave who some time earlier had run away from his master in Colossae. He had come to faith in Christ Jesus, through meeting Paul in his prison in Rome (Philem. 10). Onesimus had now come back to Colossae with this letter and with the intention of returning to his master (Philem. 12). His master's name was Philemon, and there is good reason to think that when this letter was first read to the gathered believers in Colossae, they were in Philemon's house (see Philem. 2, and the Introduction for more details of this story). Tychicus and Onesimus also carried another letter from Paul for Philemon himself, but that is another story, to which we will turn in due course. I find it moving to realize that as this letter was read on that first occasion, and particularly as 3:22–4:1 was read, among the listeners were Onesimus, the runaway slave, and Philemon, his master.

> Slaves, obey in everything those who are your earthly lords, not by way of eye-service, as people-pleasers, but with sincerity of heart, fearing the Lord. Whatever you do, work heartily, as for the Lord and not for men, knowing that from the Lord you will receive the inheritance as your

> reward. You are serving the Lord Christ. For the wrongdoer will be paid back for the wrong he has done, and there is no partiality.
>
> Lords, treat your slaves justly and fairly, knowing that you also have a Lord in heaven (3:22–4:1).[1]

The poignant situation in which these words were first heard sharpens the awkwardness I am sure all of us feel hearing this part of the letter today. Perhaps there is no part of the letter that is more difficult for us to hear now as *the Word of God*.

The problem of slavery

The Bible's treatment of the subject of slavery is not the only point at which the Scriptures offend the moral sensibilities of almost every one of today's readers. Yet it is one of the best known and, for many Bible believers, possibly the most embarrassing. It has frequently been cited as the case proving the cultural relativity of the Bible. What we now see as utterly unacceptable morally, namely, the institution of slavery, the Bible writers accepted, some would say *endorsed*. This, it is said, proves how they were bound to the culture of *their* time and place. And (so the argument always goes) just as we have come to understand (as they did not yet understand) the moral evil of slavery, so we have come to understand (more recently) the moral evil of patriarchy and the cultural limitations of the Bible writers with respect to the place and role of women in family, church and society. More recently still, the cultural limitations of the Bible's unenlightened sexual morality can be seen. The Bible's disapproval of homosexual sexual relations can now be seen as a consequence of the ignorance of the time about homosexuality (its causes, its nature) – just as the endorsement of male 'headship' can be seen as a consequence of a culture unenlightened concerning women's rights, and

---

[1] The ESV is slightly amended here to bring out one important point. 'Master(s)' in 3:22 and 4:1 has been replaced by 'lord(s)', in order to preserve the repetition of this word at the end of 3:22 and in 3:24, 25. The resulting English is a little unnatural, but helps us to see an important feature in the original.

the acceptance of slavery can be seen in the context of a culture where this dreadful institution was unquestioned.

There is a certain attraction and persuasiveness to this line of reasoning. It is not a matter of condemning the Bible writers. They were people of their times. We must not pretend that the Bible is an a-historical book. This letter to the Colossians, for instance, addresses a real historical, and therefore cultural situation. The slave Onesimus and the slave-master Philemon were listening to this! But it was not *our* culture. And just as we, no doubt, have *our* areas of culturally conditioned ignorance and blindness, so did they. It is hardly *surprising* that their moral vision (like ours) had its limits and inadequacies: the limits and inadequacies of anyone in the first-century Roman Empire. But it is very important indeed (so the argument runs) that we acknowledge those limitations, rather than perpetuate them. Otherwise we, like some earlier Christians, may find ourselves on the wrong side of history – defending the now indefensible institution of slavery. That is what many Bible believers did only 200 years ago! Or fighting a rearguard action to keep women in subordinate roles (as the conservative evangelical Christians are accused of doing today). Or unjustly mistreating homosexual people (as most Christians are still seen to be doing). All this we may do with a sense of moral superiority, for we believe we are following the teaching of the Bible.

In this way slavery is advanced as the case that proves the cultural limitations of the Bible's vision, at least in the areas of social relations. For we all agree at least that slavery is evil. I am sure that most thoughtful Christian people feel the attraction of this line of argument.

We have opened up a big subject, and it is not possible to say everything here that could or should be said. So I will attempt to say enough to clear away, if I can, some misunderstandings that may well stop us listening as we should to the Scriptures at this point.

First, we need to see that the thinking I have been referring to is itself hugely problematic. To judge the Scriptures by the standards and values of *our* culture, the understandings of *our* historic moment, is an inexcusable arrogance. It means that you refuse to allow these Scriptures to critique your times and culture, except on your own terms. Now I understand the *non-Christian* world rejecting the Bible at this point as at most other points. But for *Christians* to want to hold on to something considered to be the heart of the Bible's message, but consider ourselves superior to the apostles and other inspired writers in seeing the consequences of that truth is, if I may say so, breath-taking cultural imperialism.

Second, the subject of slavery, rather than being the test case that proves the Bible's limitations, is a very good test case for believing Christians today. Will we humbly listen to the Word of God with the confident expectation of its thorough goodness? We should know that whenever we find it hard to see God's Word as good, it will *either* be because we have misunderstood it *or* because of a mistaken moral framework we are carrying around. In our last chapter, as we thought about the offence we easily feel at Paul's words to wives in Colossians 3:18, I suggested that the offence is largely caused by two mistaken ideas that our culture has taught us. God's Word challenges these ideas, and exposes their inadequacy.

Third, having said that, I have to acknowledge that the case of slavery is difficult. Certainly we will be helped, I hope, in a few minutes as we listen carefully to what Paul actually says, rather than what we imagine he says, and as we hear what he says in the context of the whole letter, rather than taken out of that context. Furthermore, if we looked at the New Testament more widely we would discover that nowhere does the New Testament *endorse* slavery (as for example it endorses marriage and family relationships in the sense that such relationships are clearly established and given by God for the good of the human race). The awkward thing is that neither does the New Testament *condemn* slavery. Even Christian slave-masters are not told to liberate their slaves.

Fourth, there is some baggage that almost every hearer of these texts today brings with them that contributes to our problem. When we think of slavery we cannot help thinking of the nineteenth-century phenomenon, particularly in the United States of America. That was race-based slavery, dependent on an appalling slave trade, and practised, at least very often, with terrible cruelty. That shameful institution was gradually abolished, under the influence of such great Christian statesmen as William Wilberforce, beginning with the abolition of the trade of slaves. The New Testament does condemn slave *traders* (probable meaning of 'enslavers' in 1 Timothy 1:10). Yet it is a mistake to think that the institution we encounter in passages like Colossians 3 was the same as the nineteenth-century phenomenon. These would have been domestic slaves, serving within the household. Some 80-90 per cent of the inhabitants of Rome were slaves or former slaves. Slavery was not race-based. Slaves were usually prisoners of war, although a person could sell himself or herself into slavery. Slaves had certain rights at Roman law. There were various ways in which a slave might gain freedom. In some cases a slave could expect freedom after seven years. Under Roman law he or she could expect to be set free at least by the age of 30.[2] Of course, no one would dispute that freedom would normally be a preferable state of life (see 1 Cor. 7:21). Being a slave was certainly not a desirable condition, but we ought to recognize the historical context of the Bible's words, and not read into them a situation that they were not then addressing.

Fifth, we are left with the conclusion that the Bible does not directly condemn or demand the overthrow of the institution of slavery as it was practised in places like Colossae in the first century. Slaves were not called on to rise up and revolt. Masters were not expected to set slaves free. Christians generally were not instructed to agitate for the abolition of this practice even, we must notice, within the fellowship of believers.

Therefore, the word addressed to slaves and masters actually challenges my ideas of freedom and perhaps

---

[2] For these facts about slavery I am indebted to the article on 'Slave, Slavery' by A.A. Rupprecht in Gerald F. Hawthorne and Ralph P. Martin, eds, *Dictionary of Paul and his Letters* (Leicester and Downers Grove: InterVarsity Press, 1993), p. 881-83.

even of human rights. Mind you, it is *my ideas* of freedom and rights that are challenged, not freedom and rights themselves. God has set us free from the dominion of darkness, and brought us into the kingdom of his beloved Son (1:13). Redeemed is what we are (1:14). He has forgiven us all our trespasses (1:14; 2:13). The question now is, How does Christ Jesus, who has reconciled all things in heaven and on earth to himself by making peace by the blood of his cross (1:20), redeem a *slave*? How does Christ redeem a *master* of slaves? How does the person who is a slave and the one who is a master experience the good order (2:5), redemption and freedom that Christ brings? Could it be that there is a redemption and a freedom that is authentic and real, yet not dependent on the ideas of independence, liberty, and autonomy that seem to matter so much to me and my contemporaries?

Let us then join Onesimus, the slave, and Philemon, his master, and humbly listen to the word of the apostle of Christ Jesus by the will of God (1:1) concerning slaves and masters who have received Christ Jesus the Lord (2:6).

1. To slaves (3:22-25)

a. A new obedience

It is important to notice that in the gathering of believers in Colossae that day, for whom Paul always gave thanks to God (1:3-8), for whom he prayed (1:9-14), and about whom he has said so much in this letter, there were **slaves**. Onesimus (who had left Colossae some time earlier as an unbeliever, but had just now returned, as a believer) was not the only slave present. Paul addressed the slaves directly. The fellowship of believers was distinctive in this regard (see 3:11). Slaves were members of the gathering in Philemon's house, fully recognized and acknowledged, regarded as responsible for their own conduct. While advice for how a household should be conducted was common enough in the world of the time, slaves were not usually addressed on the subject.

Slaves were to **obey in everything** what their masters required. Paul is not interested here in exploring the very reasonable question as to what limits there might be to that obedience, any more than he does for children's obedience to parents a little earlier, or wives' submission to their husbands. That does not mean there would be no limit. That question is simply not his concern here.

His point is to set their obedience in a whole new context that radically changes their situation. Their masters are only **those who are your earthly lords** (literally 'the masters/lords according to the flesh'). Slaves no longer live in fear of their masters. They are only 'lords according to the flesh'. The ultimate and true Lord is Christ Jesus. Although slaves still have an earthly lord, it is very important to know the limited sphere of his power. He is only lord (master) in the realm of the flesh.

There is an important point here. It is all too easy for the Christian believer to think that allegiance to Christ *overrides* earthly allegiances. At least it is not unusual to feel that my allegiance to Christ loosens my allegiances to mere humans in this world. 'I am serving *Christ* – and, I'm sorry, but there are times when I must therefore sit a little loose to other obligations in this world.'

The extreme case of slavery is a challenge to this understanding of the relationship between the Lordship of Christ and merely earthly, this worldly, obligations. If you are a slave, your obedience to your master is not *compromised* by having Christ as Lord. On the contrary, it is put into good order. It is (if it is possible to speak like this) redeemed. Your obedience is **not** now **by way of eye-service**. That is a rather literal translation of a Greek compound word that includes the 'slave' word: 'eye-slavery'. You serve, as a slave, not just to be *seen* to be serving. You do not obey only in order to *appear* to be obedient. The quality of your obedience would then depend on whether you were being watched. Your service now is not **as people-pleasers**. Your obedience (yes, your obedience to your earthly lord and master) is now **with sincerity of heart**. This is perhaps better rendered, '*singleness* of heart'. It is simply not the case that your allegiance to the Lord Jesus pulls you one way, and your earthly obligations pull you the other. No. The

Lord Christ who is reordering the universe does not pull us out of our earthly relationships, but calls us to live *in* those relationships *under him*, **fearing the Lord**. To fear the Lord (if we remember the Old Testament teaching about 'the fear of the Lord') includes loving him and trusting him (see Deut. 10:12; Ps. 40:3; 115:11; 147:11).

We must not, of course, lose sight of the fact that these words were addressed to *slaves*. Yet as we listen to the words to slaves (just as when every freeman in Philemon's house that day listened to the words to the slaves) we must see that, if this is how Christ works, even with the slave, there are implications for us all.

b. A new life

The new obedience of the slave is now generalized, and the radically new way of life is filled out: **Whatever you do, work heartily, as for the Lord and not for men.** There is an echo here of the summary of the Christian life a few lines earlier: 'And whatever you do, in word or deed, do everything in the name of the Lord Jesus, giving thanks to God the Father through him' (3:17). Slaves (though they are still slaves) are liberated to live in this way. In the flesh they may have limited freedom. We might think that they have no freedom at all. Yet if the slave is a Christian, the slave (though still a slave) is living for the Lord Christ. His or her service, in everything they do, is serving Christ.

This is profoundly radical. Precisely because it is the extreme case of slavery to which these words are addressed, we ought to see how every obligation under which *we* labour, every burden that life puts upon *us*, every pressure under which *we* are placed, is transformed by the wonder of the Lordship of Jesus Christ. We are liberated by Christ, but not *from* those things. We are free now to do everything in the name of the Lord Jesus, giving thanks to God the Father through him (3:17). We are free to work, not under grudging compulsion, but from the centre of our being ('heartily' is, more literally, 'from the soul'!), knowing that we are living for Christ, not for men.

c. A new reward

Paul continues this astonishing line of instruction to the slaves in the gathering there in Philemon's house: **knowing that from the Lord you will receive the inheritance as your reward.** Again it is the fact that this is the extreme case of slavery that intensifies what is said. Slaves, by definition, were not normally 'rewarded' for their work. They were not paid, at least not more than a pittance. The motivation for much that we do in life is the reward we hope to receive. The rewards that motivate us are not just monetary, of course. There are all manner of 'rewards' for our efforts, from satisfaction at an achievement to approval or gratitude from others.

Can a slave be redeemed from a life of rewardless effort? Faith in Christ *changes* life, even for a slave. Here we see starkly what Paul meant at the beginning of this letter when he gave thanks to God for 'the hope laid up for you in heaven', about which 'you have heard before in the word of the truth, the gospel' (1:5). God has qualified believers in Christ (including slaves!) to share in the inheritance of the saints in light (1:12).

Can we, who still live for so many pathetic 'rewards' (what is it that really keeps you going?), learn from this word to the slaves in Colossae? Can we share the liberation they were invited to enjoy from bondage to earthly reward? Do you know (really know) that 'from the Lord you will receive *the inheritance* as your reward'? It is undeserved, of course – all of grace. It is nonetheless the most powerful and liberating motivation for living every part of life well.

d. A new master

All this is summed up by saying explicitly what has been behind everything said to the slaves so far: **You are serving the Lord Christ.** The TNIV expresses the emphasis of the Greek word order here a little better: 'It is the Lord Christ you are serving.'

'Serving' is the word for a slave's service. Here is the power that transforms the life of the slave: he or she has become a slave of *the Lord Christ*: the one who is 'the image of the invisible God, the firstborn of all creation', by whom 'all things were created, in heaven and on earth, visible and invisible, whether thrones or dominions or rulers or authorities – all things were created through him and for him. And he is before all things, and in him all things hold together. And he is the head of the body, the church. He is the beginning, the firstborn from the dead, that in everything he might be pre-eminent. For in him all the fullness of God was pleased to dwell, and through him to reconcile to himself all things, whether on earth or in heaven, making peace by the blood of his cross' (1:15-20). All of this is implied when we are told that it is *the Lord Christ* you are serving!

Whatever indignity, shame or drudgery there was in being a slave, it can never be the same once you have received Christ Jesus the Lord. It *must* never be the same now that you are serving him.

While hearing this word to the slaves in Philemon's house is deeply moving, its power extends beyond slaves. By hearing something of what the gospel means to a slave, all believers ought to appreciate afresh the wonder: It is the Lord Christ *you* are serving!

e. A new world

The word to the slaves ends with a surprise. **For** suggests that the statement in verse 25 supports the immediately preceding words. The Lord Christ (whom you are serving) cares about wrongdoing: **the wrongdoer will be paid back for the wrong he has done**.You will answer to *him* for wrongdoing. This must transform the quality of your serving. Mind you, your earthly master is also answerable to the same Lord Christ **and there is no partiality**. This must encourage the believing slave to fear the Lord Christ, not his earthly master. The life of a slave who belongs to Christ Jesus is thus profoundly changed.

This word to the slaves, who nonetheless serve the Lord Christ, again illuminates the situation of all believers. Being united to Christ changes everything: we have died with Christ; we have been raised with Christ; our life is hidden with Christ in God; when Christ appears, we also will appear with him in glory (3:1-4). But this does not mean we are taken out of the world, or the obligations of life in this world in whatever situation we find ourselves. Serving the Lord Christ deepens, it does not lessen, our obligations to those we serve in this world.

2. To masters (4:1)

Finally, there is a brief word to the slave-masters, addressed here by the word **Lords** (ESV 'Masters'). The brevity does not lessen the radical nature of the call to those who are 'lords according to flesh' (literal rendering of the phrase translated 'earthly masters' in the ESV of 3:22).

Such earthly lords are powerful. They must constrain the exercise of their power by justice and fairness: **treat your slaves justly and fairly**. The words of 3:25 should still be in our minds. Injustice and unfairness are wrongs for which the wrongdoer will be repaid by the Lord Christ.

In other words, earthly lords who are believers themselves must act **knowing that you also have a Lord in heaven**. Such lords are, in other words, themselves slaves. In the great reordering of all things in the reconciliation of creation, the power of the powerful is put in a new place (see 1:20; and cf. 2:15). Again we must see that the heavenly Lord does not do away with the earthly power. He brings it under his own rule. The powerful are still powerful, but their power must be exercised with justice and fairness. They, too, must know that it is the Lord Christ *they* are serving.

This revolutionary word to the slaves and masters gathered in Philemon's home in Colossae is an important call to today's Christian readers to see all of life's obligations and relationships (even the difficult and less desirable ones) in the brilliant light of Christ's reconciliation of all things. The key words are at the end of verse 24: 'It is the Lord Christ you are serving' (TNIV).

Study Questions

1. How would you respond to the view that the Bible's teaching about slavery is unacceptable today and therefore raises questions about the Bible's view on other subjects?

2. Why (do you think) didn't Paul insist that Christian slave masters must liberate all slaves, and all Christians should work for the abolition of slavery?

3. Does Paul's teaching in Colossians 3:22-4:1 support the institution of slavery?

4. In what ways (make a list) did faith in Jesus Christ transform life for
   a. a slave?
   b. a slave master?

   In what ways does your faith in Christ transform particular 'earthly' relationships?

5. Consider the implications today of Paul's word to slaves and slave-masters in Colossians 3:22–4:1 for
   a. a Christian politician;
   b. a prisoner who becomes a believer;
   c. the CEO of a successful business who is a Christian;
   d. a Christian policeman.

19

Pray
(Colossians 4:2-4)

There are a small number of subjects that a preacher or Bible teacher can touch on, and be almost certain to stir the conscience of at least many of his Christian hearers. All but the most insensitive of us find certain topics awkward, threatening and guilt-arousing. This is partly because all of us have secrets. What we are, what we think, what we have done are things only partly known to those who know us, even those who know us well. How could it be otherwise? Among the hidden things about us there are things we really are glad are hidden (and we would like to remain hidden forever, even from ourselves, if that were possible). The word for how we feel about these things is 'ashamed'. When a preacher or Bible teacher starts to talk about one of these things, we cringe inside. Those of us whose consciences are sensitive can be troubled, not only about the matter of which we have been reminded, but by the very fact that it is secret: that our life is at this point a pretence. If you are a serious Christian person, you may well be troubled, not only by your sense of guilt or shame, but also by your sense of hypocrisy. I am quite sure that most readers of this book know exactly what I am talking about.

I have found four subjects that are almost always like this. Whenever I speak about *forgiveness*, I know there will be some who are troubled by the secret grudges they bear. Whenever I speak about *sexual purity*, I know there will be those who are troubled by their secret thoughts or behaviour. Whenever I speak about *prayer*, I know that if my hearers are Christian, then their consciences will be very easily provoked. And whenever I speak about *sharing the gospel with unbelievers*, I know that many of my hearers are inwardly wishing I would talk about something else. I know this, not only because of those who talk to me when I have spoken about these subjects, but because of my own experience as a hearer.

These four subjects were raised at various points in the letter that Paul wrote to the Colossian believers. *Forgiveness* was an important part of the life of 'God's chosen ones' described in 3:13, based on the experience of the Lord's forgiveness (see 1:14; 2:13). *Sexual purity* was the aspect of the believer's new life in Christ emphasized in 3:5. *Prayer*, of course, was prominent very early in the letter ('when we pray for you', 1:3), and becomes the subject of the apostle's exhortation in 4:2-4. *Speaking to unbelievers* will be the theme of our next chapter as we consider 4:5, 6. It is valuable to carefully listen to the way in which the apostle deals with these subjects that we find sensitive.

As the letter draws towards a close, he speaks of prayer:

> Continue steadfastly in prayer, being watchful in it with thanksgiving. At the same time, pray also for us, that God may open to us a door for the word, to declare the mystery of Christ, on account of which I am in prison – that I may make it clear, which is how I ought to speak (4:2-4).

All the evidence suggests that Paul was a remarkable pray-er. At the beginning of this letter he spoke naturally about 'when we pray for you' (1:3), and it is clear that this was not an occasional thing: 'from the day we heard [of your faith, love and hope in Christ Jesus], *we have not ceased* to pray for you' (1:9). When you consider that Paul said something similar in letters to Christians in Rome (Rom. 1:9, 10), Ephesus (Eph. 1:16), Philippi (Phil. 1:3, 9) and Thessalonica (1 Thess. 1:2), as well as in his letters to Timothy (2 Tim. 1:3) and Philemon (Philem. 4), we can see that praying is something he took very seriously indeed. It must have taken a considerable amount of his time.

As this great man of prayer spoke of his own praying at the beginning of this letter, he now addresses his readers about their praying as the letter draws to a close.

Reading Paul's words, it is difficult for our minds not to turn to our secret *failures* in praying – how *inadequate* we feel as pray-ers – how *little* time and effort we give to prayer – how easily it is the first thing dropped from our daily activities – and so we could go on. Many Christians feel ashamed, even guilty, about their prayerlessness.

However, I want to suggest that God's Word does not work like that. Certainly here Paul is not playing on the sensitive consciences and guilt feelings of believers who do not pray as much or as diligently as they think they should. Preachers and Bible teachers take note. It is easy to achieve certain responses through playing on tender emotions in the hearers. There are various techniques, that come with just a little experience in public speaking, to manipulate the feelings of listeners. This is a significant temptation to the preacher, for the Word of God does deal with many sensitive subjects. It is ever so easy to stir up memories you know many of your hearers have (because you have them too!), to touch raw nerves you know so well (because they are raw for you too!). But is this the work of the Spirit of God? Is this what God's Word in fact does with these sensitive subjects? I am not suggesting that the Word of God does not search consciences, nor that shame and guilt are things we should ignore, deny or run away from. The Spirit of God *does* stir our emotions and our consciences by his Word. I am simply saying that the preacher's task is to ensure that God's Word does God's work rather than manipulative speaking doing the preacher's work. Faithful exposition of the Word of God allows Scripture to set the agenda, and this takes great care. As a general principle, we should understand that the Word of God has not done its work if the hearer is left *simply* feeling terrible, or *just* determined to try harder in the future.

The way in which Paul speaks to his readers about prayer is particularly striking.

1. A call to pray (4:2)

The first thing we should notice is that 4:2 is certainly a call to pray – a serious call to pray. Indeed it is a call to follow the example of Paul himself, as we heard of his praying at the beginning of the letter.

The power of this call to prayer, however, comes from its context in the letter as a whole, not just from the words here in 4:2, heard as an isolated rule or command. Like all that we have heard through chapter 3 of the letter, the call to pray comes as part of an exposition of the life of faith in Christ Jesus. Paul's theme is: 'As you received Christ Jesus the Lord, *so walk in him,* rooted and *built up in him* and *established in the faith,* just as you were taught, abounding in thanksgiving' (2:6, 7). *That* will mean praying.

Why? The answer to that question is: For the same reason that Paul himself had not ceased praying for the believers in Colossae from the day he heard about them (1:9). It is because something absolutely wonderful and extraordinary is going on. Our Lord Jesus Christ is the one through whom and for whom all things have been made, and by his death on the cross God has reconciled all things to him (1:15-20). Through Christ, God is bringing the universe back together again: order out of chaos, peace out of hostility (2:15), reconciliation out of alienation (1:20). Christ among the nations is the hope of glory (1:27)!

That is why Paul prayed, 'asking that you may be filled with the knowledge of his will in all spiritual wisdom and understanding, so as to walk in a manner worthy of the Lord, fully pleasing to him, bearing fruit in every good work and increasing in the knowledge of God' (1:9, 10). Paul prayed, not simply as a spiritual exercise or discipline, and certainly not in order to move an inactive God into action. Paul prayed *because of* the extraordinary work that God had done and that God was doing.

Yet it is even more than that. The call to pray in 4:2 comes to us because through faith in the Lord Jesus Christ God is turning chaos to order, hostility to peace, alienation to reconciliation *in our lives* (1:21, 22; 2:5). Praying is a characteristic of the reordered life. The new life in union with Christ in his death and resurrection has been the subject since 3:1. This life (see 3:12-17) is a stark contrast to the chaos (see 3:5-8). Prayer and peace with God go together. God's enemies do not pray. The reconciled pray; the alienated do not.

In other words, if we have been listening to the teaching of this letter, we will not hear the call to pray in 4:2 as an obligation that *condemns* and *threatens* and *rouses the sense of guilt*, but as a *gospel* invitation. Listen to the particular way in which the call is expressed.

a. 'Continue steadfastly'

Continue steadfastly in prayer, says the apostle. Other English translations have '*Devote yourselves* to prayer' (so TNIV). Similar expressions are found a number of times in the New Testament. It is what the apostles did in Acts 6:4: they *devoted themselves to prayer* and the ministry of the word. The three thousand who received the word on the day of Pentecost *devoted themselves* to the apostles' teaching and fellowship, to the breaking of bread and *the prayers* (Acts 2:42). Indeed it is what Jesus' disciples were doing immediately after his ascension as they waited in Jerusalem: they were *devoting themselves to prayer* (Acts 1:14).

Paul certainly calls for a *commitment* to praying. There is also a sense of *privilege*. When you know and understand the grace of God in Jesus Christ, praying is what you do. When we are conscious of what God has done and is doing and will do, we will pray. This is precisely what we heard Paul doing at the beginning of the letter. 'We *always* thank God, the Father of our Lord Jesus Christ, when we pray for you, since we heard of your faith in Christ Jesus and of the love that you have for all the saints … And so, from the day we heard, we *have not ceased* to pray for you, asking that you may be filled with the knowledge of his will …' (1:3, 9). Now he invites his readers to do likewise: Continue steadfastly in prayer. Devote yourselves to prayer.

b. 'Being watchful'

What will enable us to heed this call? It requires **being watchful in it**. Being awake. Praying is not the sleepy activity we may sometimes imagine (and perhaps sometimes practise!). It requires alertness. Yet this is not simply a call not to drift off to sleep as we pray, as the disciples did in the

Garden of Gethsemane (Mark 14:37). As on that occasion, praying requires being awake *to what is really happening.* Don't lose sight of the fact that you have been raised with Christ (3:1), that you have died and your life is hidden with Christ in God (3:3). Keep awake to what is soon to happen. When Christ who is your life appears, then you also will appear with him in glory (3:4).

This characteristic of the Christian life is worth emphasizing. Jesus taught it: 'Therefore *stay awake* – for you do not know when the master of the house will come, in the evening, or at midnight, or when the rooster crows, or in the morning – lest he come suddenly and find you asleep. And what I say to you I say to all: *Stay awake*' (Mark 13:35-37); 'Therefore, *stay awake,* for you do not know on what day your Lord is coming' (Matt. 24:42); '*Watch* and pray that you may not enter into temptation' (Matt. 26:41).

This wakeful watchfulness is alertness to the realities of which 'you have heard in … the gospel' (cf. 1:5). It is keeping our eyes of faith open. It is having the work of God in Christ and in his gospel in our consciousness. When we see life and the world in this brilliant light, when we understand what is going on, then we can properly hear this call to pray.

c. *'With thanksgiving'*

The third element in the call to pray in 4:2 settles the fact that this call is not intended to be guilt-driven. On the contrary, we are to pray **with thanksgiving**. Being watchful is not a matter of being frightened, or worried, or anxious. On the contrary, like the whole Christian life, praying is energized by thankfulness.

This has been a repeated note through this letter, which has been described as 'one of the most 'thankful' documents in the New Testament'.[1] It began with Paul's own 'We always *thank God* … since we heard of your faith in Christ Jesus' (1:3, 4). Then his prayer for the Colossian believers climaxed with the request that they would

[1] James D.G. Dunn, *The Epistles to the Colossians and to Philemon: A Commentary on the Greek Text* (Grand Rapids and Bletchley: Eerdmans and Paternoster, 1996), p. 262

be '*giving thanks* to the Father, who has qualified you to share in the inheritance of the saints in light' (1:12). Indeed the purpose of this letter includes that its readers will 'abound in *thanksgiving*' (2:7). At one point in this letter, Paul simply and starkly says, 'And be *thankful*' (3:15), and then speaks of the '*thankfulness* in your hearts to God' (3:16). Indeed the Christian life can be summed up as 'whatever you do, in word or deed, do everything in the name of the Lord Jesus, *giving thanks* to God the Father through him' (3:17).

The words of 4:2 should move us to be serious about praying, but if we hear these words rightly we will be moved, not by guilt feelings, but by being 'woken up' and by thankfulness.

2. Pray for us (4:3, 4)

Praying that is watchful and thankful will be about a range of matters. When we heard about Paul's praying in 1:9 we noted that 'praying' in the New Testament is typically 'asking'. If you are unsure what wakeful, thankful believers ask God for, a very good place to look is the prayers of Paul himself, described at the beginning of a number of his letters, not least this one.

In 4:3 he includes some specific guidance for the Colossian believers: **At the same time, pray also for us.** 'Us' means at least Paul and Timothy, the senders of this letter (1:1). Perhaps he also includes other servants of the gospel such as Epaphras (1:7; 4:12, 13). In any case, he was particularly requesting prayer for himself.[2]

Watchful, thankful praying will particularly pray about what God is doing. That is what Paul constantly did. That will mean praying for servants of the gospel who proclaim Christ (see 1:28).

a. A door

I am not suggesting that praying for other things is somehow unworthy or unimportant. It is striking, however, that the suffering, imprisoned Paul does not call for the

---

[2] Douglas J. Moo, *The Letters to the Colossians and to Philemon* (Nottingham: Apollos, 2008), p. 321.

kind of prayer that I suspect we would call for if we were in chains (see 4:18). I am sure that the believers in Colossae would have prayed for Paul's release, for his safety, and for his physical needs. They may well have been praying for these things before this letter arrived. But precisely because he was awake and thankful these were not the things uppermost in Paul's mind.

He asked them to pray **that God may open to us a door for the word**. Not that God would open the door of his imprisonment! That was relatively unimportant. Whether he remained in bondage or not, pray that God will open a door for *the word*.

Earlier in this letter, Paul spoke of the powerful work the gospel was accomplishing. This is what he means by 'the word'. He called it 'the word of the truth, the gospel' (1:5). It was 'bearing fruit' there in Colossae, and indeed in the whole world (1:6). That is, people were coming to faith in Christ Jesus, and all that flows from that. Paul has urged that this word, 'the word of Christ', should dwell among you richly as you teach and admonish one another (3:16). By this word God was doing his world-wide (indeed creation-wide, 1:23!) work of establishing the reconciliation and pacification that has been accomplished in Christ's death (1:20; 2:15; see also 1:21, 22).

This word was advancing through servants of the gospel like Paul (see 1:24–2:5): 'open *to us* a door for the word'. Obviously the work this word does is not something we humans can ourselves accomplish. God must open doors for this word if it is going to achieve its purpose: doors of opportunity for the word to be proclaimed and the doors of human hearts that the word might be received.[3] This is a reminder of how hard the work of proclaiming Christ is. In our enthusiasm we sometimes give the impression that if only we get our strategy right, if only we learn to be relevant, if only we use technology to the full, if only we learn the art of contextualization, of entrepreneurship – *then* our preaching will have an impact. Such enthusiasm is heading for disillusionment. The doors to this word are tightly shut

[3] See the similar way of speaking in Acts 14:27; 1 Cor. 16:9; 2 Cor. 2:12.

and bolted! The darkness is thick. The alienation is extreme. The hostility is intense. This word will only do its work if *God* opens a door. So pray that he will.

b. The mystery

When God does open a door, the responsibility of servants of the gospel, like Paul, is clear. He is to speak: **to declare the mystery of Christ** – God's secret plan for the whole world, to reconcile all things through Christ. We heard about 'the mystery' in 1:26. It was hidden for ages and generations but is now revealed to his saints. 'To them God chose to make known how great among the nations are the riches of the glory of this mystery, which is Christ in you, the hope of glory. Him we proclaim, warning everyone and teaching everyone with all wisdom, that we may present everyone mature in Christ. For this I toil, struggling with all his energy that he powerfully works within me' (1:27-29). Do *pray* that God will open a door for this labour to be effective. That is what we will do if we are watchful and thankful.

c. The bondage

The great work Paul is asking his readers to pray about is that **on account of which I am in prison**. With these words he reminds them of the earlier teaching about the servant of the gospel: 'I rejoice in my *sufferings* for your sake …' (1:24). The opposition and resistance, the firmness of the closed doors to the gospel, are such that the servant of this word *will suffer*. Paul's imprisonment, therefore, is a spur to pray that God will open a door for the word, for if he does not, the word will accomplish nothing *but* the suffering of the messengers. Pray, not that those who proclaim Christ will not suffer, but that as they suffer God will open a door for the word.

d. Clarity

Finally, in verse 4, we are reminded again of Paul's earlier descriptions of his labours: **that I may make it clear, which is how I ought to speak.** The apostle's God-given task was to reveal the mystery to the world, to make known God's formerly hidden and secret plan for world history, by proclaiming Christ. This is how he described his task in 1:28, 29: 'Him we proclaim, warning everyone and teaching everyone with all wisdom, that we may present everyone mature in Christ. For this I toil, struggling with all his energy that he powerfully works within me.' Pray for an open door for that work to be done and to be effective.

As we reflect on Paul's call to his readers to 'continue steadfastly in prayer', it is important to notice that his purpose has not been to make them feel bad about how much they fall short of his earnest and faithful prayer life. Yet it is clear that Paul expected his words to have an effect on the praying of his readers. How would this happen? Praying (like Paul's praying) comes not from a sense of guilt at not praying enough, or even a mere duty that 'Christians should pray', but from *watchfulness* and *thankfulness*. Watchfulness and thankfulness come, not from just being told to be watchful and thankful, but from the extraordinary thing that God has done and is doing. It is a marvellous circle. If you are filled with the knowledge of God's will (1:9) you cannot but be joyfully thanking him (1:12). If you are really thanking him, how can you not be praying that his marvellous work will have its full effect in you, in your friends, in the whole world? Continue steadfastly, devote yourselves to prayer.

Study Questions

1. Why do we find praying difficult?
2. What should motivate us to pray?
3. What difference does it make to hear Paul's call in Colossians 4:2 as a 'gospel invitation', rather than a *rule* for Christian living?
4. What advice would you give to a fellow believer who is finding it difficult to get around to praying?
5. When you pray, what are the usual subjects of your prayers? Compare the things you pray for with Paul's prayer (Col. 1:9-14) and his call to prayer (4:2-4).
6. Why is praying for the effective work of the gospel important?

20

Towards Outsiders
(Colossians 4:5-6)

There is a discussion that goes on from time to time among Christian people. To simplify both sides of the argument it goes like this. On the one side, it is said that evangelism is the duty of all who believe the gospel, and every believer ought to be taking every opportunity to share the news about Jesus with everyone they can. On the other side, it is said that this is an unnecessary and impossible burden to place on the consciences of all believers. The believer's responsibility is to live a godly life (as described, for example, in Colossians 3). Evangelism is the responsibility of those gifted as evangelists like Paul and Epaphras, and of course many more.

Both sides of the argument have a certain logic. Furthermore, both sides would make various qualifications to this simple way of stating the positions. On the one side, there is logic from the gospel itself. How could you believe this message and not long to tell it to all? How could you know of this great salvation and not want everyone else to know it? How could loving your neighbour mean anything less? Speaking the gospel to others is almost the necessary outcome of believing it (see 2 Cor. 4:13). On the other side, there is the observation that in all that is said to believers in general in the New Testament it is difficult to find direct instructions to *be evangelizing*. Certainly all believers must *care* about evangelism and *pray* for evangelists, as we saw in 4:3, but a word to all believers about their responsibility to be directly evangelizing is not easy to find.

As we come to the end of the main body of Paul's letter to the Colossians, it is interesting that his last word (in this sense) is about Christian conduct towards 'outsiders', by which he means people outside the Christian fellowship, outside of Christ. Whichever side you may take in the discussion about everyone evangelizing, Paul's words about Christians' dealings with unbelievers are important. It is helpful to take a small step back, and listen to what he says in the context of what we heard in our previous chapter:

> Continue steadfastly in prayer, being watchful in it with thanksgiving. At the same time, pray also for us, that God may open to us a door for the word, to declare the mystery of Christ, on account of which I am in prison – that I may make it clear, which is how I ought to speak.
>
> Walk in wisdom towards outsiders, making the best use of the time. Let your speech always be gracious, seasoned with salt, so that you may know how you ought to answer each person (4:2-6).

As the main body of Paul's letter closes he turns attention to the 'outsiders'. In 4:3 he urged his readers to pray that God would open 'a door for the word'. This was a door for Christ to be proclaimed to those he now describes in verse 5 as 'outsiders'. The letter began with a reference to the gospel reaching those who *had* been 'outsiders' in Colossae and bearing fruit in the whole world (1:6). It was this gospel that changed 'outsiders' into those who now believed in Christ Jesus, had love for all the saints and a hope laid up for them in heaven (1:4, 5). Those listening to this letter were no longer 'outsiders'.

'Outsiders' is an interesting general term for non-Christians.[1] Paul uses this expression, in this sense, in a number of other places in his letters (1 Cor. 5:12, 13;

[1] Peter T. O'Brien, *Colossians, Philemon* (Waco, Texas: Word Books, 1982), p. 241.

1 Thess. 4:12; 1 Tim. 3:7). It clearly suggests the very great difference between being an 'insider' and being an 'outsider'. There are those who are 'inside' and 'outside' the fellowship of God's people, 'God's chosen ones' (3:12). Believers are 'in Christ' (see, for example, 1:2, 14, 28; 2:6, 7, 10, 11); unbelievers are (by implication) 'outside' of Christ. This is the new way of seeing the whole human race. No longer Greek and Jew, circumcised and uncircumcised, barbarian and Scythian, slave and free (3:11), but now simply 'in Christ' and 'outsiders'.

Yet this way of seeing people is not intended to create a Christian ghetto, or monastery, where the 'insiders' are cut off and separated from the 'outsiders'. This is something that very easily happens. Churches develop their own community life, and the Christians have less and less contact with 'outsiders'. It is important for any Christian community to work hard at keeping up and developing contacts and interactions with the 'outsiders'.

This appears to be the assumption behind what Paul says in Colossians 4:5. There will be interactions and relationships between the believers and the outsiders. The importance of this should not be overlooked. There is inevitably some kind of distance or barrier between believers and unbelievers. The bond of love that the Spirit creates between those in Christ (see 1:8) inevitably creates a contrast with those relationships where *that* bond is not a reality. We can all think of 'outsiders' (in this sense) with whom we come into contact. There are family members, friends, work colleagues, neighbours, shopkeepers, and no doubt many others. While there are, of course, some 'outsiders' about whom we care deeply, there is nonetheless always a certain distance. They are, after all, outside of Christ, who is your life (see 3:4).

Paul's words in 4:5, 6 are about the believer's behaviour in relation to 'outsiders'. He speaks first, in verse 5, of our 'walk', and then in verse 6 of our words.

1. Your walk (4:5)

Twice already in this letter Paul has referred to the Christian life as a 'walk'. In 1:10 his prayer was that his readers shall be so filled with the knowledge of God's will that they shall '*walk* in a manner worthy of the Lord'. In 2:6, in the theme sentence of the letter, he said, 'as you received Christ Jesus the Lord, so *walk* in him'.

It is important to remember what has already been said about the Christian's 'walk' as we think about our conduct towards 'outsiders'. Whatever else needs to be said, we should remember that our behaviour towards unbelievers must still be walking 'in a manner worthy of the Lord, fully pleasing to him, bearing fruit in every good work' (1:10). Our ways with non-Christian people must still be walking 'in Christ Jesus the Lord' (2:6).

In other words, the kind of character and conduct described through chapter 3 of the letter is not suddenly to change when we move outside the Christian fellowship. It may sound unkind to suggest that any Christian would behave one way among fellow Christians, and another way towards non-Christians – that compassion, kindness, humility, meekness, and patience (3:12) might be more evident in the life of some when they are among the believers than when they are in another setting. It is worth saying, however, simply because there are too many occasions when Christian people do display one character in church on Sunday, and something quite different in work on Monday, or perhaps back at home. All that has been said about the Christian walk in this letter should still be in our minds as Paul speaks about our conduct, our walk, towards outsiders.

a. Wisdom

The first specific piece of advice about our conduct towards unbelievers is: **Walk in wisdom towards outsiders**.

Wisdom is practical. It is applied knowledge, knowing how to live and behave. Again it is valuable to remember what this letter has taught us about wisdom. Wisdom has to do with knowledge of God's will (1:9), which is to reconcile all things to Christ through his death (1:20). Wisdom characterizes the teaching and admonishing by which Paul proclaims Christ (1:28), and by which the word of Christ dwells richly among believers (3:16). Indeed, Paul has said that 'all the treasures of wisdom and knowledge' are hidden *in Christ* (2:3).

'Wisdom' is therefore not some kind of *corrective* to the Christian life, as though Paul were saying, 'It is all very well to be enthusiastic about Christ, but in your dealings with outsiders *be wise*.' On the contrary, I suspect his meaning is the very opposite. In your dealings with outsiders, there will always be pressures to conform, fit in, win approval, be thought well of. You will need *wisdom* to live out your knowledge of God's will. It will take *wisdom* to walk in a manner fully pleasing to *him*. We are to live with the wisdom found in the Lord Jesus Christ.

Certainly that will mean thinking about our behaviour and our relationships with unbelievers, and considering the consequences of our conduct. The point is that the wisdom we seek is not the wisdom to please the unbelievers, or to make ourselves look good, or any of the other kinds of wisdom we may easily find ourselves seeking. We need wisdom to please the Lord in our conduct towards outsiders.

b. Buying up time

This will mean **making the best use of the time**. The translation sounds a little lame. The phrase is rather more vivid in Greek. It suggests that time is in short supply and, like a bargain hunter in a sale, you snap up what time you find. Our understanding of 'the time' is to shape our conduct towards outsiders. 'Only one life, it will soon be past; only what's done for Christ will last.'

Notice two things about the exhortation in verse 5. First, Paul's emphasis here is on behaviour generally: how we treat people, how we speak to people, what we do and what we don't do. Such conduct matters. Before you start worrying about whether or not you should be sharing the gospel with the person who serves you coffee, consider how you are behaving. Are you walking *in wisdom*, the wisdom that comes from knowing Christ as Lord; making the best use of the time, bearing fruit in every good work (see 1:10)?

Second, I cannot think that in this context Paul has forgotten his longing that doors be opened for the word. He has just asked that these Colossian believers pray for that to happen for him (4:3), so that *he* may declare Christ. It would be hard to be praying for a door to be opened for the word in far-off Rome, and to not care about doors for the word in your dealings with unbelievers in Colossae.

2. Your word (4:6)

Therefore, I am not surprised that from the exhortation about general behaviour towards outsiders (v. 5), Paul moves to the specific behaviour of speech (v. 6).

a. Grace

Let your speech always be gracious. Over-literally we could translate: 'Let your word always be in grace.' 'Walk in wisdom,' 'speak in grace.' Wisdom is to shape our behaviour; grace is to shape our speech.

I do not think that Paul's words can be pressed to mean, 'always be speaking about *God's* grace'. On the other hand, the evangelistic context should not be missed. There seems to be an echo from verse 3 in verse 6. Verse 3: 'pray … that God may open to us a door for *the word*.' Verse 6 (literally): 'Let *your* word …' He does not say that your word, like his, must be a clear declaration of the mystery of Christ. There is a difference between Paul's declaring and the believer's speaking, to which I will return in a moment. But your word must be 'with grace', which I do not think for Paul would just mean 'polite'.

With so many links back to the beginning of the letter here at its close, how can we forget that what happened when the gospel came to Colossae is that they 'heard it and understood *God's grace* in truth' (1:6)? Your speech, then, to outsiders must always be shaped by that grace. Whatever you are speaking about, grace will be present. 'Always', says Paul.

b. Salt

As though to underline that point, he says that your speech, your word, should always be **seasoned with salt**. No one seems to be quite sure what Paul precisely meant by this image. Of course we recall Jesus' teaching about his disciples being 'the salt of the earth' (Matt. 5:13; Mark 9:49, 50; Luke 14:34). Some draw attention to idioms in contemporary Greek, where salty speech meant 'interesting, lively and colourful' speech.[2] I am inclined to think the context here is sufficient to give us the sense of the metaphor. Speech that is flavoured with your knowledge of God's grace will be salty. It will be significant, have effects, and do good.

c. Knowing how to answer

You would be right to observe that there has still been no direct instruction to believers to proclaim Christ on every possible occasion, to every outsider you speak to. Would we be right to heave a sigh of relief, and think that somehow 'the word' reaching the outsiders is not my responsibility, unless I am an evangelist (which I obviously am not!)?

No. But the wisdom of Paul does seem to recognize that many believers will not be constant evangelists. His last words here are very significant. Your conduct and your speech towards outsiders have this purpose: **so that you may know how you ought to answer each person**.

There is an important shift in emphasis from verse 4 to verse 6. Making clear the mystery of Christ is how Paul 'ought to speak'. Believers generally are to behave and speak in such a way that they will know 'how you ought to answer'.

The practical significance of this is drawn out very helpfully by Dick Lucas. In his fine exposition of Colossians, he draws the following conclusions from this passage (it is well worth quoting at length):

> We may describe this difference by saying that while the apostle looks for many opportunities for *direct* evangelism and teaching, the typical Christian in Colossae is to look for many opportunities for *responsive* evangelism.
>
> If this distinction is a correct one, it immediately commends itself by its sanity and realism. Harm can be done by sincere believing people who feel compelled to preach and testify to those with whom they mix in shop or office. Rightly aware of the importance of their message, the sad ignorance of many of their neighbours, and the

---

[2] N.T. Wright, *The Epistles of Paul to the Colossians and to Philemon* (Leicester: Inter-Varsity Press, 1986), p. 153.

urgency of the times, they plunge in bravely (whatever the temperature!). But direct assault on entrenched apathy (to change the metaphor) is seldom successful and can never be carried out by normally sensitive people without great cost to nerve and confidence. Alas, one consequence of failure in such verbal witnessing is a discouragement sufficiently severe at times to lead to disengagement from this part of the battle altogether.

Now Paul's advice to the Christians is not along the lines of possessing oneself of better techniques with which to approach people. Rather he turns the problem right around so that the Christians can see their responsibilities in a much more promising light. Their privilege, simply put, is to *answer everyone*. That is to say they are to respond to the questions of others rather than initiate conversations on leading topics; they are to *accept* openings rather than *make* them.

This is, emphatically, not to sound the retreat. Paul evidently believes that opportunities for response and explanation are to be found everywhere, for everyone is looking to discover answers about life and its meaning. And Paul evidently thinks that believing Christians should be found everywhere too, ready to take up these frequent opportunities.

It is obvious what strain this removes from conscientious Christians. The pressure to raise certain topics and reach certain people can make it difficult to live or talk normally. In any case we go to the office to work, not to evangelize. But by being ready and willing to respond the way is opened to a more serene, and successful, approach to each day's opportunities. It opens the way, too, for a greater dependence on God's leading as well as for a more relevant and sensitive witness, suited to each individual. And remember, when the outsider has chosen the time and the place and the subject, how wonderfully free is the Christian to 'open his mouth' and tell 'the good news of Jesus'.[3]

---

[3] R.C. Lucas, *Fullness and Freedom: The message of Colossians and Philemon* (Leicester: Inter-Varsity Press, 1980), pp. 173, 174.

Study Questions

1. It may be helpful to think of a small number of particular 'outsiders' with whom you are in some kind of contact. Who are they? How do you think about them? How does your relationship with them differ from your relationship with others who are Christian believers?

2. How 'wise' has your conduct been towards these 'outsiders'? How might you now 'buy up the time'?

3. In what ways do you tend to act differently towards 'outsiders' (say, your colleagues at work) compared to how you act towards fellow believers (say, members of your church)? (How are you different at work on Monday from in church on Sunday?)

4. Can you think of occasions in which your conduct towards outsiders has 'opened a door' for the gospel? How has that happened?

5. In what ways ought our knowledge of God's grace affect our speech, particularly to 'outsiders'?

6. What would you now (having listened to Col. 4:2-6) like to say in a discussion about whether evangelism is the responsibility of all Christians or only those gifted as evangelists?

21

Concluding Words
(Colossians 4:7-18)

We come at last to the concluding words of Paul's magnificent letter to the believers in Colossae. In these closing lines we hear names, greetings and references to particularities about the situation of both Paul and his readers.

It is not unusual, of course, for Paul to close his letters with this kind of personal and situation-specific detail. Both the Bible reader and the Bible teacher are conscious that the relevance and importance of this part of Paul's letters is rather less obvious than some other parts. If I were to choose one section of Colossians to recommend for reading, I doubt that it would be 4:7-18! Consequently, the concluding sections of the letters are often passed over with scant attention.

That being said, like so many other parts of the Bible, if only we will listen carefully and thoughtfully, and put aside our assumptions about what *we* think will be interesting and important, there is gold to be found here. Let us look at some of the gems in the details, and then make some observations about this letter concluding in this way.

There are four parts to the closing section of this letter. In verses 7-9 Paul says something about the men who carried the letter from him to Colossae. In verses 10-14 he passes on greetings from others who were with him in Rome.

In verses 15-17 he issues some specific instructions to the people in Colossae. Finally in verse 18 he takes the pen from his scribe (Timothy?, see 1:1) and adds a greeting in his own hand.

1. The bearers of Paul's letter (4:7-9)

First, we hear about the postmen.

> Tychicus will tell you all about my activities. He is a beloved brother and faithful minister and fellow servant in the Lord. I have sent him to you for this very purpose, that you may know how we are and that he may encourage your hearts, and with him Onesimus, our faithful and beloved brother, who is one of you. They will tell you of everything that has taken place here (4:7-9).

The letter had arrived in Colossae by the hand of Tychicus, who was accompanied by Onesimus. The letter has told us (and likewise the Colossian believers) very little about Paul's own circumstances. That was not the purpose of this letter. That, by the way, is why we cannot be certain about just where Paul was as he wrote, or when it was. In my opinion the limited evidence favours a date in the early 60s, from his imprisonment in Rome, as we learn of it at the end of the book of Acts. Yet simply because he says so little about his own situation in the letter, we cannot be certain.

a. Tychicus

The Colossian believers knew where Paul was, and were no doubt keen to know details of his circumstances. Paul left it to the bearer of the letter to fill them in. **Tychicus will tell you all about my activities.** That is a slight over-translation. The emphasis is not on Paul's *activities*, just (more literally) 'all the things about me'. If only we had access to what Tychicus told them, one of the minor debates in New Testament studies would be resolved!

Tychicus was a man who had accompanied Paul on his missionary adventures for some time. We hear of him in the Book of Acts. He had been with Paul on the Greek campaign and travelled with him to Troas at the end of the so-called third missionary journey (Acts 20:4). He was probably included in the 'we' of whom Luke speaks in Acts, travelling with Paul after that journey. Therefore he may have accompanied Paul to Jerusalem with the collection from the churches for the needy believers in Jerusalem. He is mentioned in four of Paul's letters (as well as here, Eph. 6:21; 2 Tim. 4:12; Titus 3:12), and was clearly a loved and trusted colleague, entrusted with a number of important tasks.

Although he was from Asia Minor (and so from the general region of Ephesus and Colossae, Acts 20:4), he was apparently not known in Colossae, and so Paul introduces him to the Colossian believers. In the words he chooses we can sense the affection and high regard Paul had for this man. Tychicus came to Colossae with an impressive letter of recommendation!

He is a beloved brother. We should remember what a remarkable thing it was for Paul the Jew to be speaking like this of a gentile (as Tychicus probably was). Paul had described the believers in Colossae, mainly Gentiles whom he had never met, as 'faithful brothers' at the beginning of this letter (1:2). Such is the historic wonder of the gospel of Christ Jesus.

Tychicus was a *loved* brother: in this context, loved by Paul. There was every reason, therefore, that the Colossians should regard him as a dear brother too.

He was also a **faithful minister** or better, 'faithful servant'. We should remember what Paul said earlier about his own role as a servant: a servant of the gospel (1:23) and thus a servant of the assembly (or 'church', 1:25), through whose hard and suffering labour Christ was proclaimed (1:28). Tychicus was also a faithful servant. What a commendation that word 'faithful' carries! He is a servant you can trust.

Stronger language still is used. He is a **fellow servant**, (literally, 'a fellow slave'). We know there were slaves and slave-masters among the believers in Colossae (3:22–4:1). We know that in Christ Jesus the distinction between slave and free has been broken down (3:11). Paul was so far from elevating himself above others who served Christ with him that he saw Tychicus and himself as 'fellow slaves' of the Lord Jesus Christ.

The phrase **in the Lord** could be linked to all three nouns, 'brother', 'servant', and 'slave'.[1] It connects the thought here about Tychicus both to the extensive teaching in this letter about the believer's life 'in Christ' (see especially the theme sentence in 2:6, 7) and the repeated use of 'L(l)ord' in the preceding exhortations (the Greek term occurs eleven times in 3:13–4:1).[2]

Tychicus had been sent to Colossae on a mission: **I have sent him to you for this very purpose, that you may know how we are** [literally, 'that you may know the things about us'] **and that he may encourage your hearts.** Encouraging hearts is what Paul's gospel work aimed to do (2:2). As Tychicus brought news of Paul and his colleagues, how could he not bring news of the gospel, and therefore encourage the hearts of the Colossians? No doubt Tychicus, the letter bearer, Paul's fellow slave in the Lord, was expected to not only read the letter, but also to explain whatever needed explaining. In that way too he would encourage their hearts. Tychicus was the first, therefore, in a long line of expositors of this great letter, all of whom have the same mission: to encourage hearts with the riches of Christ (2:3).

b. Onesimus

Tychicus arrived in Colossae with another man, who *was* known to the Colossians: **and with him Onesimus.** Here is one of the truly remarkable characters of the New Testament and one of the truly remarkable stories. I will refrain from telling much of his story here, because there was another letter that Onesimus himself was carrying as he arrived in Colossae. It was addressed to Philemon, the man in whose home the Colossian believers met. We will turn our attention to that letter in due course.

Here we may note that from the available evidence it seems that Onesimus was a slave whose master had been Philemon. Onesimus had apparently run away, and somehow had come into contact with Paul. Through that contact he had come to faith in Christ Jesus. As a result he was now returning to Colossae, and to his master, with the

---

[1] So Eduard Lohse, *Colossians and Philemon* (Philadelphia: Fortress Press, 1971), p. 171.

[2] The Greek expression translated here 'in the Lord' occurs in 3:18, 20; 4:17.

letter from Paul to Philemon. (For Onesimus's story in a little more detail, see the Introduction.)

What is wonderfully striking is the description Paul gives of Onesimus the runaway slave: **our faithful and beloved brother.** The Colossian believers (including Philemon, in whose house they met) were to receive this returning offender as a brother. He was as much a brother as Tychicus (v. 7), or even Timothy (1:1), as indeed they were all themselves 'brothers' (1:2). Onesimus was a brother loved by Paul, and to be loved by them too.

Onesimus was therefore **one of you** in a double sense. The obvious sense is that he was from Colossae, but now he was 'one of you' because he was a brother in Christ.

Onesimus must have been nervous in coming back to Colossae. It was a brave thing to do. Paul's words testify to the power of Christ to make that situation very different. (We will hear more about that in the letter to Philemon.) Along with Tychicus, Onesimus was a trusted messenger from Paul: **They will tell you of everything that has taken place here.**

2. Greetings from others with Paul and Timothy (4:10-14)
Having clarified the affection and regard in which he held the two men who had brought this letter to Colossae, Paul turns to pass on greetings to the Colossians from no fewer than six of those who are with him at the time he was writing: three Jewish and three gentile believers.

> Aristarchus my fellow prisoner greets you, and Mark the cousin of Barnabas (concerning whom you have received instructions – if he comes to you, welcome him), and Jesus who is called Justus. These are the only men of the circumcision among my fellow workers for the kingdom of God, and they have been a comfort to me. Epaphras, who is one of you, a servant of Christ Jesus, greets you, always struggling on your behalf in his prayers, that you may stand mature and fully assured in all the will of God. For I bear him witness that he has worked hard for you and for those in Laodicea and in Hierapolis. Luke the beloved physician greets you, as does Demas (4:10-14).

a. Aristarchus

The first mentioned is Aristarchus: **Aristarchus my fellow prisoner greets you**. Aristarchus was from Thessalonica (Acts 20:4), another of Paul's companions in his travels that we meet in the book of Acts (Acts 19:29; 20:4; 27:2). He accompanied Paul to Jerusalem, and then on his journey to Rome.[3] We now learn that he was apparently imprisoned with Paul there in Rome.

b. Mark

The second of Paul's companions mentioned is **Mark the cousin of Barnabas (concerning whom you have received instructions – if he comes to you, welcome him).** This was John Mark, from Jerusalem (Acts 12:12, 25). He had travelled with Paul and Mark's cousin Barnabas to Cyprus on the so-called first missionary journey. Mark, however, pulled out and returned to Jerusalem (Acts13:13). This led to a rather sharp disagreement between Paul and Barnabas some time later, when Paul was not willing to have Mark join them on a return visit to the new churches they had founded. Barnabas and Paul went their separate ways: Barnabas with Mark, Paul with Silas (Acts 15:36-41).

That happened probably about 12 years before the writing of this letter.[4] How good it is to read here of Paul's renewed confidence in John Mark, who was now there with him in Rome! The Colossians had already received instructions from someone about Mark. Perhaps the earlier falling-out with Paul had taken some living down. Paul here adds his word of instruction. If Mark were to come to Colossae, they were to welcome him.[5]

This is the Mark who spent time with Peter, and who is traditionally considered to be the author of the second Gospel, thought by some to have been written in Rome.

---

[3] See Peter T. O'Brien, *Colossians, Philemon* (Waco, Texas: Word Books, 1982), p. 249.

[4] Douglas J. Moo, *The Letters to the Colossians and to Philemon* (Nottingham: Apollos, 2008), p. 339.

[5] Further on John Mark, see 2 Tim. 4:11; Philem. 24; 1 Pet. 5:13.

c. Jesus (Justus)

The third companion to send greetings from Rome to Colossae was **Jesus who is called Justus.** Of this companion of Paul we know no more than we learn here.

Paul says of Aristarchus, John Mark and Jesus Justus: **These are the only men of the circumcision among my fellow workers for the kingdom of God.** That is, these are the only Jewish Christians who have remained faithful companions of Paul through all his trials.[6] Is that not astonishing? At this late stage in Paul's life and ministry, there were just three Jewish fellow workers still with him working for God's kingdom. The struggle for the gospel of grace had been tough. It had cost Paul dearly: only three of his fellow countrymen had stayed the course! Yet he was not complaining: **they have been a comfort to me.** They had no doubt encouraged him with the grace of God they all loved and taught.

d. Epaphras

There may have only been three *Jewish* companions still working with Paul, but there were other companions. He mentions three.

Epaphras, who is one of you, a servant [or, slave] **of Christ Jesus, greets you.** We learned at the beginning of the letter that Epaphras, a Colossian himself (like Onesimus), had apparently been converted during Paul's ministry in Ephesus, and had brought the gospel of Christ to Colossae and the nearby towns of Laodicea and Hierapolis (see the Introduction). The believers listening to this letter had heard the gospel and understood 'the grace of God in truth' from Epaphras (1:6, 7). For reasons that are not entirely clear, Epaphras had more recently travelled from Colossae to Paul in Rome with news of the firm faith in Christ, the ordered lives and the Spirit-given love of the Colossians (2:5; 1:8).

Epaphras was still with Paul, but he was **always struggling on your behalf in his prayers.** I wonder whether Paul and Epaphras, and perhaps the others whose names

---

[6] The Greek of this sentence is somewhat ambiguous, but the ESV is probably correct. See Douglas J. Moo, *The Letters to the Colossians and to Philemon* (Nottingham: Apollos, 2008), pp. 340-342.

we hear in this passage, met together regularly to pray earnestly for the Colossian believers. I suspect that it was so.

Remarkably, Paul saw Epaphras's agonizing efforts in prayer alongside, and in the same terms as the agonising efforts of his own serving the gospel (see the similar language in 1:29; 2:1). The purpose of Epaphras's praying was the same as the purpose of Paul's gospel labours. Paul proclaimed Christ, 'warning everyone and teaching everyone in all wisdom, that we may present everyone mature [perfect] in Christ' (1:28). Epaphras prayed to the same end: **that you may stand mature** [or, perfect]. This maturity or, better, perfection if Paul is thinking eschatologically, involves being **fully assured in all the will of God.** This is the firm confidence that comes when God's will, his purpose in Jesus Christ for the totality of all things, is clearly and certainly known in mind, heart and life (cf. 2:2b). Epaphras prayed, as Paul himself constantly prayed, 'that you may be filled with the knowledge of his will' (1:9).

What a wonderful servant of Christ Epaphras had turned out to be! The apostle wanted the Colossians to appreciate that fact, as he did. **For I bear him witness that he has worked hard for you and for those in Laodicea and in Hierapolis.** Laodicea and Hierapolis were two other nearby towns where Epaphras had apparently also planted the gospel, and for whom he now earnestly prayed.

It has been a concern of this letter (we saw it particularly in 1:24-29 and 2:1-5) to draw careful attention to God's way of working through servants of the gospel, who suffer, and work very hard in prayer to the Lord for people and in speaking to people about the Lord. We do well to remember this, and appreciate the servants whom the Lord is using for his kingdom.

e. Luke

There are two more of Paul's companions who want to get a word in: **Luke the beloved physician greets you, as does Demas.** Luke, of course, is a well-known person to New Testament readers, as the author of the third Gospel and the book of Acts and as a companion of Paul to the end (see 2 Tim. 4:11). Only here do we learn that he was a physician, and only here do we have evidence (which is not in fact conclusive) that he was a gentile. Luke sent his greetings to the Colossians.

f. Demas

About Demas we know very little, except that some time later he deserted Paul in rather sad circumstances. In Paul's last letter he mentions that 'Demas, in love with this present world, has deserted me' (2 Tim. 4:10). Here, however, he joined those with Paul greeting the believers in Colossae.

It was a notable little prayer group there in Rome, interested, concerned and thrilled about the gathering of believers in Colossae, giving thanks to God for the wonder the gospel had accomplished in these lives and praying for their growth and maturity. Among them, if tradition is correct (and it may well be) were three of the writers of the New Testament: Mark, Luke and Paul! They send their greetings to the brothers and sisters in far-off Colossae.

3. Specific requests from Paul (4:15-17)

Having mentioned those who were with him sending greetings, Paul then has three final specific requests or instructions to make.

> Give my greetings to the brothers at Laodicea, and to Nympha and the church in her house. And when this letter has been read among you, have it also read in the church of the Laodiceans; and see that you also read the letter from Laodicea. And say to Archippus, 'See that you fulfil the ministry that you have received in the Lord' (4:15-17).

a. Greet the brothers at Laodicea

Give my greetings to the brothers at Laodicea and to Nympha and the church in her house. As the believers in Colossae met in Philemon's house (Philem. 2), it seems the believers in Laodicea gathered in the house of a woman named Nympha.[7] We see in the next verse that Paul had

[7] On the question of whether this was Nympha (a woman) or Nymphas (a man), see Peter T. O'Brien, *Colossians, Philemon* (Waco, Texas: Word Books, 1982), p. 256.

written a letter to Laodicea. It is not clear why he asked the Colossians to pass on his greetings, unless it was to encourage their relationship with one another.

b. Exchange letters with Laodicea

In any case he wanted them to be in touch with one another so that they could exchange their letters from Paul. His second instruction is: **And when this letter has been read among you, have it also read in the church of the Laodiceans; and see that you also read the letter from Laodicea.**

This is an important insight as to how Paul's letters began to be copied and distributed among the Christian fellowships. We almost certainly no longer have the letter to the Laodiceans, just as we do not have a lost letter to Corinth (1 Cor. 5:9).[8] Notice, that from the beginning Paul's letters were intended to be read aloud in the gatherings of believers.

c. Tell Archippus

Third instruction: **And say to Archippus, 'See that you fulfil the ministry that you have received in the Lord.'** The Colossians knew Archippus, and what his ministry was. We don't. Had Paul heard that Archippus was discouraged, under some pressure, growing weary? We don't know. We simply hear Paul giving this word of encouragement to one member of the Colossian fellowship to complete his God-given ministry.

4. Last word from Paul (4:18)

At last the letter is done. Paul takes the pen from his scribe, and in his own hand writes the last line: **I, Paul, write this greeting with my own hand. Remember my chains. Grace be with you.** Indeed. And may the grace of which he speaks be known among us, as it was known among this wonderful assortment of ordinary people – like us – whom we have glimpsed through the window of the letter's conclusion.

---

[8] It has been suggested that the letter known to us as Ephesians was the letter referred to here. This is unlikely. See Peter T. O'Brien, *Colossians, Philemon* (Waco, Texas: Word Books, 1982), p. 258.

I would like to conclude our reflections on Paul's letter to the Colossians with three observations about the fact that this letter concludes like this.

First, here we glimpse the specific, real, historical situation of Paul as he wrote and the real situation to which the letter was addressed. Here are a number of the actual people, mentioned by name, who were either with Paul as he wrote, or gathered (as we have imagined) in Philemon's house that day as Tychicus read this letter that he had just brought all the way from Paul in Rome to Colossae. The people mentioned are ordinary people, just like you and me. They are individuals, who have come to faith in Christ Jesus, some of them eagerly engaged in ministries of various kinds, all of them needing to hear what Paul has written in these pages. They are people with their life-situations, their anxieties and their dreams, their fears and their joys, their disappointments and their surprises. The concluding words of Paul's letter give us a window through which to glimpse some of these people, and should remind us that our names could well have been included at the end of this letter – if we had been there.

Second, we have this window into the situation because of Paul's evident heart for people. This letter of his pulsates with the most powerfully stretching theology. We have taken twenty-one chapters to think our way through his teaching – and what we have done has been somewhat superficial! In particular, this letter is famous for its exalted Christology (remember 1:15-20!). Furthermore, in these brief pages Paul presents a cosmic understanding of the cross (remember 1:20, unpacked in 2:11-15). In the context of these grand doctrines he outlines the richest theology of the Christian life (see 3:1–4:6). Indeed, as we have seen, that was the purpose of the letter (2:6, 7). The point we see from the way the letter concludes is how his rich theological understanding was not an escape from people! His theological depth and strength does not cause him to withdraw from people. It is evident that he cared deeply for so many of those he names in this and other letters. If he rejoiced in the news of the love the Colossian believers had by the Spirit (see 1:4, 8), he too was a man who loved much – not in theory, but he loved real people.

It is a travesty when the study of theology at a high level of thought and understanding causes a person to love less. Mind you, it is a travesty no smaller when great love for people is thought to prohibit serious study of God. Somehow in our day these options seem to be set over against one another. For Paul, all his great theological knowledge served the purpose of working ever so hard to see hearts encouraged, knit together in love, and full of the rich assurance that comes with knowing Christ (see 2:2).

Third, Paul displays his warm support for the ministry of others. It is perfectly clear that Paul was no one-man band. He was not full of his own importance (or indeed taken up with his own difficulties) so that he neglected the labours of others. He appreciated them, and said so. He cared for them. How good it is to see him reconciled to John Mark! If Demas will one day desert him, I do not believe it will be because Paul did not support and encourage him.

We find ourselves as believers in Christ Jesus today among those for whom Paul's letter was written (see 2:1b). May the grace of which he has taught us so richly in these pages fill our lives, and continue to do so.

Study Questions

1. Make a summary of all that we learn from Colossians 4:7-18 about Paul's circumstances at the time of writing the letter. Look back over the whole letter. Is there anything more to add?

2. Paul introduces Tychicus by telling his readers three things about him (Col. 4:7). What is the importance of these things? What effect would you expect this introduction to have?

3. From the teaching of the whole letter, how do you think Tychicus would go about his task of 'encouraging hearts' in Colossae?

4. Remembering who Onesimus was, what is the importance of the three things Paul tells his

readers about Onesimus (Col. 4:9)? What effect would you expect this commendation to have?

5. Make a brief summary of all we have learnt about Epaphras (see Col. 1:3-8 as well as 4:12, 13), and consider the ways in which he seems to have taken Paul as his example.

6. In what ways does the concluding section of Paul's letter to the Colossians (Col. 4:7-18) help us not to treat the letter as merely abstract theory?

Philemon

Effective fellowship

22

Effective Fellowship
(Philemon 1-7)

The fellowship of believers in Jesus Christ is remarkably powerful for good. I wonder whether that has been your experience. It may have been, without your fully appreciating just how good it has been. Too easily we take familiar things for granted. It is also possible for the fellowship of believers to be less in our experience than it ought to be. What we call *fellowship* might be no more than a loose association of people who occasionally assemble for something we call 'church'. Or it may be that what we think is 'fellowship' is just human friendship – itself a wonderful thing, but not the same as *the fellowship of believers*. It is possible that the concept of Christian 'fellowship' is in danger of being underestimated or undervalued. Could it be that as Christian churches focus on *worship*, or *ministry*, or even on *discipleship*, we lose sight of the basic and wonderful goodness and power of *the fellowship of believers*? If you are wondering what I am talking about – perhaps that is evidence that my concerns have some basis!

What is Christian 'fellowship'? What is good about it?

In a corner of the New Testament is a very short letter – not quite the New Testament's shortest, but in most Bibles it fits on one page. It is a gem. It is about the power of the fellowship of believers. The letter has become known by the name of the man to whom it was written, Philemon.

Behind the letter is a remarkable story. It too, in its own way, is a story of the power of the fellowship of believers. The letter itself – that is, the preservation of the letter, its very existence in the New Testament – is eloquent testimony to the power of the fellowship of believers – and, as we will see, to hear this letter is to hear a deeply moving call to know and experience the power of that fellowship.

The story behind the letter was told in the Introduction to this commentary. There we saw that the available evidence indicates that the letter to Philemon had been brought to Colossae along with the longer letter (the one we know as 'Colossians') that was addressed to all of the Christian believers who would meet there in Philemon's house. I have imagined the day on which the believers gathered there to hear the letter from Paul that had been brought all the way from Rome by Tychicus. At the conclusion of the reading of the longer letter I see (in my mind's eye) Tychicus saying, 'Brothers, I do have another letter from Paul that he wants you all to hear. It is brief, but important.'

As the assembly waited in silence, I imagine that Tychicus began to read again: 'Paul, a prisoner for Christ Jesus, and Timothy our brother, To Philemon our beloved fellow worker and Apphia our sister and Archippus our fellow soldier, and the church in your house: Grace to you and peace from God our Father and the Lord Jesus Christ' (vv. 1-3).

He kept reading, but now there was a change of tone. We miss it in English, but in the original Greek text the word 'you' wherever it occurs from verse 4 onwards through to verse 21 is singular.[1] As Tychicus read, he may have lifted his eyes from time to time to look directly at his host, Philemon, for these words were directly for him. We can convey something of the effect of the singular 'you' by adding Philemon's name as indicated in square brackets:

---

[1] 'Your' in verse 2 is singular, referring to Philemon, but 'you' in verse 3 is plural, referring to 'the church' that gathered in Philemon's house. 'Your' in 'your prayers' in verse 22 and in 'your spirit' in verse 25 is plural again, but 'you' in verse 23 is singular. These movements from singular to plural strongly suggest that the letter was certainly addressed directly to Philemon himself, but was expected to be read publicly and heard by the whole gathering of believers in his house.

> I thank my God always when I remember you [Philemon] in my prayers, because I hear of your love and of the faith that you have towards the Lord Jesus and for all the saints, and I pray that the sharing of your faith [Philemon] may become effective for the full knowledge of every good thing that is in us for the sake of Christ. For I have derived much joy and comfort from your love, my brother, because the hearts of the saints have been refreshed through you (vv. 4-7).

I suspect that everyone in the room was now listening very carefully. What was it that Paul was going to say to their esteemed host? What was so important that a separate letter had been written to him? I have no doubt that Philemon was listening *very* carefully.

We are going to wait until our next chapter to hear the answers to the questions that must have been in all their minds, because the profound importance of this careful letter's introduction deserves attention. It prepares us, as it prepared Philemon, to hear the rest of the letter.

1. The introduction (vv. 1-3)

There is no surprise that the letter begins with the standard form of identifying the senders, identifying the recipients, and a word of greeting. That is how the other letter had begun (Col. 1:1, 2); it is how most of Paul's letters begin, and it is how letters in that world normally began. As usual, however, there are some surprises with how Paul employs this form for this particular letter.

a. The writer(s)

First, he introduces himself as **Paul, a prisoner for Christ Jesus.** Not, notice, 'an apostle of Christ Jesus by the will of God' as he had said at the beginning of the longer letter (Col. 1:1). Paul draws attention in this letter, not to his apostolic authority, but to his bondage, suffering, and humiliation.

We could translate this 'a prisoner *of* Christ Jesus'. From the very first words of this letter there is a hint of what is to come. Christ Jesus changes all human situations and relationships. You might think that Paul was in bondage for offending the Roman authorities in some way. No. He was there because he had been proclaiming Christ. You might think that he was being punished for some wrong. No. He was there for the sake of Christ and his gospel. You might think that he was under the power of the soldier who was guarding him. No. He was a prisoner who belonged to Christ.[2]

As with the longer letter, Paul adds, **and Timothy our brother** (cf. Col. 1:1). Timothy, no doubt known to some in Colossae (almost certainly known to Philemon), joins Paul in the sending of this letter, although it is quite clear that Paul himself is the author.

b. The recipient(s)

The next surprise is that Paul singles out a particular person as the main addressee of the letter, and then adds some others.[3]

(i) Philemon

Paul's letter is addressed first **to Philemon our beloved fellow worker.** Most of the believers in Colossae had never met or seen Paul in the flesh (see Col. 2:1). But Philemon, of course, had (see the Introduction). If we have got the story right they had worked together in Ephesus after Philemon had become a believer. How good it must have been to hear this affirmation of Paul's love for him – after the years that had passed.

(ii) Apphia

A second name is included: **and Apphia our sister.** It is a reasonable guess that Apphia was Philemon's wife. This letter is going to concern matters to do with their household, and so the inclusion of Apphia's name is understandable.

(iii) Archippus

A third name is added: **and Archippus our fellow soldier.** Archippus had been singled out for special mention in

---

[2] Cf. Douglas J. Moo, *The Letters to the Colossians and to Philemon* (Nottingham: Apollos, 2008), p. 380, note 8.

[3] 'In Graeco-Roman letters it is virtually always the first-named individual who is the main recipient of the letter.' Douglas J. Moo, *The Letters to the Colossians and to Philemon* (Nottingham: Apollos, 2008), p. 382.

the longer letter, where Paul encouraged the believers to say to him, 'See that you fulfil the ministry that you have received from the Lord' (Col. 4:17). He may have been a son of Philemon and Apphia, and for that reason included here. He may have had some leadership in the gathering – that may be why his name appears. Certainly he and whatever his ministry was were known to Paul.

(iv) The assembly

Perhaps the biggest surprise at this point in the letter is that the whole assembly of believers is included in those addressed in what will turn out to be a very personal letter to Philemon: **and the church** [or, assembly] **in your house** – that is, in Philemon's house.

This is strange, particularly from the point of view of our sensibilities about how we distinguish private and public matters. When we get to the main part of the letter, we will see that this *is* a particularly personal word to Philemon. Yet it seems that it was delivered to him in the hearing of the whole assembly. The greeting in verse 3 is plural, and seems to address the whole gathering. Likewise in verse 22 Paul will refer to 'you' and 'your' prayers – plurals referring to all the believers there. Also the closing greeting in verse 25 is directed to them all.

I do not think that this should be regarded as a tactic to increase the pressure on Philemon to do what Paul will be proposing in the letter.[4] It is certainly not a public rebuke, or anything of that kind. Philemon has done nothing at all wrong. Rather we should recognize the corporate nature of the Christian fellowship. If Philemon's wife and son were rightly included in the matter to be raised with Philemon, then so was the whole household of God in that place.[5] The matter that Paul will raise with Philemon was not (despite our natural first impressions) a private matter. Much that we tend to think of as private, should perhaps be recognized as less so – if we take the fellowship of believers seriously. More of that shortly.

---

[4]*Contra* Douglas J. Moo, *The Letters to the Colossians and to Philemon* (Nottingham: Apollos, 2008), p. 383.

[5]Cf. *Ibid*, p. 384.

c. The greeting

The greeting echoes the greeting in the longer letter (cf. Col. 1:2b): **Grace to you and peace from God our Father and the Lord Jesus Christ.** This is what God the Father and the Lord Jesus Christ give to those who believe: grace and peace.

2. The thanksgiving (vv. 4-5)

At this point the letter becomes a word to Philemon himself. It is addressed to him in the hearing of the gathering in his house, but it is to him.

Dear brother, Philemon, **I thank my God always when I remember you in my prayers.** Paul was a serious pray-er. We saw that in the longer letter (see Col. 1:3-14; cf. 4:2-4). Here is another glimpse. Philemon was on Paul's prayer list. He may have been included in Paul's prayers for some years, but now news about Philemon had come to Paul in Rome by Epaphras (see v. 23 and Col. 1:7, 8; 4:12, 13). Paul *thanks God,* no doubt because his prayers for Philemon over these years have been graciously answered.

What news had Epaphras brought? **because I hear of your love and of the faith that you have towards the Lord Jesus and for all the saints.** How brilliant! The man who had come to faith in Christ in Paul's company in Ephesus, was continuing strong in his faith, and in his love for God's people. Paul was thrilled.

The way in which this is expressed here is a little unusual. Paul often refers to faith in Jesus Christ and love for fellow believers (see Col. 1:4). This may be his meaning here, although the word order is a little unusual with 'love' and 'faith' separated from their objects in reverse order: 'the Lord Jesus' and 'all the saints'. It is also possible that in this letter whose key idea (as we are about to see) is the effective power of believers sharing in the faith (see v. 6), Paul hints here at the fact that just as Philemon's love is directed to *both* God's people *and* the Lord Jesus, so his faith connects him to *both* the Lord Jesus and to all God's people. One of those people with whom he shares this faith will shortly become the central subject of this letter (see v. 10).

3. The prayer (vv. 6, 7)

The news of answered prayers did not mean that Paul stopped praying (as we also heard in the longer letter, see Col. 1:9). What did he pray for Philemon? I assume that Philemon was included in Paul's prayers for all the Colossian believers (see Col. 1:9-14). Nonetheless Paul had a particular prayer for him.

The ESV of verse 6 puts it like this: **and I pray that the sharing of your faith may become effective for the full knowledge of every good thing that is in us for the sake of Christ.** The verse is very difficult to translate, but what it says is magnificent. 'The sharing of your faith' translates a Greek expression that may, more literally, be rendered 'your fellowship (*koinonia*) of the faith'. The best translation I have found is 'your participation in the faith' (HCSB).[6] This is the reality of Christian fellowship: sharing in faith in Christ Jesus. This is what we believers have in common: our faith in the Lord Jesus. Our sharing in this faith, our participation in this faith, is our 'fellowship'.

I began this chapter by saying that the fellowship of believers in Jesus Christ is remarkably powerful. That is what Paul prayed for Philemon: that his fellowship in the faith, his participation in the faith, his sharing in the faith (with Paul, with his brothers and sisters there in Colossae and, very importantly as we will see in the rest of this letter, with one particular believer named Onesimus) *may become effective*. This will be a test case of the power of the fellowship between believers.

Onesimus (as we saw in the Introduction) had been a slave in Philemon's household. He had run away, possibly robbing Philemon in the process (see v. 18). Subsequently Onesimus had become a Christian believer, apparently through meeting Paul in Rome. Onesimus had now accompanied Tychicus back to Colossae with the two letters (see Col. 4:7-9). How will Philemon's and Onesimus's participation in the faith affect what happens between this wronged master and this returning runaway slave?

---

[6] Cf. 'your partnership with us in the faith' (TNIV).

We are getting ahead of Paul, and anticipating more than the hearers would grasp at this point in the letter, where Paul simply, but profoundly, says, 'I pray that your fellowship in the faith may become effective.'

The rest of verse 6 is also difficult to translate, although the ideas are clear enough. Paul's prayer is that the fellowship will be effective (again translating quite literally) 'in knowledge of every good thing which is among us for Christ.' While that sounds a little strange to our ears, I suspect that Paul's meaning was close to what he prayed for all the believers in Colossae, namely, that they would be filled with the *knowledge* (same word as here) of God's will, bearing fruit in every *good* work, and growing in the *knowledge* of God (Col. 1:9, 10). It is in the context of knowing and understanding the astonishing good that God is doing among us, by uniting us with Christ, that Philemon's fellowship in the faith will become effective.

This is not to suggest that Philemon's fellowship in the faith was not already powerfully effective, as far as Paul was concerned. **For I have derived much joy and comfort from your love, my brother, because the hearts of the saints have been refreshed through you.** The fellowship had been working! Paul was delighted and comforted by Philemon's love. This was not simply his love for Paul, but his loving ministry to the believers who met in his house – the news of which Epaphras no doubt had brought to Paul (see Col. 1:7, 8).

We must read on to hear where this is leading. What does Paul have to say particularly to his dear friend Philemon? In what way is he hoping and praying that the fellowship of the faith will now become effective? Even at this point we may pause to consider whether *our* fellowship in the faith, our participation in faith in Christ, is *effective*.

Paul described more fully the effects of this fellowship in the longer letter to the Colossians. We may look back to that letter and recognize the following words as a description of the powerful effects of our fellowship in the faith:

> Put on then, as God's chosen ones, holy and beloved, compassionate hearts, kindness, humility, meekness,

and patience, bearing with one another and, if one has a complaint against another, forgiving each other; as the Lord has forgiven you, so you also must forgive. And above all these put on love, which binds everything together in perfect harmony. And let the peace of Christ rule in your hearts, to which indeed you were called in one body. And be thankful. Let the word of Christ dwell in you richly, teaching and admonishing one another in all wisdom, singing psalms and hymns and spiritual songs, with thankfulness in your hearts to God. And whatever you do, in word or deed, do everything in the name of the Lord Jesus, giving thanks to God the Father through him (Col. 3:12-17).

Study Questions

1. How are the relationships between Christian believers affected by our participation in the same faith?
2. Consider how participating with others in your faith in the Lord Jesus Christ has had effects. What have some of these effects been?
3. Can you think of situations where a matter that might otherwise be considered 'private', should (like the matters Paul wrote about to Philemon) be dealt with openly before the Christian fellowship? (Note that we are not talking about discipline or reprimand. Philemon had emphatically not done something wrong.)
4. What do you think would have been the effect of Paul's *public* report of his thanks to God for Philemon (Philem. 4, 5)?
5. Consider the passage from the longer letter quoted at the end of this chapter (Col. 3:12-17). Which of the qualities mentioned have been exhibited by Philemon already? With the return of Onesimus, which qualities might become particularly important?

23

The Fellowship at Work – I
(Philemon 8-16)

'I pray that your fellowship in the faith – your participation in the faith, your sharing in the faith – may become effective' (Philem. 6a, my translation). That was Paul's prayer for Philemon, his dear friend, and the host of the gathering of believers in Colossae.

The *effectiveness* of the fellowship believers share is seen most clearly in difficult situations, where this fellowship changes things in unexpected ways. There was a difficult situation in the Colossian fellowship on the day this letter from Paul to Philemon was read out before the believers gathered in his house.

We have heard Paul's confidence that Philemon's participation in the faith *would* be effective, because of Philemon's track record in the fellowship of believers. 'I have derived much joy and comfort from your love, my brother, because the hearts of the saints have been refreshed through you' (v. 7). Philemon was a man who cared for his fellow Christians. In his words, his acts, and (I am sure) in his prayers, he cared about their welfare, especially *their* faith in Jesus, their love for each other, and their hope. Paul had little doubt that Philemon's *fellowship in the faith* would *become effective* in the difficult matter his letter was going to raise with him.

How does this work? How does the fellowship of believers 'become effective' – particularly in difficult situations?

By difficult situations I mean situations where, if it were not for the fellowship of believers, things really would be different. We do not see the power of the fellowship of believers simply when like-minded people, who share a great deal in common, enjoy one another's company and friendship. There is nothing wrong with that, of course, and it will always be part of the reality of our fellowship. But the fellowship of the faith is more powerful than that. It is more than 'the new friends I make at church'! It is important for believers to know the power of their fellowship for the difficult situations.

The situation in Colossae on the day that this letter from Paul was being read for the first time was at the extremities of difficulty. Philemon was the man from Colossae whom Paul had led to faith in Christ some years earlier in Ephesus. Paul was now under house arrest in Rome, where he had met Onesimus, the slave who had run away from Philemon. We will learn a little more about the difficulties between Philemon and Onesimus shortly. But Paul had now led Onesimus to faith in Jesus Christ. For these three men (all now believers in Christ Jesus), how was the fellowship of the faith to be effective among them? They were different in so many ways: the apostle, the slave and the master – the master who had been wronged, perhaps robbed by the slave; the slave who had run away from the master, having stolen from him, and the apostle who had led them both to Christ. How will their *fellowship in the faith* 'become effective'?

As we take up the letter again, remember two things. First, we are to imagine it being read aloud before the whole gathering of believers meeting in Philemon's house. Second, from verse 8 to verse 21 the person addressed is Philemon himself (the 'you's are singular).

> Accordingly, though I am bold enough in Christ to command you [Philemon] to do what is required, yet for love's sake I prefer to appeal to you – I, Paul, an old man and now a prisoner also for Christ Jesus – I appeal to you for my child, Onesimus, whose father I became in my imprisonment. (Formerly he was useless to you, but now

> he is indeed useful to you and to me.) I am sending him back to you, sending my very heart. I would have been glad to keep him with me, in order that he might serve me on your behalf during my imprisonment for the gospel, but I preferred to do nothing without your consent in order that your goodness might not be by compulsion but of your own accord. For this perhaps is why he was parted from you for a while, that you might have him back for ever, no longer as a slave but more than a slave, as a beloved brother – especially to me, but how much more to you, both in the flesh and in the Lord (vv. 8-16).

Those who share faith in Jesus Christ are brought into a very remarkable relationship with one another. To understand the particular example of the fellowship of the faith at work spoken of in this passage we need to see the various relationships involved.

1. Paul's relationship to Philemon (vv. 8, 9)

a. As apostle

First, look at Paul's relationship with Philemon. Paul draws attention to two aspects of the relationship. On the one hand, he says, **Accordingly,** [he is drawing a conclusion from what we saw previously: Paul's prayer in verse 6 and his confidence in verse 7] **though I am bold enough in Christ to command you to do what is required ...**

Paul is the apostle. That, of course, is how he introduced himself at the beginning of the other letter to the Colossians (Col. 1:1). He is, moreover, the apostle who brought Christ to Philemon and Philemon to Christ. As an apostle of Christ Jesus by the will of God, Paul was never timid about issuing instructions, warnings, rebukes and, yes, even commands – when the occasion warranted it.

This occasion did warrant something. Something was 'required' of Philemon. One of the marvels of this little letter is how Paul holds back from *explicitly* telling Philemon what he should do. He simply refers to 'what is required' (or 'what is fitting' or 'what is proper'). Yet it is clear that there is *something* that he is hoping and expecting Philemon will do.

We may well feel that it would be a lot easier for all concerned if Paul would just come out and tell Philemon what it is he expects of him. It would certainly make the life of commentators and preachers easier! Much speculation and guesswork has gone into trying to work out exactly what Paul meant by 'what is required' at the end of verse 8. In fact, Paul had good reason for not simply telling Philemon what to do – not yet, anyway.

b. As brother

Although he could have directly issued a command to Philemon he continues, **yet for love's sake I prefer to appeal to you**. Paul hopes that the fellowship in the faith will not become effective through a command. That is not to say that there is no place for commands in the Christian fellowship. But there is something better than a command. 'I appeal,' says Paul. I encourage. I exhort. The reason is 'for love's sake' – because of love.

He has spoken already of Philemon's love for God's people in verses 5 and 7. Paul's love for Philemon is mentioned in verse 1 ('our beloved fellow worker') and implied in verse 7 ('my brother'). Those who share faith in Christ know the love of God and so are to love one another. Paul and Philemon did. 'Because of love,' says Paul, 'I prefer to appeal to you.'

As though to underline the lack of coercion in this he adds: **I, Paul, an old man and now a prisoner also for Christ Jesus.** For the second time Paul refers to his imprisonment (see v. 1a), and in addition mentions his age. Paul was not coming down on Philemon with a heavy hand. This was an old man speaking – an old man in chains.

Ministers of God's Word – who are rather less important than the apostle, and much less in a position to be giving commands among God's people – would do well to take note of this. There may be a time and place to wield authority, but that was never Paul's preferred way. It should never be our preferred way either. 'Because of love, I prefer to appeal to you.'

2. Paul's relationship to Onesimus (vv. 10-13)

Still we wait for some indication of what Paul wanted Philemon to do.

a. His son

The first hint comes in verse 10, where Paul speaks of a second relationship: **I appeal to you for my child, Onesimus, whose father I became in my imprisonment.** In the original he does not mention the name until the end of the sentence: 'I appeal to you for my child, whose father I became in my imprisonment, Onesimus.'

I imagine an awkward silence in the gathering at the mention of that name. Everyone knew, no doubt, of his escape from Philemon's household, and perhaps of the robbery. His presence with Paul's envoy, Tychicus, must have caused quite a stir when the two of them arrived in Colossae. There must have been at least some tension and difficulty with Onesimus present in the gathering as the first letter had been read out. I imagine the nudges and whispers when Tychicus read, towards the end of the longer letter, 'with [Tychicus I have sent to you] Onesimus, our faithful and beloved brother, who is one of you' (Col. 4:9a). Whatever people may or may not have guessed about Paul's letter to Philemon, this is the first hint that it had to do with Onesimus.

Not to put too fine a point on it, Onesimus represented a difficult situation. Yet what Paul wanted to underline about Onesimus was that Paul had brought him to faith in Christ, to new birth. He was, therefore, Paul's 'child'. In his imprisonment Paul had become his father, by being instrumental in him receiving new life. Onesimus had left Colossae a criminal. He was returning a different man.

b. 'Useful'

Indeed, **Formerly he was useless to you, but now he is indeed useful to you and to me.** His name, 'Onesimus', means 'profitable' or 'useful'. It was a common name for slaves, perhaps given to them by masters in the hope that they would live up to it. Apparently this Onesimus had not. Here is a glimpse of the earlier relationship between this master and this slave. 'Useless'. Perhaps he was a troublemaker.

Perhaps he was lazy. Perhaps he was dishonest. Perhaps all of these things. We have every reason to think that Philemon (certainly after becoming a believer) would have been a fair and just master who knew very well that he had a Master in heaven (see Col. 4:1). Apparently Onesimus was a very unsatisfactory slave. It is possible that Philemon was not particularly distressed when Onesimus ran away, except that he seems to have robbed him as well.

Paul insists that the man returning to Colossae is a different man. Now he is 'useful' – both 'to you and to me'. There is more to say about his usefulness in a moment.

Today's readers of this letter understandably have difficulty with all of this because of the serious problems we rightly have with the very idea of slavery. We gave some thought to the questions raised by slavery in the New Testament when this subject was raised in Colossians 3:22-25. I do not propose to revisit those matters now, except to point out again that the very difficulties raised by slavery make it a particularly powerful case study in the power of Christian fellowship. Here we see not just two men who have become Christians, but two men who have a very difficult history: the useless slave and his master, now both believers in Jesus. How will the fellowship of the faith 'become effective'?

c. His heart

Paul's appeal is not finished. He clearly wants Philemon to be under no misapprehension about Paul's relationship to Onesimus. **I am sending him back to you, sending my very heart.** *This* is the fellowship of the faith at work. Let's put the difficulties between Philemon and Onesimus to one side for a moment. Consider *Paul* and Onesimus. Consider the improbability of the Jewish prisoner of Rome and the fugitive gentile slave finding anything in common. Yet, he is 'my very heart', said Paul. This is astonishing! The affection of Paul for Onesimus was deep and strong. This *is* the fellowship of the faith at work.

d. His 'servant'

Furthermore, **I would have been glad to keep him with me, in order that he might serve me on your behalf during**

my imprisonment for the gospel. Paul was certainly not sending Onesimus back to Philemon because he wanted to. If it were a matter of Paul's preference, he would have kept Onesimus with him. Perhaps Onesimus had been caring for Paul himself in some way during his imprisonment. More likely, given the words Paul uses here, Onesimus helped Paul in his gospel work during his confinement in Rome. They were working well together as partners in the gospel! Onesimus was indeed 'useful' to Paul! In a sense he was standing in for Philemon, who had (in all probability) similarly served with Paul in Ephesus (see the Introduction).

3. Paul and Philemon, concerning Onesimus (v. 14)

Notwithstanding all of this, Paul's relationship to Onesimus was not the only reality of the fellowship of the faith. We have already seen something of Paul's relationship to Philemon. This relationship had consequences for Onesimus. So Paul continued, **but I preferred to do nothing without your consent in order that your goodness might not be by compulsion but of your own accord.**

We are back to where we began in verses 8 and 9. Paul did not want Philemon's hand to be forced, either by an apostolic command (v. 8), or an apostolic pre-emptive action (v. 14). What Philemon was to do, literally 'the good thing', was to come from his heart, not from forced necessity. The picture of how the fellowship of the faith 'becomes effective' is becoming clearer.

We still have not heard exactly what Paul expects or wants Philemon to do. He just calls it in verse 14 (literally) 'the good thing', which may remind us of verse 6, where the fellowship of the faith becomes effective in the knowledge of every 'good thing' that is in us, with a view to Christ. That might remind us of Paul's prayer in the other letter that believers would so be filled with the knowledge of God's will that they would bear fruit in every *good* work (Col. 1:10).

The point, however, is that the good thing (whatever it might be!) must come from Philemon's believing heart, not from external compulsion – if it is going to be the fellowship of the faith becoming effective.

4. Paul, Philemon, Onesimus and the Lord (vv. 15, 16)
Before Paul actually tells Philemon what he expects of him (and, yes, he will do that before the letter is done) he has one more observation. Onesimus may well have been useless previously. He may well have caused some difficulty for Philemon by his running away. He may also have stolen from him. All of these actions were wrong.

Paul knew who rules over the affairs of men and women. We cannot infallibly discern *God's* purpose, particularly in events involving wrong human actions. Sometimes, especially with the benefit of hindsight, we can guess at God's purpose in what happens to us, in the difficult situations that life brings. Paul suggests the possibility of an extraordinary purpose in what has happened! **For this perhaps is why he was parted from you for a while, that you might have him back for ever**.

The useless slave was lost to Philemon for a time. It is not clear that Philemon was particularly anxious to have him back. Yet God's purpose in this may well have been precisely that Philemon would have Onesimus *for ever*! This would be **no longer as a slave** (that would no longer be their defining relationship; that is not the relationship that would go on for ever), **but more than a slave, as a beloved brother**, just as he had become a loved child to Paul (v. 10): **especially to me, but how much more to you.**

Both in the flesh and in the Lord probably means, not just in a spiritual sense ('in the Lord'), but in the reality of human relationships ('in the flesh'), these two men were now to be *loved brothers* to one another! That is the fellowship of the faith at work.

So what exactly did Paul hope Philemon would do? With all the preparation of the letter to this point, he is ready to tell him – and he does from verse 17.

Study Questions

1. Have there been any difficulties lately in the relationships in any fellowship of Christians to which you belong? What was the trouble? Did participation in the faith – sharing the same faith

in Jesus Christ – make a difference? How *should* participation in this faith have made a difference?

2. Why did Paul not simply tell Philemon what to do? When might it be appropriate for 'commands' to be given among Christian people?

3. Reflect on what we have heard about the relationships between Paul and Philemon, and between Paul and Onesimus. How did the *faith* they shared shape these relationships? What relationships have you known that have developed out of a shared faith in Christ?

4. As Philemon (and the others) listened to this letter, by the time they had heard verse 16 what might they have thought Paul was hoping Philemon would do? What are the possibilities?

24

The Fellowship at Work – II
(Philemon 17-25)

Paul's letter to Philemon has been about the powerful effectiveness of the fellowship of the faith ('the sharing of your faith', in the ESV, v. 6). This has not been discussed in the abstract, but presented in the concrete situation of Philemon, the man in whose home the Colossian believers met (v. 2). Philemon's fellowship in the faith with Paul (who had introduced him to Christ years earlier), Paul's fellowship in the faith with Onesimus (whom he had much more recently led to Christ), and therefore Philemon's fellowship in the faith with Onesimus are the dynamic forces at work through this short letter. The fact that Onesimus had been Philemon's slave, who had run away, possibly robbing him in the process, creates one of those situations where the supernatural power of God's grace is needed if the fellowship of the faith is to become effective.

There are, of course, many such experiences in the life of any fellowship of God's people. The story of this runaway slave, now himself a man of faith in Christ, returning to his Christian master in Colossae, is about the real and practical power of the fellowship of faith in Jesus Christ to transform the most difficult of situations between people. Relationships, even between Christians, are easily dominated by wrongs that have been done. People often treat one another and regard one another in the light of past hurts or injuries. Rejection, resentment, and distrust or shame, embarrassment and insecurity can govern these relationships. What can happen if these difficult relationships are renewed by shared faith in Jesus Christ becoming the dominant factor? Then fellowship in the faith can become effective. This is what Paul prayed would happen with Philemon and Onesimus (v. 6).

Up to this point in the letter Paul has prepared the way for the remarkable thing that he expects Philemon to do, but has not yet spelled out exactly what he has in mind. He has referred to Philemon's own genuine faith in the Lord Jesus (v. 5), and prayed that his participation with other believers in this faith will become effective (v. 6), as indeed it already has (v. 7). He has then spoken of the relationships between himself, Philemon and Onesimus, with a clear indication that the fact that Onesimus is now (like Philemon) a much-loved brother in Christ to Paul must make all the difference to the relationship between the wronged master and the runaway slave (see vv. 8-16).

1. The fellowship of the faith becoming effective (vv. 17-22)

At last Paul is ready to tell Philemon explicitly what he is asking of him:

> So if you consider me your partner, receive him as you would receive me. If he has wronged you at all, or owes you anything, charge that to my account. I, Paul, write this with my own hand: I will repay it – to say nothing of your owing me even your own self. Yes, brother, I want some benefit from you in the Lord. Refresh my heart in Christ.
>
> Confident of your obedience, I write to you, knowing that you will do even more than I say. At the same time, prepare a guest room for me, for I am hoping that through your prayers I will be graciously given to you (vv. 17-22).

So (or 'therefore') connects this appeal to what has been said. The appeal flows out of the argument about the remarkable relationships between the apostle and these two men that has been discussed in verses 8-16, as well as the Christian experience, character and conduct of Philemon himself which was the subject of verses 4-7. Here we reach the point of the whole letter.

a. Paul's appeal

In verse 17, then, Paul at last makes his appeal to Philemon direct and clear. Once more, however, he mentions the motivation he has been presenting in all that he has said so far: **if you consider me your partner**. 'Partner' does not convey the sense of the Greek word at this point. Although the word could be used of 'partnerships' of various kinds, including business partnerships, in this context the Greek word clearly echoes the word translated 'sharing' in the ESV of verse 6, the word we have been rendering as 'fellowship' or 'participation'. Paul is emphasizing again Philemon's relationship to the apostle. Quite literally he says, 'If you have me as a fellow (believer)'.

Of course there is no doubt that Philemon does have this relationship to Paul. 'If' does not suggest otherwise, but draws Philemon's attention to the importance of this relationship, and invites him to affirm it. Paul has called Philemon a 'beloved co-worker' (v. 1) and 'my brother' (v. 7, cf. 20). These are both expressions of the basic relationship of those who participate, share or have fellowship in the same *faith*.

On the basis of their fellowship, then, Paul calls on Philemon to **receive him** [Onesimus] **as you would receive me.** This is the remarkable outworking of the astonishing threefold bond between Paul, Philemon and Onesimus, as fellow believers in Christ. Small wonder that Paul has taken some time to prepare for this extraordinary exhortation.

We might imagine the way in which Philemon would 'receive' Paul, the 'apostle of Christ Jesus by the will of God' (Col. 1:1), should he come to visit Colossae. Consider the respect that would be shown, and the many appropriate kindnesses that would be extended to the deeply loved teacher. Indeed in a few lines' time we will hear that Paul *was* planning to visit Philemon in the near future! His very reasonable expectation was that Philemon would prepare a guest room for him (v. 22). We can be sure that Paul's visit would be highly anticipated, and very warmly welcomed by his dear friend and (actually more importantly) *fellow believer*, Philemon.

The welcome that Philemon would soon extend to the apostle was to be the standard by which he was to welcome Onesimus, the slave who had betrayed him. We who have not experienced the stratification of society as it was in Philemon's world can hardly appreciate the breathtakingly radical call of verse 17. Onesimus would now be a member of the gathering of believers that met in Philemon's house. He would be a 'brother' (v. 16) and fellow believer *just like Paul*! Here was an application of the far-reaching principle that Paul had proclaimed in the longer letter to Colossae: 'Here there is not Greek and Jew, circumcised and uncircumcised, barbarian, Scythian, slave, free; but Christ is all, and in all' (Col. 3:11).

b. Paul's grace

In the case of Philemon and Onesimus there was not only the division between master and slave that was generally expected by the apostle to be transformed by faith in Christ (see Col. 3:22–4:1), but there was the serious matter of the wrong that had been done to Philemon by Onesimus. This is acknowledged by Paul: **If he has wronged you at all, or owes you anything**.

The 'if' of verse 18 does not suggest that there is any doubt about the fact that Onesimus had wronged Philemon (any more than the syntactically identical 'if' clause of verse 17 suggested uncertainty about the matter mentioned there). Philemon, as well as the other believers who listened to the reading of this letter, would have known well what Onesimus had done. Readers today are less well informed of the details. Paul may be referring simply to the fact of Onesimus's running away from his master for no good reason. Philemon had, in this way, been 'robbed' of Onesimus's service. It is also possible that Onesimus stole from Philemon at the time of his flight. This has an inherent probability if we imagine the desperate situation of a runaway slave.

What, we might imagine Philemon asking, is to be done about the debt Onesimus owes me, the wrongs he has committed against me? Paul's answer is stark, simple and profoundly Christ-like: **charge that to my account.** It is not too much to see Paul here acting out the role that Christ himself has played in the saving of sinners. Paul owed Philemon nothing (on the contrary, see 19b), just as Jesus Christ was not in debt to God. Yet Paul takes the debt of Onesimus and promises to pay what is due to Philemon, just as Jesus took on the debt of sinners and paid it in full on the cross. Therefore Philemon should now regard Onesimus as owing him nothing at all, just as the debt we sinners owe to God has been completely expunged by the death of Jesus (see Col. 2:14!).

As far as Paul was concerned this was not mere rhetoric. He meant it, literally. **I, Paul, write this with my own hand: I will repay it**. The statement is very emphatic. In the Greek 'I' is repeated in a form that underlines Paul's personal assurance here. Paul often took the pen from his scribe and added words at the end of a letter in his own hand (see Col. 4:18; also 1 Cor. 16:21; Gal. 6:11; 2 Thess. 3:17). It is possible that Paul wrote the whole of this short and particularly personal letter to Philemon in his own hand. Whether or not that was the case, his writing of the words in verse 19 is more than his signature to authenticate the letter. It was his personal guarantee to Philemon that the debts of Onesimus would be paid in full by Paul himself. This was Paul's fellowship in the faith becoming effective!

c. Paul's claim

Without stepping back from this firm commitment, Paul adds a qualification that should set his gracious offer in proper perspective for Philemon: **to say nothing of your owing me even your own self.** Once again Paul sees the whole situation and the relationships involved in the brilliant light of Paul, Philemon and Onesimus participating in faith in Christ. In that context Philemon must be conscious of his profound debt to Paul. 'To say nothing of' is an indication that Paul does not want to 'use' Philemon's debt to him manipulatively to pressure Philemon into acting unwillingly. Nonetheless it is a matter that should not be forgotten. So he mentions it.

It seems clear that Paul is referring here to his own involvement in Philemon's coming to faith in Christ. In our reconstruction of the story (see the Introduction), we have concluded that Philemon was most probably converted to Christ while visiting Ephesus during Paul's extended three-year ministry in that city. There, through Paul's proclamation of Christ (see Col. 1:28), Philemon had come to know 'all the riches of full assurance of understanding and the knowledge of God's mystery, which is Christ, in whom are hidden all the treasures of wisdom and knowledge' (Col. 2:2, 3). What a debt he owed the apostle!

The one to whom Philemon was infinitely and eternally indebted was now going to pay what was owed (by another) to Philemon. This was grace in action!

Surely Philemon could not be unmoved by all of this. Yet the strength of Paul's appeal to Philemon in the letter as a whole should cause us to see that what Paul was asking was far from a simple matter. There are indications that in addition to the social gulf between slave and master, as well as the offence of whatever ways in which Onesimus had wronged Philemon (v. 18), the relationship between these two had always been difficult ('Formerly he was useless to you,' Paul acknowledged in verse 11!).

This accounts for the persistent way in which Paul presses his point, not assuming that Philemon's response will be easy. **Yes, brother, I want some benefit from you in the Lord.** There is nothing new here. Paul is simply, but powerfully, pressing the astonishing exhortation of verse 17. Again he uses an emphatic form of 'I', underlining everything that he has said about Philemon's relationship to Paul. If Onesimus has a debt to Philemon (which Paul has just taken on himself), Philemon has a debt to Paul, which Paul is now calling in – ever so gently, but firmly. The 'benefit' Paul asks of his debtor is that he accept the additional generosity that has just been extended. Only 'in the Lord' can sense be made of such thinking! The 'benefit' to Paul is Philemon receiving Onesimus as he would receive Paul.

This gracious action by Philemon would be entirely consistent with the love for which he was well known to Paul. Earlier Paul had recalled the joy and comfort that he derived from Philemon's love, 'because the hearts of the saints have been refreshed through you' (v. 7). Now he urges Philemon to apply such conduct to the matter at hand: **Refresh my heart in Christ.** Once again we must see that Paul's heart will be refreshed by Philemon's gracious conduct, not directly towards Paul, but towards Onesimus (whom he has described in verse 12 as 'my very heart'!). As Paul, Philemon and Onesimus participate in the blessings of their faith in Christ, all benefit.

d. Paul's confidence

Although the letter is brief, we have seen that Paul has brought a great deal to bear on what might appear to us (reading these words far removed from the circumstances of Philemon) to be quite a straightforward request, namely, that Philemon extend a kind welcome to the returning Onesimus. We have understood, however, that this was anything but a straightforward request, and it is fair to say that if Philemon did what Paul asked of him in verse 17 it would be a remarkable work of God's grace. Where, but in the fellowship of believers, could you expect to see such conduct?

Paul, however, does not doubt that his brother and fellow worker will do as Paul has asked. **Confident of your obedience, I write to you**. While 'obedience' may seem a little strange here, where Paul has so deliberately avoided 'commanding' Philemon in this matter (see v. 8), Philemon's response to the whole powerful exhortation presented in this letter would be 'obedience', not exactly to a 'command' of Paul, but to the imperative that arises from the fellowship of faith (see, again, v. 6). Paul is confident in the reality of Philemon's love and faith (v. 4) and its active expression (v. 7). He has not written with doubts and uncertainties about the response his letter would receive. He has written fully 'confident'.

While this confidence should not undermine either the magnitude of Paul's request, or the necessity for the powerful reasoning he has advanced, it may suggest that one purpose of the letter was to teach the believers who met in Philemon's house so that they would understand the master's unconventional conduct towards his returning delinquent slave. If (as seems to be clearly indicated) the letter was to be read out in the hearing of the whole assembly, we may suppose (from the confidence that Paul expresses here) that this was not in order to put pressure on Philemon to do the right thing. On the contrary, it is far more likely that it was in order to make the 'right thing' understandable and acceptable to the whole body of believers, who themselves may have been inclined to resent their host's excessive generosity towards Onesimus. If Philemon took Paul's words in verse 17, 'as you would receive me', quite literally there may have been many who were seriously shocked at such outrageous treatment of a criminal. The letter, read aloud to them all, may have done much to address their outrage.

Indeed Paul expected that there would be even more reason for people to be shocked at Philemon's conduct. He did not only write this letter confident that Philemon would do all that had been suggested, but **knowing that you will do even more than I say.** There have been several suggestions as to what Paul may have been hinting at here. Did he expect Philemon to release Onesimus from slavery altogether (as some think is suggested in verse 16)? Did he hope that he might even return him to Paul as a 'fellow worker' in the service of the gospel (see verse 13)? Since Paul does not make either of these suggestions explicit, it is probably best not to read between the lines. Paul may well be simply indicating that he is sure that Philemon will exhibit grace towards Onesimus beyond anything Paul has actually said in this letter – without having any particular expectation of what that will be. This seems more likely than the expectation that Philemon would be able to read more between the lines (in this case) than we can.

e. Paul's plans

Finally, the section that began with a reference to 'receiving' Paul (v. 17) closes with the news that Philemon may soon have the opportunity to do just that. **At the same time, prepare a guest room for me**. There is no sense here that Paul's visit should be regarded by Philemon as an intimidation. The warmth of the whole letter, as well as the genuine confidence expressed in verse 21, suggest that this anticipated visit will be a joyous occasion both for the apostle, for Philemon and for the Colossian believers generally.

Yet, 'at the same time' (admittedly a rather more vague expression in Greek) may well function to make a powerful connection between the treatment of Onesimus and the preparations undertaken 'at the same time' for the visit of Paul. What could draw attention more starkly to the exhortation of verse 17 that both Onesimus and Paul should be 'received' in like manner?

If there is any lingering doubt that the coming visit is regarded by Paul in an entirely positive light (and that he is confident it will likewise be seen in Colossae), the following words settle the matter: **for I am hoping that through your prayers I will be graciously given to you.** Paul was writing from an imprisonment, which we have supposed was in Rome (see the Introduction). His release was not yet a certainty, but it was his hope. Just as he was praying for both the Colossian believers in general (Col. 1:9), and for Philemon in particular (vv. 4 and 6 of this letter), he knew that they were praying for him. In verse 22 the imperative 'prepare' is singular (addressed, like everything that has been said since verse 4, to Philemon himself), but 'your' and 'you' are plural, addressed now (like v. 3) to the gathered believers listening to the letter being read. Presumably Epaphras had reported to Paul the earnest prayers of these brothers and sisters (see Col. 1:8), most of whom Paul had never met (see Col. 2:1). Should the Lord grant their prayers, then Paul's anticipated visit would be (both from his point of view and theirs) a gracious gift. That he sees it like this underlines the bonds of affection Paul felt for Philemon himself and those who met in his house. This, too, was the fellowship of the faith at work.

This section (vv. 17-22) is the heart of the letter. The appeal to Philemon for which the letter had been written has been clearly made (v. 17). The difficulty in the way of that appeal being enacted has been graciously dealt with (v. 18, 19a). This has been put in the proper perspective of who owes what to whom (vv. 19b, 20). Paul has declared his confidence in Philemon (v. 21). Finally Paul's own visit to Colossae has been anticipated, and acts as a reminder of the terms of the appeal (v. 22, cf. v. 17).

2. The wider fellowship of the faith (vv. 23-25)

It only remains for Paul to include other believers who are with him in Rome in the greetings conveyed by his letter. This too is the fellowship of the faith at work. Philemon, described by Paul in verse 1 as 'our beloved fellow worker', is reminded of others in Rome with Paul whom he calls 'my fellow workers' in verse 24. The bond that this group has with Paul (and more importantly, of course, with Christ Jesus), whether there with him in Rome or in far-away Colossae, is another expression of the profound power of participating in the faith that this letter has explored in detail with respect to Paul, Philemon and Onesimus.

The longer letter to Colossae had expressed greetings from each of these (and one other, Jesus Justus) to the wider fellowship in Colossae (see Col. 4:10-14). The greetings in verses 23, 24 of this shorter letter are personally addressed to Philemon (the 'you' in verse 23 is singular). This may account for small differences between the otherwise corresponding sections of the shorter and longer letters (Philem. 23, 24 and Col. 4:10-14). Paul's own greeting in verse 25 is addressed to the whole fellowship ('your' in v. 25 is plural), corresponding neatly to the similar greeting in verse 3.

> Epaphras, my fellow prisoner in Christ Jesus, sends greetings to you, and so do Mark, Aristarchus, Demas, and Luke, my fellow workers. The grace of the Lord Jesus Christ be with your spirit (vv. 23-25).

a. Epaphras

It is no surprise that the first mentioned here among Paul's companions in his imprisonment is **Epaphras**. Behind the whole correspondence with the believers in Colossae was this faithful servant of Christ. He was a Colossian himself (Col. 4:12) and was the one who had taught them 'the grace of God in truth' (Col. 1:6, 7). It was Epaphras who had brought news to Paul of the Colossian believers' thriving faith, love and hope (see Col. 1:4, 5, 7, 8) and there in Rome was agonizing in prayer for them all (Col. 4:12, 13). For more of his story see the Introduction and the exposition of Colossians 4:12, 13.

Here Paul describes him as **my fellow prisoner in Christ Jesus**. This probably means that he was literally sharing in Paul's physical imprisonment (rather than being a 'prisoner' in some metaphorical sense). Details of why or when this occurred are unknown. The important thing here is that this faithful servant of Christ **sends greetings to you** (Philemon). The two men would have known one another well. A greeting from Epaphras would no doubt have meant a great deal to Philemon.

b. Mark

The second companion mentioned was also the second in the longer letter (see Col. 4:10). He is John **Mark**, the one-time travelling companion of Paul and Barnabas. We noted some details of his story in our discussion of Colossians 4:10, in particular the fact that his mention there (as here) testifies to a restoration of good relations between this younger man and the apostle after a rather serious falling-out more than a decade earlier. Now he is included again among Paul's 'fellow workers'. We might note (although Paul makes nothing of the point) that the restored relationship between Paul and Mark was evidence of the same power that Paul expected to accomplish great things in the relationship between Philemon and Onesimus.

c. Aristarchus, Demas and Luke

Aristarchus was the first mentioned of Paul's companions in Colossians 4:10, There he was described (as Epaphras is described here) as Paul's 'fellow prisoner'. He too had been involved with the apostle in numerous adventures (see the exposition of Col. 4:10). With the benefit of hindsight, **Demas** stands as a reminder to readers of the New Testament that present good relations between believers is no guarantee that all will be well in the future. Some time later, Demas will desert Paul (2 Tim. 4:10). That, however, was not yet known to anyone in the situation of this letter.

Finally, Paul mentions greetings from **Luke**, described in the other letter as 'the beloved physician' (Col. 4:14).

The designation given to Mark, Aristarchus, Demas and Luke is **my fellow workers.** The phrase picks up and echoes the reference to Philemon at the beginning of the letter as 'our beloved fellow worker', and draws Philemon into this group by virtue of this relationship with Paul. No doubt these fellow workers, there in Rome with Paul, with their direct knowledge of Onesimus's new faith in Christ, stand with Paul as silent supporters and encouragers to Philemon to do what Paul has asked.

d. Paul

The final word of the letter is a greeting from Paul himself to the whole body of believers who were to hear this letter. **The grace of the Lord Jesus Christ be with your spirit.** While the greeting is conventional, in the sense that Paul often closed his letters in similar terms (see Col. 4:18), the appropriateness of these words on this occasion should not be missed. If Philemon is to act in the way that Paul expects towards Onesimus, and if the believers in Colossae are going to understand and support him in his generous welcome to the one who had wronged him, then it will be a remarkable display of grace. But grace is what the Lord Jesus Christ is all about! As the letter began with a word of gospel grace (v. 3), so it closes. It has been a letter drawing attention to grace experienced by believers, and calling for grace to be shown by believers. May all who read these words (not just in first-century Colossae) know 'the grace of the Lord Jesus Christ' in the depths of our being and in the lives that we live.

The survival of this letter is evidence enough that Philemon heeded its appeal. Indeed, history has a tantalizing fact that we cannot certainly connect with all this, but it is just possibly an amazing sequel to all we have heard. At the beginning of the second century there was a bishop of Ephesus named Onesimus![1] Is this the remarkable conclusion to one of the Bible's amazing stories?

---

[1] Ignatius, *Letter to the Ephesians* 1:3, 6:2.

Whether or not the Ephesus bishop was this Onesimus, something remarkable happened in Colossae. The fellowship of the faith between Philemon and Onesimus became effective. We who read this letter so many years later must be stirred not to rest content with our fellowship in the faith being as unreal as it can very easily become, wherever Christian fellowship is no more than the context for friendships that may well have happened anyway, for like-minded people with much in common to enjoy one another's company. The fact that there may be no slave- masters reading these words today, and no runaway slaves returning, does not mean that we can remain unaffected by this letter. Our fellowship in the faith can work in the *difficult* situations that life brings to the relationships between believers today. Wherever Christian people have good reasons to *not* get on, where there is perhaps an unfortunate history of wrongs that have been done, the word from Paul to Philemon suggests powerful possibilities.

Let us pray that our fellowship of the faith will become more and more effective.

Study Questions

1. Paul expects Philemon's fellowship with *him* (Paul) to radically affect his (Philemon's) treatment of *Onesimus*. Why?
2. What might have made it difficult for Philemon to accept Paul's generosity with regard to Onesimus's debt?
3. In what ways might the believers in Colossae have been put out by Philemon's behaviour towards Onesimus (when Philemon heeded Paul's appeal)? How would Paul's letter help?
4. Has your fellowship in the faith been effective (or failed to be effective) in a relationship with someone who has wronged you in some way (or someone you have wronged)? How has Paul's letter to Philemon been relevant?

Subject Index

Scripture Index

Colossians

Christian Focus Publications

Our mission statement

Staying Faithful

In dependence upon God we seek to impact the world through literature faithful to His infallible Word, the Bible. Our aim is to ensure that the Lord Jesus Christ is presented as the only hope to obtain forgiveness of sin, live a useful life and look forward to heaven with Him.

Our Books are published in four imprints:

CHRISTIAN FOCUS

Popular works including biographies, commentaries, basic doctrine and Christian living.

MENTOR

Books written at a level suitable for Bible College and seminary students, pastors, and other serious readers. The imprint includes commentaries, doctrinal studies, examination of current issues and church history.

CHRISTIAN HERITAGE

Books representing some of the best material from the rich heritage of the church.

CF4KIDS

Children's books for quality Bible teaching and for all age groups: Sunday school curriculum, puzzle and activity books; personal and family devotional titles, biographies and inspirational stories – because you are never too young to know Jesus!

Christian Focus Publications Ltd,
Geanies House, Fearn, Ross-shire,
IV20 1TW, Scotland, United Kingdom.
www.christianfocus.com